Criminal Justice Responses to Maternal Filicide

Criminal Justice Responses to Maternal Filicide: Judging the failed mother

BY

EMMA MILNE
Durham University, UK

United Kingdom – North America – Japan – India – Malaysia – China

Emerald Publishing Limited
Howard House, Wagon Lane, Bingley BD16 1WA, UK

First edition 2021

Reprints and permissions service
Contact: permissions@emeraldinsight.com

British Library Cataloguing in Publication Data
A catalogue record for this book is available from the British Library

ISBN: 978-1-83909-621-1 (Print)
ISBN: 978-1-83909-620-4 (Online)
ISBN: 978-1-83909-622-8 (Epub)

Printed and bound by CPI Group (UK) Ltd, Croydon, CR0 4YY

ISOQAR certified
Management System,
awarded to Emerald
for adherence to
Environmental
standard
ISO 14001:2004.

ISOQAR
REGISTERED
Certificate Number 1985
ISO 14001

INVESTOR IN PEOPLE

To women everywhere, whether pregnant or not, mothers or not.
Keep fighting, and surviving, and living.

Content

List of Tables

About the Authors

Dr Emma Milne is Assistant Professor in Criminal Law and Criminal Justice at Durham University. Her PhD in Sociology from the University of Essex was funded by the Arts and Humanities Research Council. Her research is interdisciplinary, focussing on criminal law and criminal justice responses to newborn child killing and foetal harm. The wider context of her work is social controls and regulations of all women, notably in relation to pregnancy, sex, and motherhood. She co-authored *Sex and Crime* (SAGE, 2020) and co-edited *Women and the Criminal Justice System: Failing Victims and Offenders?* (Palgrave, 2018).

Acknowledgements

This book is the product of research conducted for my doctoral studies and during the following three years. It has been a labour of love, as well as being simply laborious a good deal of the time. There are numerous people/organisations to whom I owe my thanks for their support to enable me to complete the research and produce this book: these are but a few, and I hope the rest know who they are.

The PhD research would not have been possible without the support and guidance of my supervisors, Professors Jackie Turton and Pete Fussy. Particular thanks to Jackie for over a decade of encouragement, support (emotional and academic), and friendship, and for persuading me to 'go for it' and start the PhD in the first place. Dr Marisa Silvestri (truly the greatest external examiner anyone could ask for!): her continued support since completion of the PhD has been invaluable, and I am so grateful. Further thanks to Jackie and Marisa for their incredibly helpful comments on the book proposal.

Thanks to Dr Karen Brennan, for her friendship, instigated when we both discovered we have a thing for (the study of) infanticide. Bouncing ideas off each other, discussing how the law works, and how the law *should* work, and continuing to share and develop ideas with her is nothing but a joy! Karen, your friendship and all the fun only make it sweeter.

Sadly, more often than not, academic research is only possible with a wad of cash – this book is no exception. So, thanks to the Consortium for the Humanities and the Arts South-East England (CHASE), Grant No. AH/L503861/1, and Arts and Humanities Research Council (AHRC) International Placement Scheme for funding the PhD and research fellowship at the Library of Congress, USA. It was only possibly to obtain additional court transcripts for the post-PhD research due to funding provided by the Socio-Legal Studies Association (SLSA) Research Grants Scheme, so my thanks to the SLSA for both the money and the ongoing academic engagement facilitated by the society.

A number of people have assisted this research and this book through their professional activity. I would like to offer my thanks to all the court clerks in England and Wales who helped me with access to court transcripts – especially the two clerks who trolled through court listings and schedules in order to identify two anonymised cases. Particular thanks to Michelle Sisson, my proofreader: dyslexia can make a tough job so much harder, but Michelle helps to ameliorate this with her compassionate and helpful corrections of my (sometimes incomprehensible) English. Thanks, too, to Durham Law School for agreeing to pay for Michelle's services without fuss or query – it's lovely to see this sort of disability support so readily and willingly given. I also owe a great deal to my counsellor, Caroline Hodgeson, who helped me through the difficulties of 2020. Professional support for mental health and well-being is essential at the best of times, but particularly in the context of the events of 2020 (on a global and personal level). I'm aware that to be able to afford such support is, regrettably, a privilege of the few. Nevertheless, I am deeply grateful to Caroline for her compassion, support, and care over the last 12 months. Caroline, I'm not sure I could have made it if you hadn't been there.

Particular thanks go to those who read sections of this book or this book in its entirety and commented upon my ideas; their feedback on my work and assistance in developing these thoughts was invaluable: Dr Lynsey Black, Dr Alexandra Fanghanel, Professor Clare McGlynn, Dr Elizabeth Chloe Romanis, and the anonymous reviewer. Others assisted me in unpacking and/or considering key ideas; I have noted and thanked these people in the text to denote their contribution to that thought/idea.

To my cheerleaders (you know who you are), thanks for your encouragement from the sidelines. Thanks also to the friends who provided day-to-day support throughout the analysis and writing stages – through the painful labour and delivery of this book: specifically, but not exclusively, Dr Alexia Caesel, Dr Emma Watkins, and Dr Janet Weston.

Finally, my thanks to Dr Orlando Goodall, who kept me sane during 2019/2020 with his regular text communication which ranged from being beautifully banal to powerfully political, radically resistant, and, always, hilariously funny! Nolite te Bastardes Carborundorum, comrade!

Chapter 1

The 'Problem' of Maternal Filicide of Newborn Children

How could a mother kill her own child? Particularly her newly born child who has developed inside her and is so new to the world as to be seen as nothing but innocent and deserving of love and care? Such questions reflect popular sentiment towards women who are suspected of killing their newborn children. These sentiments perhaps explain why criminal law and justice have focussed on women who are believed to have committed such acts, and why such women are the subject of innumerable research studies. These studies span the disciplines of sociology, criminology, law, history, psychology, medicine, and psychiatry. Most attempt to answer the question 'Why does she do it?': Why does a woman hide a pregnancy, give birth alone, and behave in a way that leads to the death of the child?

The focus of the question, the desperate desire to understand *her*, I contend, is wrong. This question is fixated on the woman, as an individual. It is determined to discover who she is, and what she does, in the hope to understand why *she* did 'it'. Such an approach starts from the premise that the behaviour of accused women is 'wrong' – that it is 'unthinkable', 'unnatural' – embodying the principle that this is a behaviour that society does not expect and cannot accept. Therefore, the natural consequence of such analysis is to conclude that her behaviour should be seen and understood as criminal and so deserving criminal law and justice intervention and, consequently, punishment. As I outline in this book, not only is this an unhelpful approach to these cases, but it also leads us to a false conclusion as to how and why women behave in such ways towards their pregnancies, foetuses, and newborn children, and how and why criminal justice should be involved.

This study throws cases of suspected newborn child killing on their head. Rather than asking 'Why would a woman do such a thing?', the focus of my inquiry is upon society, and what society does. What is society's role in creating a situation whereby a woman experiences her pregnancy as a crisis, to the extent that she feels she cannot accept and respond to her pregnancy, so she conceals and/or denies it to herself and to those around her? What factors in society lead women to take steps to illegally end their pregnancy or to not seek help when they realise that they are about to birth a child? And what responsibility does society bear when a woman 'decides' that ending the life of her late-term foetus or newly born baby is her only viable option? When considering the hand society

Criminal Justice Responses to Maternal Filicide: Judging the Failed Mother, 1–26
Copyright © 2021 by Emma Milne
Published by Emerald Publishing under an Exclusive Licence
doi:10.1108/978-1-83909-620-420211003

has in the outcomes of these cases – the hardships of motherhood, the controls and regulations on women's sexuality and motherhood, the substantial burden of pregnancy placed on women – the natural question is not 'Why did she do it?' but 'Why wouldn't she do it?'. And perhaps even 'Isn't it surprising that more women don't do it?'. In light of these revised questions, we need to critically analyse the role of criminal law and criminal justice in sanctioning women when they take extreme steps to remedy the harms of pregnancy and motherhood that occur due to social structures.

This is precisely what this book does: it takes 15 cases of women who are suspected of causing the death of their newborn children and who have been convicted in England and Wales of a criminal offence connected to this behaviour from 2010 to 2019. In assessing these cases, I analyse the nature of each one with a strong focus on the social causes, so moving the centre of analysis away from women as individuals. I evaluate the social norms and ideas that underpin the assessment of these women and their behaviour – specifically ideals of mother-hood and expectations of being the 'responsible' pregnant women. I then unpack how English and Welsh law works to criminalise the actions of these women. Through this analysis, it becomes clear that women who are suspected of causing the death of newborn children collide with immovable expectations that society holds about motherhood – of who should be a mother, when, where, and how. These expectations are not new and have long and complex histories. They are also not universally experienced and are deeply impacted by perceptions on race, class, sexuality, disability, and other intersecting identities.

In evaluating the function and operation of criminal law and justice in cases of suspected newborn child killing, what becomes clear is that the desire to crimi-nalise the behaviour of suspected women, and to sanction them for their 'failure' as mothers and as pregnant women, is incredibly strong. Such a desire operates despite the position of the women who stand accused. The women in these cases, as with other women who have been the subject of other research in this field,[1] are incredibly vulnerable. When I use the term vulnerable here, I am specifically referring to the work of theorists such as Martha Albertson Fineman (2008):

> Because we are all positioned differently within a web of economic and institutional relationships, our vulnerabilities range in magni-tude and potential at the individual level … it is experienced uniquely by each of us and this experience is greatly influenced by the quality and quantity of resources we possess or can command. (p. 10)

The vulnerabilities of women who are suspected of causing the death of their new-born child are substantial. To be blunt, a woman does not come to the situation of giving birth alone, scared to call for help, and deciding that the death of the infant is the only option, if she is *not* vulnerable. To make such a claim is not to essen-tialise women who have such experiences but to acknowledge that newborn child

---

[1]Explored in Chapter 2.

killing in the circumstances explored in this book is a product of desperation and hardship.[2] The vulnerabilities of these women are directly connected to their interpretation, understanding, and engagement with their pregnancies. As argued in Chapter 2, a woman's experience of her pregnancy as a crisis is closely connected with her social and cultural circumstances (Oberman, 2003; Vellut et al., 2012). Within the context of cases of women suspected of causing the death of newborn children, being pregnant when it is perceived by the pregnant woman, and possibly those around her, that she should not be, adds a distinct level of vulnerability to women who are already disadvantaged (Ayres, 2007).

Despite the apparent vulnerabilities of accused women, the push to criminalise their actions is strong. Why this push exists is explored throughout this book. What becomes clear through the analysis is that the desire to sanction women, to hold them accountable and label their actions as criminal, results in criminal law being contorted and reshaped so that it fits with the circumstances of the cases and so can be applied to capture the behaviour exhibited by the women. Laws are applied in ways never intended by legislators when enacted, and so offences are reinterpreted to fit new scenarios. Such use of the law is common and uncontroversial within criminal justice practice.[3] However, the manner in which it is done in the cases assessed here tells us a great deal about how women who hide pregnancies and labour alone, resulting in the death of the foetus/child, are understood and assessed.

The clearest examples of the stretching of the criminal law in these cases can be seen in the approach to the legal principle of the born alive rule. In England and Wales, if you are not born alive, then you are not a legal person who can be a victim of crimes against the person, such as homicide or non-fatal offences. If not born alive – if *in utero* or in the process of being born – then a human does not have legal personality and, thus, does not have the same level of legal protection as all other born humans. Accordingly, foetuses have limited legal protection.[4] The courts have determined that to be born alive means the body of the child is entirely out of the birth canal,[5] and so the child has a separate existence.[6] The umbilical cord and afterbirth (placenta) do not need to have been delivered nor

---

[2]The vulnerability of women who have their behaviour controlled and sanctioned by criminal law and criminal justice is widely recognised in feminist literature. See, for example, Carlen and Worrall (1987), Barlow (2016), Milne et al. (2018), and Singh (2017).

[3]See, for example, McGlynn et al. (2017) in their analysis of using voyeurism laws to facilitate prosecution of defendants for non-consensual sharing of explicit images and image-based violence.

[4]Foetus is not the correct term for all periods of gestational development, with different terms associated with different periods of development: zygote (at fertilisation), blastocyst (during the period leading up to implantation, 6–10 days after ovulation), embryo (following adherence of the cells to the uterine wall), and foetus (from 8 weeks until birth). The term foetus is used throughout this book to indicate a human *in utero* from conception to the completion of birth. This term is used for ease of the narrative and not to indicate a specific period of gestational development.

[5]*Poulton* [1832] 5 C&P 329; *Enoch* [1833] 5 C&P 539; *Crutchley* [1837] 7 C&P 814.

[6]*Paton* v. *British Pregnancy Advisory Service Trustees* [1979] QB 276.

severed from the child.[7] Separate existence is evidenced by the child breathing after birth.[8] However, as Romanis (2020b) makes clear in her analysis of the born alive rule, these measures are potentially subject to change in line with medical developments.[9]

In many respects, the cases analysed here should be simple: if there is evidence of live birth then the child is treated like any other victim of crime, if not, then limited liability exists for the pregnant woman as it is a foetus, not a born person, who has died. However, as will be illustrated through the course of this book, the application of criminal law in this area is anything but simple. Criminal offences relating to conduct against a foetus/newborn child are a medley of different pieces of statute that have developed from the late sixteenth century to the early twentieth century. As a result, the laws in this area have a long, complex history and are saturated with the legacy of the control and regulation of women's sexuality and ideas around who can and should be a mother. The end result is that prosecutors – the Crown Prosecution Service – have a 'menu' of offences from which they can select the one that works best to fit the facts of a particular case and so criminalise the conduct of the suspected woman. The menu is made up of the following offences:

Evidence of Live Birth Required:

- Homicide, including infanticide. Infanticide is both a homicide offence and a partial defence to murder, under the Infanticide Act 1938. Infanticide prevents a woman from receiving the mandatory life sentence for murder if she kills her own child within a year of its birth, and at the time of the killing, 'the balance of her mind was disturbed by reason of her not having fully recovered from the effect of giving birth to the child or by reason of the effect of lactation consequent upon the birth of the child'.[10]
- Child cruelty.[11]

---

[7]*Reeves* (1839) 9 C&P 25; *Trilloe* (1842) 2 Mood CC 260; *Crutchley.*

[8]*C* v. *S* [1988] QB 135; *Rance and Another* v. *Mid-Downs Health Authority and Another* [1991] 1 QB 587.

[9]For example, foetal surgery, whereby the foetus is removed from the uterus and body of the pregnant woman, operated on and then returned to the uterus to continue gestating. Has this 'baby' been born alive and thus garnered the rights and legal protections of a born person? If so, what are the legal implications for the woman whose body that 'born alive person' is within?

[10]According to Ministry of Justice data (Freedom of Information Request 200908003), of the 26 women who were sentenced at the Crown Court 2000–2020, only 1 received an immediate custodial sentence: imprisoned for four years. It is not known if this woman killed a newborn child or an older infant.

[11]Children and Young Persons Act 1933, s1. This offence is not explored in detail; however, comments are made in a number of the court hearings that the behaviour of women in these situations does not fit neatly into the definition of the offence or the sentencing guidelines; thus, suggesting this offence also operates as a 'makeshift' in light of more suitable offences.

Evidence of live birth not required:

- Concealment of birth – concealing the dead body of a baby in order to conceal the fact it was ever born.[12] Hereafter 'concealment'.
- Procuring a miscarriage – criminalising attempts to end a pregnancy at any stage of gestation, other than for the purpose of saving the life of the pregnant woman. It does not matter if the foetus dies or is born alive or if the attempts to end the pregnancy fail.[13]
- Child destruction criminalises the killing of a child capable of being born alive; so, a foetus that has passed viability. The foetus has to die before birth for this offence to be committed.[14]

In assessing the menu of offences and how they are applied, in this book, I am analysing a range of cases that, on the face of the criminal outcome, are vastly different: ranging from women convicted of homicide offences and sentenced to serve a minimum of 18 years' imprisonment, through to women convicted of a miscellaneous crime against society (the category in which the offence of concealment sits in police data) and receiving a 12-month community order. My decision to look across the criminal conviction outcomes, rather than at a specific offence, arose from the fact that, in many respects, the circumstances, contexts, and outcomes of these cases are the same: the woman 'hides' her pregnancy, gives birth alone, and at some point around the time of birth the foetus/baby dies. This is a distinctly feminist approach to assessing deviant/criminal behaviour: taking the experiences of women as the starting point and demonstrating that the law often does not work with or fit for the lives of women.

As will become clear over the course of this book, legal professionals also appear to see the actions of the women as bearing similarities, whether she violently killed a newborn child or not. The impact of these perceptions is that the criminal law is being applied to criminalise the actions of the women despite the specific circumstances of the cases. The women and their actions (or inactions) are not seen as different, and the born alive rule ceases to have the meaning it is (officially) proscribed in law. The differences lie in which offences can be applied to the conduct of the women and so the label that is attributed to the 'crime' committed. I have also included two cases of women who abandoned live born children but resulting in the babies being found soon after they were left and so surviving. These cases were included on the basis that the outcome may easily have been different and the survival of the child occurred through happenstance, rather than due to the actions of the women; thus, they are similar in

---

[12]Section 60 of the Offences Against the Person Act 1861 (hereafter OAPA 1861).

[13]OAPA 1861, s58. Discussed in detail in Chapter 6. Abortion remains illegal unless conducted within the parameters of the Abortion Act 1967.

[14]Infant Life (Preservation) Act 1929, s1(1). The origins of the offence are analysed in Chapter 5. See also Sheldon (2016).

nature to the other cases.[15] In analysing the cases together, I am not suggesting that the women acted in exactly the same way or that their behaviour is comparable. I am illustrating that this is how criminal law and justice is approaching these cases – same behaviour, different outcomes, and so a different choice from the menu of offences.

As will become clear throughout this book, the menu might be working for criminal justice, and perhaps also for wider society, as it allows us to lay the blame for foetal and newborn child death firmly at the door of accused women. It allows us to individualise women's behaviour and hold them, and them alone, responsible for what occurs: for their 'failure' as mothers and pregnant women. This approach to these cases reflects society's beliefs about women more broadly. It is saturated by misogynistic ideas about women, embodying the control and regulation of women's bodies, sexuality, and motherhood. Such regulation of women – as adult female humans – underpins sex-based discrimination and oppression and is one of the cornerstones of heteronormative, capitalist, racist patriarchy.[16] Women are controlled because they can become pregnant. But as outlined in Chapter 3, the ability to become pregnant does not mean motherhood is natural or inherent. Such perceptions of the role of caring for children are driven by discriminatory ideas about women and their role in society. This book is not alone in making such observations about motherhood and pregnancy, and about criminal law and criminal justice approaches to women; it joins a chorus of vibrant and sophisticated feminist voices, providing yet more evidence that criminal law and justice (as well as the structures of life under patriarchy) do not serve women.

The text is best read sequentially, as the early chapters provide details of the cases that underpin the analysis of the law in the latter part of this book. The remainder of the first chapter explains how the research was completed and provides a summary of the cases analysed. Chapter 2 explores the women's experiences of pregnancy and previous research into similar cases, thus offering an explanation for how a woman comes to a concealed/denied pregnancy that results in the

---

[15]While we have very little data to tell us exactly how frequently infants are abandoned, Sherr et al. (2009) estimate that an average of 16 babies are abandoned yearly. The two cases assessed here provide examples of this response to a crisis pregnancy.

[16]It is beyond the scope of this book to explore these complex and incredibly important forms of oppression in any detail. My inclusion of this descriptive 'list' of the nature of contemporary society in the Anglo-American world is to acknowledge that the discriminations and oppressions experienced by women go beyond patriarchy – the social organisation whereby men and male power are privileged over women, resulting in the oppression of women. The world is not simply all men on top equally enjoying power, domination, and control, and all women equally experiencing the consequences of subordination. The nature of gender- and sex-based oppressions are shaped and constructed by the expectations that the 'normal' sexuality is heterosexual, that the 'normal' mode of financial operation is capitalist, and the 'normal' race is white. This list is also not exhaustive and could include (dis)ability, nationality, immigration status, educational level, and more. The consequence is that oppression is multifaceted and experienced by individuals differently depending upon their intersecting identities.

death of the foetus/child. Chapters 3 and 4 take a critical look at the ideologies of motherhood and 'responsible' pregnancy and how these play out in the courtroom. Chapter 5 provides a historical analysis of the menu of offences, illustrating the misogynistic legacy that surrounds the laws that continue to operate today. Finally, Chapter 6 outlines how the menu works to defeat the born alive rule, so facilitating criminalisation of women who fail as 'good' mothers and 'responsible' pregnant women, operating despite the principle of legal personhood. In this chapter, I also turn to the United States, to illustrate the potential consequences that could occur if foetuses officially gain legal protection as has been granted in most states. I conclude the text by reflecting on the role of criminal law and justice in protecting newborn children and foetuses and in controlling and regulating women.

Suspicious Perinatal Deaths

Much of our understanding of women suspected of causing the death of a foetus/ newborn child is shaped by the language we use to describe what occurs. Within academic literature, 'filicide' is defined as the killing of a child by its parent, including a stepparent, and 'maternal filicide' is used when the perpetrator is the child's mother. 'Infanticide' is popularly used to refer to the killing of an infant, usually under one year old, by its mother. A further term that is often used within the literature is 'neonaticide', coined by Phillip J. Resnick (1969), defined as the killing of a child within 24 hours of its birth. Resnick noted neonaticide as a distinct form of child homicide, most often committed by the mother following an unwanted pregnancy, thus different from other forms of maternal filicide due to the context, motive, and psychological state of the perpetrator. This distinction between the killing of newborn children and older infants has subsequently been embraced within the literature (see, e.g., Bourget et al., 2007; d'Orbán, 1979; Friedman & Friedman, 2010; Meyer & Oberman, 2001; Pitt & Bale, 1995).

Exploration of language, and the meaning and preciseness of the terms used to describe the events that occur, is essential for this study. The nature of the cases analysed is such that often we do not know exactly what happened: exactly when the foetus/child died, exactly how it died, and exactly the role of the woman in the death. As will become clear through this chapter and the course of this book, this level of uncertainty and what this means for the application of law is of immeasurable importance. Therefore, it is crucial to be as precise with language as possible when describing the death of a foetus/newborn child.

As is no doubt already clear, I distinguish between a born child and a not born child: a foetus. I also distinguish between women who kill their newly born children and women who exhibit other behaviour that may result in the death of the foetus/child (such as not taking steps to 'save' the baby after live birth).[17]

---

[17]While in a legal sense, failure to save a newborn child could also constitute a homicide offence, and murder and infanticide can be committed through an omission, such a failure is more difficult to prove beyond reasonable doubt. For example, if no witnesses are present at the birth and death of the child, how do prosecutors demonstrate

Consequently, I do not use the terms 'filicide' or 'neonaticide' in this study. By their nature, both terms indicate an act of killing, which have implications in terms of how we discern and view the behaviour of the 'perpetrator'. For example, the term 'neonaticide' comes from the Latin *neos*, meaning new, and *caedere*, meaning to kill – implying action and possibly intent. Examination of cases, both in this study and others (Amon et al., 2012; Beyer et al., 2008; Meyer & Oberman, 2001; Vellut et al., 2012), highlights the extent to which we often do not know who or what caused the death of the 'baby', nor if it had been born alive. Difficulties in determining live birth and cause of death have a substantial impact on the criminal law and criminal justice responses to suspected women, as is exemplified throughout this book. Out of the 15 cases assessed here, only 7 women were convicted of a homicide offence. However, as will become clear, in most of the cases, it is presented that the woman was responsible for the child's failure to survive, even if it cannot be proven she legally killed it or, in fact, if it had been born alive and, thus, could have been unlawfully killed.

For these reasons, the term 'neonaticide', and by extension 'filicide', is inadequate in capturing the nature of these cases and the legal and criminal justice responses.[18] Consequently, I have developed two alternative phrases to cover killings or suspicious deaths in the period surrounding birth: 'suspicious perinatal death' or 'suspected perinatal killing'. Perinatal refers to the period immediately surrounding birth.[19] Inclusion of this wider window in the definition of these forms of infant death is important as it reflects the legal regulations of women's pregnant bodies as well as the nature of the cases. As outlined in Chapter 2, the death of the infant around the time of birth is prefixed by a difficult experience of pregnancy by the woman; thus, it is important to take this period into account when examining these cases. For the definition used in this book, the perinatal period commences after 24 completed weeks of gestation (24 + 0, as referred to in medical terms) and ends 24 completed hours after live birth. I have specifically chosen the parameters of this period to reflect key aspects of English and Welsh criminal laws. Section 1(1)(a) of the Abortion Act 1967 places legal limits on medical professionals' abilities to provide women with abortions if

---

a woman purposefully did nothing to save the child with the intent to kill, rather than that she did nothing due to panic or falling unconscious after the birth? The cases I have analysed, those presented here and others that are not examined, indicate that homicide convictions are reserved for women who took actions to kill the born alive child, rather than those instances where the child could be said to have died due to an omission of the woman post-birth.

[18] I also reject use of the term 'infanticide', outside of discussion of the specific criminal offence of infanticide and in the context of popular understanding of women suspected of killing newborn children during the nineteenth century, who were popularly referred to as 'infanticidal women', discussed in Chapter 5.

[19] Different timescales are used for the 'perinatal' period; for example, the World Health Organisation (n.d.) defines the perinatal period as commencing at 22 completed weeks of gestation and ending 7 completed days after birth. However, the principle is that it is the period surrounding birth.

the continuance of the pregnancy would involve risk, greater than if the pregnancy were terminated, of injury to the physical or mental health of the pregnant woman or any existing children of her family.

Prior to 24 weeks of pregnancy, women can request an abortion.[20] Following this gestational stage, an abortion can only be legally provided if to prevent grave permanent injury to, or death of the pregnant woman, or due to foetal abnormality.[21]

At the other end of the time period, the first 24 hours post-birth marks a critical period in the life of a child that is born alive; it is the time during which a person is most likely to be killed (Bortoli et al., 2013; Porter & Gavin, 2010). Consequently, the period between 24 completed weeks of pregnancy and the end of the first day of life captures the time when a foetus/child may be at risk of dying as a consequence of the pregnant woman's actions. The phrases 'suspicious perinatal death' and 'suspected perinatal killing' cover the broad range of actions or inactions that occur in these cases, as well as the breadth of legal and criminal justice responses.

Incidence of Suspicious Perinatal Deaths

It is difficult to know how many cases of suspicious perinatal death occur each year in England and Wales. No official record is kept for how many children are suspected to be victims of homicide within the first day of life, nor are there records reflecting suspicious deaths that occurred prior to live birth. Therefore, to attempt to calculate how many incidents of suspicious perinatal death occur every year, it is necessary to piece together information from data that *are* collected and reported.

The Homicide Index, collated and reported by the Home Office, provides some insight into the occurrence of suspected homicide where the victim was born on the same day that the homicide occurred; frequency of such cases can be seen in Table 1.1. The average number of newborn child deaths recorded each year is two cases of suspected homicide, resulting in an average of one case per year ending in a homicide conviction, and one case each year acquitted or convicted of a lesser offence than homicide. However, as indicated, infants where the date of birth is unknown are excluded. The consequence of this is that cases where the body is found years after the birth and death will not be included in these statistics due to the inability to determine live birth and/or date of death. Similarly, if it is later determined the baby was stillborn, then they will be excluded from these statistics, and if the cause of death is unascertained, then they may be removed from the statistics if the police determine that no crime took place.[22]

---

[20]Although she may find it more difficult to access the medical procedure the closer her pregnancy is to the 24th week of gestation.

[21]Abortion Act, s1(1)(b-d).

[22]With thanks to Katherine Piedrahita, Crime and Policing Analysis at the Home Office, for support with these statistics.

Table 1.1.   Offences Initially Recorded as Homicide by Outcome, for Victims Who Were Born on the Same Date the Homicide Occurred.[a,b,c]

Year	Number of Offences Initially Recorded as Homicide	Number of Offences With No Suspect Charged	Number of Offences Where a Suspect Is Convicted of a Lesser Offence or Acquitted on All Counts	Number of Offences With a Conviction for Homicide
April 1999–March 2000	8	3	2	3
April 2000–March 2001	3	1	0	2
April 2001–March 2002	0	0	0	0
April 2002–March 2003	3	2	1	0
April 2003–March 2004	2	1	0	1
April 2004–March 2005	0	0	0	0
April 2005–March 2006	3	1	2	0
April 2006–March 2007	4	1	0	3
April 2007–March 2008	2	0	2	0
April 2008–March 2009	5	3	0	2
April 2009–March 2010	0	0	0	0
April 2010–March 2011	2	0	1	1
April 2011–March 2012	1	1	0	0
April 2012–March 2013	0	0	0	0
April 2013–March 2014	2	1	0	1
April 2014–March 2015	1	0	0	1
April 2015–March 2016	2	1	1	0
April 2016–March 2017	2	0	0	2
April 2017–March 2018	1	1	0	0
April 2018–March 2019	2	2	0	0
Yearly average	2	0	1	1

[a]Data obtained from The Home Office – Homicide Index. Obtained through a Freedom of Information Request: FOI 58992.

[b]As at 5 December 2019; figures are subject to revision as cases are dealt with by the police and by the courts, or as further information becomes available.

[c]When the police initially record an offence as a homicide, it remains classified as such unless the police or courts decide that a lesser offence, or no offence, took place.

[d]Excludes offences where the date of birth is unknown.

A further potential measure of occurrences each year can be gleaned from police and courts' activities relating to other offences, namely the offence of concealment. Table 1.2 shows an average of seven offences recorded each year.

As identified in this book, a number of other offences are used to criminalise the behaviour of women in such cases. However, there is limited benefit in using available statistics for these offences to attempt to determine the incidence of suspicious perinatal deaths each year. As will be outlined in Chapter 6, procuring a miscarriage and child destruction have been used to convict women suspected of causing the death of their viable foetus. But as Sally Sheldon (2016) concludes, supported by this research, the vast majority of convictions are of men who assault pregnant women, either by inflicting violence against her abdomen

Table 1.2. Police-recorded Statistics for the Offence of Concealment of Birth.[a]

Year	Number of Offences Recorded by Police
1999/2000	4
2000/2001	9
2001/2002	4
2002/2003	7
2003/2004	6
2004/2005	6
2005/2006	8
2006/2007	4
2007/2008	8
2008/2009	8
2009/2010	6
2010/2011	9
2011/2012	5
2012/2013	2
2013/2014	2
2014/2015	5
2015/2016	4
2016/2017	9
2017/2018	12
2018/2019	19
2019/2020	8
Yearly average	7

[a]Data from 1999/2000 to 2012/2013 obtained from Home Office (2016); data from 2013/2014 onwards obtained from Home Office (2020).

or by administering her an abortifacient without her knowledge, rather than of women illegally ending their pregnancies/killing their foetuses.[23] Police-recorded data between 2002/2003 and 2014/2015 show an average of six cases of procuring a miscarriage and four of child destruction recorded each year (Home Office, 2020). While it is possible that some of these police-recorded offences could relate to women ending their own pregnancies, both Sally Sheldon and I agree that it seems unlikely that these cases would not have been recorded in the media.

Further offences under which suspicious perinatal death could be recorded include preventing a lawful burial,[24] cruelty to a child, and abandoning a child under the age of two years.[25] However, with each of those offences, it is impossible to determine if the statistics relate to a case involving a newborn child or an older person, thus they are unable to be used for the purpose of determining incidence. Therefore, we must rely upon the homicide index data and police recordings of the offence of concealment of birth to indicate yearly instances of suspicious perinatal death. It is not possible to determine if each dataset includes any cases that are duplicated in the other set, so this caveat must be borne in mind. If we assume there are no duplicates, then these numbers, when collated, bring an average number of cases to nine per year, as can be seen in Table 1.3.

Numerous scholars researching newborn child homicide have commented on the inaccuracy of official statistics; Ania Wilczynski (1997) argues there is a large 'dark figure' of crime for child killing (victim aged under 16 years), estimating that true incidents of child homicide are three to seven times higher than official statistics report. It is arguably easier to conceal the death of a newborn child compared to that of an older infant as the concealment/denial of the pregnancy (as discussed in Chapter 2) means it is possible that no one knows of the existence of the foetus/baby and so would not miss the child if the body is disposed of in secret after its birth/death. It is not fanciful to believe undetected perinatal homicide may be occurring, as a number of the cases assessed here only came to light due to the woman needing medical attention after the birth or by happenchance discovery of the body years after the birth/death. Using this logic, and Wilczynski's estimates, the rough calculation presented above could potentially be converted to between 27 and 63 cases of suspicious perinatal death per year.

---

[23]Two cases of women convicted of procuring a miscarriage have been recorded, and both are assessed here. I am aware of one case of a woman convicted of child destruction; this case has not been included as the court transcript had been destroyed prior to the research commencing.

[24]A common law offence. See Jones and Quigley (2016) for explanation and analysis of this crime.

[25]OAOP 1861, s27.

Table 1.3. Police-recorded Offences of Concealment of Birth and Homicide Index Data of the Number of Offences Initially Recorded as Homicide for Victims Who Were Born on the Same Date the Homicide Occurred.[a]

Year	Police Recorded	Homicide Index	Total
1999/2000	4	8	12
2000/2001	9	3	12
2001/2002	4	0	4
2002/2003	7	3	10
2003/2004	6	2	8
2004/2005	6	0	6
2005/2006	8	3	11
2006/2007	4	4	8
2007/2008	8	2	10
2008/2009	8	5	13
2009/2010	6	0	6
2010/2011	9	2	11
2011/2012	5	1	6
2012/2013	2	0	2
2013/2014	2	2	4
2014/2015	5	1	6
2015/2016	4	2	6
2016/2017	9	2	11
2017/2018	12	1	13
2018/2019	19	2	21
Yearly average	7	2	9

[a]2019/2020 excluded as Homicide Index data are unavailable for this year.

Approach to the Research

One of the key challenges of studying perinatal killings lies in how to access suitable data to assess both the nature of the cases and the application of law. As outlined above, very few cases are reported each year, meaning that there are a limited number of opportunities to study this form of women's behaviour and criminal law and justice responses. Thus, analysing court transcripts from criminal hearings of past cases was identified as a very good means through which to understand what transpires in these cases and how the criminal law and criminal justice respond.[26]

The process of using court transcripts from England and Wales criminal cases for the purpose of research is long and expensive. Permission must be obtained from the judge who heard the case through an application for that case to the court in which it was heard. If that judge is unavailable due to retirement, for example, then another judge will make the decision as to whether access will be granted.[27] Speculative enquiries are not sufficient to obtain permission, so it is necessary to know the details of the case prior to seeking permission. Hence, cases were identified through media reporting. The consequence of this is that there is no doubt that the sample of cases I have accessed and used for this research is incomplete. I believe I have considered the vast majority of cases that are available or at least those that received national media attention. However, I am aware of cases that are missing from my analysis. For example, through informal discussion with a solicitor, I am aware of a woman convicted of two counts of unlawful burial of her newborn children, which I do not believe made national news, and so, is not included in this research. I am also aware of cases that were heard in the Magistrates' Court rather than the Crown Court. Hearings in the Magistrates' Court are not recorded, and so it is not possible to conduct this type of research on cases heard in this lower court. This also applies in cases of concealment of birth where a defendant is sentenced in the youth court.[28]

Once permission is obtained to access the transcript, a fee is payable to the transcription company for their services to transcribe the recording. This fee can be prohibitive to research, particularly in instances where a full trial has

---

[26]Interviewing women who are accused of crimes connected to the suspicious death of their foetus/child is potentially another approach that could have been taken. However, this approach was not adopted due to the few cases each year, and the significant moral and ethical challenges of approaching accused and/or convicted women. A further avenue would be to interview professionals who work in the criminal justice system, to determine their views on the law and how it is applied. Such research would complement the findings of this study.

[27]Applications can be refused with no reason provided. My request to view the transcripts and use them for research was provided in all but one case: I was granted permission to view the sentencing remarks but not the rest of the sentencing hearing in 'Sally's' case. It is not clear why access was refused, as no reporting restrictions apply to the case.

[28]If a young person is convicted of a more serious crime, then they will be sentenced in the Crown Court and so a transcript would be available. However, for the offence of concealment of birth, the case is likely to remain in the youth court. See, for example, the case of a teenage girl who was originally charged with infanticide, manslaughter, and concealment of birth. She was convicted of concealment of birth after entering a guilty plea on that charge. This case is not included in the research due to no transcript being available from the youth court.

occurred.[29] As a consequence, in the case of 'Jessica', I only obtained a copy of the judge's summing up (at the exclusion of the prosecution and defence closing speeches and the sentencing hearing). I have indicated below what portion of the transcript I have accessed for each case.

I am aware that in countries in mainland Europe and in the United States, it is far easier and cheaper to access recordings and/or transcripts of cases than it is in England and Wales. While criminal hearings do not occur for the purpose of research, and the cost of transcription must be borne by someone, the cost of these cases raises the question as to the appearance of justice having been done after the fact. A further restriction on accessing transcripts is that the recordings can only be held for five years by the transcription company and must be destroyed if not already transcribed by that point. The result is that research can be limited, and a number of the cases I identified were excluded due to no transcript being available.

The nature of the challenges around researching this area and using court transcripts as the source of data means that the study is a mosaic, or a patchwork, of information.[30] Cases that are included are the ones that I have been able to identify and then been able to access. There is no doubt that cases are missing, and so this is not a complete sample of cases heard in English and Welsh courts over the period of 2010–2019. However, the nature of the cases – how few there are each year and the different legal circumstances in each – means that a larger sample will not necessarily result in a clearer picture of how and why criminal law is applied as it is.[31] It is not the aim of the study to provide a comprehensive and systematic picture of how the law operates each and every time a woman is suspected of killing her foetus/newborn child. Instead, this book provides an assessment of how the law has been applied and therefore what such applications tell us about how women are viewed in relation to their pregnancy and motherhood. Consequently, a complete sample is not required. The analysis presented

---

[29]The fee for a full trial for murder could be at least £3,000. During informal discussions with a former colleague about her work around rape trials, she advised that her research team had calculated it would be cheaper to pay a research assistant to make detailed notes of what was said in court during a hearing, rather than pay for transcripts. However, this approach would be unworkable in relation to cases of suspicious perinatal deaths, due to the limited number of cases heard each year.

[30]With thanks to Dr Daniel Grey for suggesting I use this terminology to describe the nature of evidence available for a study such as this. In his study of infanticide in the nineteenth and twentieth centuries, Grey (2014) has also found identification and inclusion of cases a challenge.

[31]The role of individual prosecutors, defence barristers, solicitors, and judges in the application of the law in these cases is a factor, such as why certain charges were brought and not others, advice given to defendants by barristers and solicitors to plead guilty, and the acceptance of guilty pleas for particular charges over others; see, generally, Henham (2001), Jeremy (2008), and Tague (2007). It is not possible to comment on the impact of the discretion of individual legal professionals in these cases. Such research would be of huge value to the understanding of the application of law in this area.

here provides a good overall picture of the nature of cases of suspicious perinatal death and the criminal law and justice responses.[32] From these cases, we can extrapolate dominant views on the position and role of women in relation to pregnancy and motherhood and assess how these ideas impact the criminal law and justice outcomes in these cases.

Approach to the Cases

The transcripts have been analysed thematically to allow for assessment of the differing perspectives expressed and to identify unanticipated insights (Braun & Clarke, 2006; Spencer et al., 2013a, 2013b). The analysis focussed on how the women and their acts are discussed by members of the court during their hearings, and how the crimes of which they have been convicted have been applied in these cases. The analysis of discussions around both – the discourse – was conducted with the goal of identifying 'institutionally supported and culturally influenced interpretive and conceptual schemas (discourses) that produce particular understandings of issues and events' (Bacchi, 2005, p. 199). In so doing, the research is focussed on the meaning of the narratives that are constructed and what they tell us about the wider issues. Consequently, it is not the aim of this research to attempt to determine why the women did what they did (or perhaps better phrased as why they did not do anything to stop the outcome that occurred). Such analysis is beyond both the scope of the data available and my discipline-specific expertise, falling into the realms of psychiatry and psychology. It also needs to be borne in mind that the transcripts cannot reveal the 'truth' of the events surrounding the birth and death of the foetus/child. Putting aside the question as to whether or not an objective truth truly exists in terms of what occurred in these cases and the 'crimes' committed (Cohen, 1985), the version(s) of events told during court proceedings are constructed narratives. They are not an accurate reflection of what occurred. Instead, they are reconstructions of what happened to whom and when for the purpose of winning an argument: storytelling with a purpose, a 'contest of stories that transpires' (Olson, 2014, p. 371; see also, Gewirtz, 1996; Jackson, 1996a; Rackley, 2010). As a result, what is said, how, and why, depends on who is speaking and what they are aiming to achieve through their speech, for example, the prosecution barrister aiming to justify the acceptance of the plea and convince the judge to hand down a particular sentence, the defence barrister attempting to ameliorate the damage done to the defendant's character by the evidence presented, either the Crown or the defence trying to convince the jury that their narrative of events is more compelling than the other, and the judge justifying the sentence. What is contained in the transcripts is very much shaped by the events that occur within the courtroom and so is both partial and incomplete. For this reason, transcripts of trials are different

---

[32]The copyright of the transcripts belongs to the Crown. I have permission from judges at corresponding Crown Courts to include sections of the transcript in this publication.

in nature from transcripts of sentencing hearings, as convincing a jury involves a different process than providing a submission for sentencing.

The version of events retold during the criminal hearings, and how they are retold, forms the basis of the analysis presented here. I have assessed the cases to see what ideas are drawn upon, what is emphasised, downplayed, and used to support a position. I have also specifically looked for wider social ideas or ideals that are assumed by the legal professionals, thus reflected in how they underpin the presentation of the actions and characters of the women defendants. As Lizzie Seal (2010) illustrates in her analysis of gender representations of women who kill, the narratives constructed around violent and criminal women, particularly those considered to have committed the most abhorrent of crimes, reflect wider concerns and anxieties that operate within and across societies. Consequently, the narratives constructed around these 15 individuals and their 'criminal' acts tell us a great deal as to what is valued in and by society, and how it is assumed that women are supposed to act. Thus, the transcripts offer a fascinating lens through which to view perceptions of women as mothers and pregnant women.

Throughout this book, I have offered a critical assessment as to how the women and their actions have been depicted and 'judged'. In doing this, I am in no way suggesting that any miscarriage of justice has occurred. I am also not criticising the legal professionals involved for how they have approached the cases, the tactics used to construct their lines of argument, or their interpretations of the events they are narrating for the court. Legal professionals work with the tools they have been given: in relation to women who are suspected of criminal acts, the tool kit consists of gender norms (discussed further in Chapter 3). By analysing the impact of gender norms as constructed and represented in the narratives in these cases, I am not critiquing the legal approach taken by barristers and judges per se. Instead, I am unpacking the narratives constructed in the courtroom to understand how these women and their behaviour are understood and also what this says about socially accepted ideas and ideals assumed for all women.

In discussing the women in these cases, I have refrained from providing details that will make the defendants, their families, and the legal professionals involved identifiable. I have provided pseudonyms for the defendants and excluded details of exact age, geographical location, and the court in which the case was heard, and have withheld information about the identities of legal professionals, witnesses, and other parties. This decision was made in line with the permission provided by the courts to view the transcripts and to include extracts of the transcripts in this publication and in line with the ethical approval received for the research.[33]

The decision to anonymise cases was also taken due to the nature of the data used for this research. Permission from the women involved in these cases, to include their experiences as the basis of this research, is not needed, nor am I

---

[33]Ethical approval was granted by the Department of Sociology at the University of Essex for the research conducted during my doctoral studies. Further research completed for the project (analysis of eight transcripts) received ethical approval from the School of Law at Middlesex University.

advocating it should be needed; thus, no such permission has been sought. However, the nature of research means that personal details about a woman's life are being dissected and examined without her consent. Considering this, in my mind, the ethical approach is to obscure the identities of the women involved as much as is possible.[34] This approach is not one that is often taken by legal researchers and indeed is argued against by some on the basis of open justice.[35] From my perspective, as a feminist scholar, the key issue here relates to the ways in which research can be and, in many instances, is exploitative of the people who are studied (Bloom, 1998; Kelly et al., 1994; Letherby, 2003; Roberts, 1981; Stanley & Wise, 1990). The power imbalance between subjects of research and the researcher is one that feminist scholars grapple with and attempt to readdress.

My own reflections on the research I present here are that a power imbalance clearly exists. As I outline throughout this book, these women are incredibly vulnerable, their experiences around their pregnancies and the aftermath have been immensely difficult, and they have been publicly sanctioned for their actions by the criminal law and criminal justice. The nature of the legal system and the principles of justice require that their case is made public (unless specific reporting restrictions exist). However, this research is not an element of the justice process. The study is not part of society's judgement of their conduct. What I am doing here is assessing the law and the application of that law. Doing this does not require sharing the women's identities and details of their lives. As my conclusions in this work show, in many respects, the outcomes of these cases are not about these women as individuals but rather about their 'failure' to adhere to the social standards of maternal conduct. Thus, we do not need to know who they are to complete a detailed analysis of the outcomes in their cases.

Some may argue that the vulnerability of the women is a reason not to study such cases. However, as argued by Julia Downes et al. (2014), in their reflections on completing research with sexual violence survivors, assumptions about the vulnerability of participants and thus decisions to not conduct research with them can have a harmful impact upon women and children and leave specialised violence and abuse services facing a precarious future. Instead, they advocate that a positive empowerment approach is needed, which is premised on the principle that victim-survivors and perpetrators are active agents and can contribute. While the research presented in this book does not involve working with accused women through interviews, the principles of Downes et al. are nevertheless relevant. Furthermore, if researchers fail to assess experiences such as these, the result may be a failure to truly scrutinise legal processes and potential injustices. In her recent, groundbreaking work, Michele Goodwin (2020) illustrates how the lack of academic and campaigner attention to the arrest and detention of women of colour who used drugs during pregnancy meant that limited critique of the law and criminal justice in these cases was offered. As a consequence, these women were 'canaries in the coalmines' – the test cases to detect risk of and opposition to

---

[34]Such a process is not entirely possible as these cases were reported in the media.
[35]*Cape Intermediate Holdings Ltd* v. *Dring* [2019] UKSC 38.

state protection of foetal life and criminalisation of pregnant women and so the control and regulation of female conduct. The end result was,

> A medical and political culture that devalues women's reproductive autonomy, privacy, and basic dignity [that] could potentially respond unjustly to all women regardless of race and class. (Goodwin, 2020, p. 100)

While I am not attempting to suggest that this research is of the same magnitude as Goodwin's, the principle is surely the same: feminist scholars cannot shy away from researching tough subjects where women have faced oppression and discrimination, particularly if our aim is to ultimately make women's lives better.

One of the challenges of analysing court transcripts as a methodological approach to any research topic is that the intersecting identities of the individuals who pass through the criminal courts are often obscured. Due to the notion that justice is blind and judges all people against the standard of the (white) 'reasonable man',[36] it is incredibly difficult to determine the class, race, and other elements of identity from the transcripts or even media reporting of cases. If I were to engage in such a process of attempting to determine race and class, this would be, at best, an unsatisfactory assessment of the women based on images in media reports, if provided, and judgements from the limited information about their employment and education history. At worst, I would be engaging in a discriminatory process, attempting to draw conclusions on the basis of what I believe I witness.

Nevertheless, women's lives are not the same and are shaped by more than sex and gender. Intersections of identity have a dramatic impact on women's experiences, both in terms of how they lead their lives and the hardships they face (Crenshaw, 1989). Furthermore, we have countless studies that show us that women's race, ethnicity, and class play a substantial role in how they are perceived by the world and thus responded to by institutions of power and the people within them. Ideological narratives that surround motherhood and pregnancy are shaped by race and class, as well as other aspects of identity, as explored in Chapters 3 and 4. Consequently, these factors are inseparable from the narratives presented about women as mothers and pregnant women, in wider society and the courtroom. Furthermore, we have clear evidence that women from ethnic minority groups, particularly black women, are criminalised at a much higher rate than their white sisters (Prison Reform Trust, 2017; Sudbury, 2002). Therefore, it is not a stretch to conclude that the race and class of the women would have had an impact on the outcomes of these cases, and there is no doubt that this study is limited by the inability to present a meaningful assessment of these dynamics.

Despite the concerns and limitations noted above, from my limited observation of images of the accused women, I can suggest that out of the 15 cases, 10 of the women are white women, 2 are women from ethnic minority groups, and in 3 cases

---

[36]A principle that has been widely critiqued, including in this text. See, for example, Curry (2011), Harris (1994), MacKinnon (2005), Naffine (1990), Smart (1998), and West (1988).

I am unable to tell due to reporting restrictions. I have chosen to not advise the reader which of the women are from minoritised ethnic communities. This decision reflects the comments I make above but also my commitment to anonymise the cases. As I have outlined, the cases are so few and far between that carefully chosen keywords typed into a search engine will likely lead the reader to a news article that they may deduce corresponds to one of the cases assessed here. By identifying which of the women are from minoritised ethnic communities, I would only increase the likelihood of her identity becoming apparent. It seems to me that an increased likelihood of being identified due to race or ethnicity is yet another example of the discrimination that minoritised ethnic women face and so goes against my attempts to limit the potentially exploitative nature of this research.

I conclude this chapter with a retelling of the events that surround the cases assessed in this research. The below versions of events are as much a construction of what occurred as are the court transcripts. My purpose here is different from those of legal professionals during court hearings – I am explaining the background information I believe you, as the reader, need to know to understand the analysis presented throughout this book. Recapturing and reconstructing narratives is a key element of feminist ethics (Bacchi, 2005; Maynard & Purvis, 2013; Raynor, 2016). I have employed such principles when constructing the below stories about the experiences of the women studied in this book.

Cases

Alice

Elements of hearing accessed: judge's sentencing remarks
After feeding and clothing her newborn infant, Alice left her in a carrier bag in a park, where she was later found by a member of the public. Although it was initially believed the baby would die of hypothermia, she recovered and was released into foster care. In her mid-twenties, Alice had other children, fathered by a man with whom she had been in a long-term relationship. Following the break-up of that relationship and believing she could not cope with a further child, Alice concealed her pregnancy and gave birth alone. She left the child in the park hoping she would be found quickly. After pleading guilty to child cruelty by wilfully abandoning or exposing a child, the judge accepted evidence from the psychiatrists that Alice had experienced a severe depressive episode while suffering from a major depressive disorder. She was sentenced to six months' imprisonment, suspended for two years with supervision. Although her older children were removed from her care, at the time of sentencing social services were working with Alice to implement a long-term plan to return all four children to her care.

Bethany

Elements of hearing accessed: prosecution and defence counsels' closing speeches, judge's summing up, and sentencing remarks
In her mid-twenties, Bethany gave birth to her child in her bathroom. The child was born into the toilet, after which Bethany removed her from the bowl

and stabbed her to death with scissors her boyfriend had retrieved for her. While Bethany was in labour, killing the baby, and cleaning up the mess in the bathroom, her partner sat in the next room playing computer games, apparently oblivious to Bethany's actions. After placing the body of the baby in the bin, Bethany joined her partner before they went to bed. Two days later, Bethany attended hospital due to a retained placenta, telling the medical team she had experienced an early miscarriage at approximately nine weeks of gestation. Upon examination, the medical team determined she had given birth and informed the police of a missing baby. From the evidence given by Bethany, and her recorded internet searches, it is not clear when she knew she was pregnant. The prosecution, who argued Bethany was deceptive and a seasoned liar, maintained she knew long before she gave birth, and, due to not wanting a baby, concealed the pregnancy, intending to kill the child after its birth. The defence argued Bethany discovered her pregnancy a few weeks prior to the birth, believing she was only in the first trimester of pregnancy; consequently, the birth came as a shock and Bethany acted in a daze. Psychiatric consultants acting for the defence argued that Bethany experienced underlying mental health conditions, which were exacerbated by the birth and so, at the time of the killing, was not acting rationally, supporting a defence of manslaughter by diminished responsibility or infanticide. At trial, Bethany was convicted of murder and sentenced to life imprisonment, serving a minimum of 20 years.

Elizabeth

Elements of hearing accessed: prosecution and defence counsels' closing speeches, judge's summing up, and sentencing hearing

Elizabeth was rushed to hospital after losing a significant amount of blood. It was suspected she had given birth, but no baby could be found. Three days later, Elizabeth's sister, whom she lived with, suspected the baby's body was hidden in Elizabeth's bedroom due to a smell coming from the room. The police were called, and the body was found. Elizabeth was arrested and tried for murder. At her trial, Elizabeth, who was in her early thirties, was determined by a psychiatrist to be of low intellect, amounting to a mild mental illness. The defence argued that the child was not born alive and so homicide had not been committed: evidence of live birth was not conclusive, but even if the jury believed the child had been born alive, then Elizabeth did not realise it when she placed tissue in the baby's mouth. Furthermore, the defence argued, she was acting as a consequence of a mental illness, pathological denial of pregnancy, a systematised dissociative amnesia, and so was irrational and not in control of her actions during labour and in the post-partum period when she placed tissue in the baby's mouth. The jury returned a verdict of guilty of manslaughter by reason of diminished responsibility. She was sentenced to a community order for two years, with supervision.

Fiona

Elements of hearing accessed: sentencing hearing

At the age of 16, Fiona gave birth alone, leaving the body of the baby in a public place, where it was discovered soon after. The baby was full term and born alive. Fiona stated that she had no knowledge of her pregnancy prior to giving birth. Following the birth, Fiona stabbed the baby 27 times with a penknife. Media publication of the details of the birth and death were broadcast in the local area. Fiona's parents saw the reports and spoke with Fiona who acknowledged the baby was hers and that she was responsible for the death. They informed the police and sought medical attention for Fiona. A psychiatric assessment concluded that Fiona seemed to be 'genuinely unaware of her pregnancy', that there was no evidence of any real criminal intent, and that her actions were driven by panic and the effects of both mental and physical shock. Fiona was charged with and pleaded guilty to infanticide. She was sentenced to a youth rehabilitation order for 12 months.

Gwen

Elements of hearing accessed: plea hearing and sentencing hearing

While away from home on a family trip, Gwen, who was in her early thirties, gave birth to a baby in a public toilet. The baby was delivered alive into the toilet bowl; then Gwen left, without touching her and after closing the lid of the toilet. The prosecution claimed Gwen also flushed the toilet, which Gwen states she does not remember doing. The baby was found alive by cleaning staff and recovered well in hospital. After the police released CCTV images of the assumed mother of the child, Gwen's mother asked Gwen if it was her, having suspected a pregnancy and noticing Gwen had been unwell around the time the baby was left in the toilet; Gwen later acknowledged that she was the baby's mother. Upon contacting the police, Gwen was taken to hospital for medical attention and arrested for attempted murder. In police interviews, Gwen stated that she acted out of panic, shock, and fear after being surprised by the birth, and that she regretted leaving the baby, believing she would be found alive soon. Gwen was charged with attempted murder and child cruelty, pleading guilty to child cruelty. She was sentenced to 8 months' imprisonment, suspended for 18 months.

Hannah

Elements of hearing accessed: sentencing hearing

Hannah concealed her pregnancy from her family and gave birth alone in her home. Following her arrest and subsequent medical examination, she told a nurse that she passed out after the labour. The child was born alive and died within two hours of birth. There were no signs of injury to the child and no cause of death could be ascertained. In her mid-twenties, Hannah's family disapproved of her relationship with her boyfriend. After not attending two appointments to terminate the pregnancy, Hannah carried the child to full term. The morning after giving birth to the child, Hannah left the body in the front garden of a friend's house; the friend later discovered it. The police traced Hannah after identifying her boyfriend, through his DNA, as the father of the baby. Hannah pleaded guilty to concealment and child cruelty due to not seeking medical assistance for the child. She was sentenced to 26 weeks' imprisonment, suspended for 2 years.

Hayley

Elements of hearing accessed: sentencing hearing and judgment from appeal of sentence

After being unable to access an abortion through a medical provider due to being over 24 weeks' gestation, Hayley, who was in her early thirties at the time, sought means to end the pregnancy. After arrest, Hayley's internet browsing history revealed that she purchased misoprostol (a drug used to start labour or an abortion) from an internet provider. It is believed the drug was taken at, or close to, full term. Hayley claimed that the child was stillborn; the body was never found. Her arrest occurred after medical professionals raised concerns about her not seeking medical care for her pregnancy and labour and delivery. Hayley was charged with and pleaded guilty to administering poison with intent to procure a miscarriage. The judge sentenced her to 12 years' imprisonment with a reduction by a third due to an early guilty plea. The sentence was appealed and the Court of Appeal ruled for the appellant, determining that the starting point should be 5 years. Honouring the sentence reduction for the plea, Hayley was imprisoned for 3½ years.

Imogen

Elements of hearing accessed: sentencing hearing

When in her late twenties, Imogen discovered she was pregnant. Although first presenting to her doctor within the legal time frame for an abortion, her delay in seeking the procedure meant she was denied a termination. She carried the baby to term, her family and friends unaware she was pregnant. She gave birth to the child alone in her bathroom, stating the child was stillborn. At some point over the following few days, she drove to her parent's house and left the baby's body in a drain. The body was discovered a number of years later. Forensic examination showed that the child was born full term, but live birth and cause of death could not be ascertained. After a lengthy police investigation (which included Imogen stating she became pregnant after being raped by a taxi driver, later disproven as DNA tests revealed her partner was the father of the child, leading Imogen to advise that the attack never happened), Imogen provided a full account of the birth, death, and burial of the child. She was charged and pleaded guilty to concealment of birth and sentenced to one year of imprisonment.

Jessica

Elements of hearing accessed: judge summing up of evidence

When in her late twenties, Jessica gave birth to a baby girl into the toilet bowl. It is believed the baby lived for between 2 and 12 hours, though likely to be closer to 2 hours. The baby is estimated to have been born at approximately 32 gestational weeks. The baby experienced numerous injuries that contributed to the cause of death: skull fracture, head injuries, bleeding in the brain and a brain stem injury, neck and throat injuries, and general abrasions and bruises. At trial, Jessica accepted the baby was born alive but argued that she believed it to be stillborn. The prosecution argued that the nature and severity of the injuries illustrated intent to kill; that Jessica must have known the child was alive due to the noises and movements it would have been making, that she went into the outdoor toilet to give birth after concealing her pregnancy as she wanted privacy from her family to kill the baby. The defence accepted that Jessica must have caused serious injuries to the child, although she stated she did not remember inflicting them and believed the child was born dead, and the injuries sustained could have been inflicted without murderous intent. Thus, the defence argued the jury could not be sure that, at the time of the relevant acts, Jessica intended to kill or cause the baby really serious harm. No evidence of mental disturbance was provided, and so, Jessica was considered to be of sound mind. From communication with Jessica's solicitor, I am aware that the offence of infanticide was withdrawn from the jury as the consultant psychiatrist who had been instructed for the defence changed his mind during the trial and declined to give evidence in support of that defence. Jessica was convicted of murder, receiving a mandatory life sentence, required to serve a minimum of 18 years' imprisonment.

Lily

Elements of hearing accessed: sentencing hearing

Lily was in her mid-thirties when she discovered she was pregnant. Although a termination of the pregnancy was scheduled, she did not attend the appointment, claiming that her abusive partner, the father of the baby, prevented her from attending. Police records and hospital admissions evidence her reports that their relationship was abusive and violent. Four years later, the body of a full-term baby was discovered in the grounds of a house in which Lily had previously resided. Identification of Lily's former partner through DNA, followed by a media campaign on the BBC's programme *Crimewatch*, resulted in Lily being arrested 10 years after giving birth to the child. Lily states she gave birth to the baby following an assault by her partner, which caused stomach pains, bleeding, and the baby 'falling out'. Lily pleaded guilty to concealment and preventing the lawful burial of the corpse. At the same hearing, Lily was also sentenced for numerous offences of fraud and dishonesty. Lily's barrister maintained that all offences committed were done so in the context of intimate partner violence and abuse, and that Lily was acting under the influence of her partner and in fear of him and what he may do to her and their young child. In sentencing, the judge concluded that an immediate custodial sentence would be unproductive and harmful to her children, as it would be for no more than a couple of months due to the deduction of time from Lily's period in custody and year of curfew while on remand. For all indictments, Lily was sentenced to a one-year community order with supervision.

Nicole

Elements of hearing accessed: sentencing hearing

Following the breakdown of her relationship with her partner, with whom she resided and worked, Nicole began an affair. In her late twenties at the time, Nicole discovered she was pregnant, telling no one about the pregnancy except the father of the child, the man with whom she was having an affair. She gave birth alone in her bathroom and was found later by her ex-partner in a pool of blood. She stated the blood was caused by her period. He helped her into bed and, due to concern for her health and level of blood loss, pressed her to call an ambulance, which she refused stating she had been pregnant and had done something terrible. He phoned an ambulance, and Nicole was taken to hospital with substantial bleeding, undergoing emergency treatment to remove part of the placenta that had been retained. Later, police attended the property and found the baby's body. The baby had been born alive and had died of ligature strangulation, resulting from a ligature compression of the neck after Nicole used her hands to strangle the child. Nicole was charged with both infanticide and murder; she pleaded guilty to infanticide. She received a 24-month community sentence, with a requirement for rehabilitation activity.

Olivia and Michael

Elements of hearing accessed: sentencing hearing

When in their early twenties and having been in a relationship for approximately 18 months, Olivia gave birth unexpectedly. She claims she only discovered she was pregnant a month before giving birth, and Michael claims he did not know about the baby until the birth. Michael took the body of the baby and left it in a bag near railway tracks. Two years later, following Michael's arrest for offences of violence, he told the police of the birth of the baby and abandonment of the body. The pathology report indicated that the child was born eight weeks premature; due to the prematurity, it was not possible to determine if it was born alive nor the cause of death. Both Olivia and Michael were charged with and pleaded guilty to concealment of birth. Each received a prison sentence of 10 months, suspended for 2 years. The judge stated the sentence was suspended due to early guilty pleas, their youth, and the context of lack of support at the time of the pregnancy and birth.

Sally

Elements of hearing accessed: judge's sentencing remarks

Sally was convicted of four counts of concealing the birth of a child. While in her thirties, Sally gave birth to four babies, all of whom, she claimed, were still-born. Sally hid the bodies in her bedroom. The pregnancies and births occurred within a 10-year period following Sally's divorce from her second husband, who was reportedly violent towards her. Sally is reported to have abused alcohol and marijuana during this period and to have neglected her three living children. The bodies of the dead infants were discovered over 10 years after the births, and Sally was arrested and charged with four counts of concealment. She pleaded guilty and received a community sentence with supervision for a period of two years.

Sophie

Elements of hearing accessed: sentencing hearing

Sophie, in her early twenties, called an ambulance due to heavy bleeding, telling the call handler and paramedics she was having a miscarriage. After looking in the toilet bowl, paramedics discovered the body of a baby, between 32 and 34 weeks of gestational development; their attempts to resuscitate the child did not work. The conclusion of the pathologist is that the baby was stillborn. The cause of death was profound antenatal foetal hypoxia, or oxygen deprivation, secondary to acute placental abruption, determined as the consequence of self-administration of misoprostol. A police search of Sophie's flat led to the discovery of a large quantity of the drug, misoprostol, which causes contractions. Review of Sophie's internet search history revealed she ordered the drugs online, taking them shortly after they arrived. The prosecution argued that, while she did not know exactly the gestational age of the foetus, based on her internet searches, Sophie was aware that the foetus was capable of being born alive. The defence maintained that Sophie had no idea how far along she was, and so this factor should be considered a significant form of mitigation. In sentencing, the judge concluded that the seriousness of the offence meant that a suspended sentence would not be appropriate. She was sentenced to two years and six months' imprisonment, taking account of a reduction by a third due to an early guilty plea.

Tanya

Elements of hearing accessed: sentencing hearing

Tanya gave birth to her live born child at the age of 16. Immediately following the birth, she pushed tissues into the baby's airway, suffocating him. Following her arrest and being charged with murder, Tanya reported to a psychiatrist that she had conceived the baby after being raped. The court did not share this opinion, determining that while she may have not wanted to have sex with the man who is five years older than her, she did consent. Regardless of the legal nature of the sexual encounter, Tanya experienced flashbacks to the attack and was treated for depression prior to giving birth (although her GP was unaware of the attack or that she was pregnant). Tanya also experienced flashbacks of the rape during the birth and reported feeling dazed and confused during the labour and after the birth. She told the psychiatrist that her actions in placing the tissue in the baby's mouth were out of a desire to stop the gurgling noises the baby made following the birth, while experiencing flashbacks of the attack. Tanya pleaded guilty to infanticide and was sentenced to a 24-month youth rehabilitation order with supervision.

Chapter 2

Mothers in the Courtroom I: Suspicious Perinatal Deaths in Context

> In closing his case to the jury, [defence barrister] said that the jury
> would want to know why this had happened. And so they would,
> and so would I. The answer is there is no way of knowing why this
> happened, only that it did, and that it was a deeply distressing –
> almost dreadful – crime. (Bethany, judge sentencing)

Why would a mother do such a thing? How could a mother do such a thing? To kill her own child, specifically her newly born child, is often presented as the most hideous behaviour a woman could exhibit: to go against her natural instincts to mother and love her child. Such a view is reflected in the comments made by the judge as he sentenced Bethany to serve a minimum of 20 years' imprisonment following her conviction for the murder of her newborn baby.

Public representations of women who kill have been a significant area of study for feminist scholars, analysing depictions of women defendants in court and in the media (see, e.g., Basilio, 1996; Jones, 2003; Morrissey, 2003; Wee, 2011). Such analysis illustrates that women who kill their children are represented as 'good' or depicted as 'mad', 'sad', or 'bad' (Milne & Turton, 2018; Morris & Wilczynski, 1993; Weare, 2016). The portrayal of a woman as 'good' or 'bad' lies in how closely her behaviour is aligned with gender norms. As will be explored in Chapters 3 and 4, in cases of suspicious perinatal death, this means how clearly the suspected woman can be assimilated with ideals of motherhood and motherly behaviour. However, before we consider the representation of the defendants during their court hearings, we need to assess and consider the situations and context of the cases – specifically how a woman comes to giving birth alone and in secret and resulting in the death of the baby.

The purpose of this chapter is to present evidence to illustrate that it is possible to understand the situation that ends with a woman killing, or being believed to have caused the death of, her newborn baby. It is possible to appreciate the factors that surround these cases: the wider context of both individual women's lives and social factors relating to women's sexuality, pregnancy, and motherhood. This chapter will not be outlining individual psychological or psychiatric factors that impacted the women's behaviour; these are beyond the scope of the study,

Criminal Justice Responses to Maternal Filicide: Judging the Failed Mother, 27–50
Copyright © 2021 by Emma Milne
Published by Emerald Publishing under an Exclusive Licence
doi:10.1108/978-1-83909-620-420211004

which does not profess to attempt to, nor want to, examine the women's psyche. Assessment of women's mental states is a process conducted by the courts using psychiatrists and psychologists as a means of facilitating justice for individual women.[1] Instead, this chapter does something more fundamental and more helpful by understanding the context of cases of suspicious perinatal deaths. I will present the academic evidence relating to concealed/denied pregnancies and reflect on the factors of the 15 cases analysed here in relation to that literature. I then propose a new way of conceptualising these cases and the women's experiences of their pregnancies – understanding the events leading up to the birth as a crisis pregnancy. Finally, I outline how crisis pregnancies are interpreted, understood, and represented during the criminal proceedings against the accused women.

Concealed/denied Pregnancy

One of the features of the cases analysed in this study is that none of the women announced their pregnancies to the majority of friends or family, nor did they seek medical assistance with their pregnancy, labour, or delivery. For example:

> Hannah knew she was pregnant and attempted to access an abortion in the weeks leading up to the 24th week of her pregnancy. She sought medical assistance for a pulled muscle on her left side and pain in her chest less than a week before she gave birth. During this medical appointment, she confirmed that she was pregnant. However, none of her family, whom she lived with, were aware of her pregnancy until she was arrested on suspicion of murder.

A further example:

> Tanya's family suspected she was pregnant and asked her about it on a number of occasions. She denied any possibility of being pregnant, including when her doctor asked her, and declined to take a pregnancy test. Tanya's body showed signs of pregnancy, with her abdomen swelling, and Tanya began wearing baggy clothes to hide her figure. She attributed the physical symptoms of pregnancy she experienced – the sickness when she would have been between 8 and 12 weeks pregnant, amenorrhea (the absence of menstruation), and weight gain – to stress due to her exams and her relationship with her father. The night before she gave birth her mother believed her to be in labour, which Tanya denied. The next day when asked about the blood in the bathroom and her bedroom Tanya explained it as due to her period. In the first interview with the police, Tanya stated she realised she was having a baby when her waters broke. In a later interview with police, she stated the baby

---

[1]On the basis that a person should be of sound mind to be held criminally liable for their unlawful acts.

was not breathing following birth. Both interviews were conducted soon after the birth and death of the baby. Later, Tanya would report she had no memory of the events from the time when her waters broke to the time when she woke up in the hospital. Analysis of Tanya's computer showed that she had searched for terms related to her pregnancy: 'Night Nurse day and night capsules, take whilst pregnant', 'How early in pregnancy does milk production start?', 'Why do I not have a baby bump?', 'How to cause a miscarriage at 4 months', 'Is it safe to have a tattoo during pregnancy?'. It was not until eight months after the death of the baby that Tanya was able to tell a psychiatrist that she had blocked knowledge that she might be pregnant, which was confirmed as she gave birth.

Women who conceal and/or deny pregnancy are conceptualised from a biomedical perspective, with the perception that women who experience pregnancy in such a way may have a psychiatric disorder (Murphy Tighe & Lalor, 2016). This approach is evident in the description of concealed/denied pregnancy as a 'reproductive dysfunction' by Klaus M. Beier et al. (2006). As will be discussed in Chapters 3 and 4, it is perceived that there is a 'normal' behaviour 'expected' of women when they become pregnant, which involves recognising the pregnancy and announcing it to family, friends, and medical professionals. Such expectations perhaps explain the volume of academic studies that have been produced since the 1970s on concealed/ denied pregnancies. While the perception that concealing/denying a pregnancy is 'abnormal' perhaps is not displaced, it nevertheless signifies the extent to which declaration of pregnancy and pursuit of medical advice is now deemed to be the norm. Consequently, any other behaviour has been pathologised and thus believed to require explanation, the subject of literature that is explored here.

Within academic literature on this topic, cases where women do not announce their pregnancies are most often referred to as concealed and/or denied pregnancies. Such experiences of pregnancy have been the focus of substantial medical, psychological, and psychiatric literature, as attempts have been made to understand and explain such behaviour. The central questions in the literature focus on whether a woman can truly not know she is pregnant and what factors lead a woman to experience a pregnancy in such a way. As a consequence, debates exist around the appropriate terminology to describe this experience.

One distinction that is clearly drawn in the literature is between psychotic and non-psychotic denial of pregnancy. Psychotic denial of pregnancy is often related to schizophrenic disorders. Scholars argue that bodily changes due to pregnancy are apparent, such as the development of a baby bump, and that people around the woman are conscious that she is pregnant. As part of her psychotic state, the woman may interpret the pregnancy as a form of illness, and the movements of the foetus in a delusional manner, such as the perception of an insect living inside of her or her liver moving around (Gonçalves et al., 2014; Miller, 2003; Slayton & Soloff, 1981). None of the women in the cases experienced this form of pregnancy denial.

Disputes lie within the parameters of behaviour considered to be non-psychotic, notably in the distinction between 'denied' pregnancy and 'concealed' pregnancy, the two terms used most often within the literature. Those who use the terminology of 'denial' argue that women have an initial recognition and awareness of their pregnancy, but that this is followed by a refusal or inability to accept the situation and so denial of the pregnancy occurs (Brezinka et al., 1994; Spinelli, 2001). Laura J. Miller (2003), for example, identifies two forms of non-psychotic denial of pregnancy: 'affective denial', when a woman intellectually knows she is pregnant but experiences none or few of the emotions or behavioural changes, and 'pervasive denial', which occurs when a woman is not consciously aware she is pregnant.

Other scholars have drawn a distinction between 'denied' and 'concealed' pregnancy, perceiving them as two distinct concepts, arguing that denial is an unconscious awareness of pregnancy, while concealment is being aware of pregnancy but actively hiding it from the wider world (Dulit, 2000; Friedman & Resnick, 2009; Friedman et al., 2007; Wessel et al., 2007). Others have used the two terms interchangeably or do not draw a distinction (Milstein & Milstein, 1983; Spielvogel & Hohener, 1995; Wessel et al., 2003). However, Laura J. Miller (2003) argues that to deny a pregnancy is also to conceal it, thus suggesting they are the same phenomenon. Similarly, Cheryl L. Meyer and Michelle Oberman (2001) refute the idea that the two phenomena are mutually exclusive, arguing that women can go through both types at any stage in their pregnancy. Further, scholars have also documented the co-occurrence of denial and concealment and so have used the phrase 'negation' of pregnancy (Amon et al., 2012; Putkonen et al., 2007). As Klaus M. Beier et al. (2006) argue:

> [...] denial and concealment of pregnancy are not separate identities. Instead, they represent different intensity levels of a flawed inner psychological rationalisation of pregnancy that may have many different reasons. (p. 726)

One element of the debate about whether a woman has knowledge of her pregnancy and so conceals it or denies it, relates to the extent to which her cognitive recognition and acknowledgement of her pregnancy are conscious or unconscious. A number of scholars argue that women in these situations experience a fluid transition between unconscious and conscious denial of pregnancy (Brezinka et al., 1994; Green & Manohar, 1990). Similarly, Margaret G. Spinelli (2001) argues that to be able to deny something, one must have prior knowledge of the existence of the reality being denied, even to the self.

As is apparent from this brief summary, there is no consensus as to whether women can and do completely lack conscious awareness of their pregnancies, with some research indicating that most women have some knowledge of the possibility they are pregnant, even if only fleetingly, while others have no knowledge. One conclusion from this body of literature is that women's awareness of their pregnancies in these cases does not seem to be clearly definable. Undetermined and varying levels of awareness do not appear to be uncommon, and knowledge and awareness that is possessed appears to be transient and changing in nature. As a consequence, the language employed in describing women's awareness of pregnancy is important and has symbolic value. Natacha Vellut et al. (2012) make this point in reporting the findings of their study of women who committed neonaticide in France. Rather than 'concealment' or 'denial', they propose the use of the terms 'secret' and 'undiscovered' pregnancy, arguing that secret is a more objective term than 'concealed', which has pejorative connotations and potential legal implications, as it can suggest premeditated homicide if the outcome of the pregnancy is death of the infant. Similarly, they argue, undiscovered is more appropriate than 'pervasive denial' and should be solely reserved for women who have no realisation that they are pregnant. While their point about the negative connotations of the word 'concealed' is important, the evidence from court cases outlined below would suggest that 'secret' may be viewed in a similarly critical light. As 'concealed' and 'denied' are the two most common phrases in use in the literature, and as the distinction between the two is unclear, I will use the term 'concealed/denied' when discussing these types of experience of pregnancy.

From the cases assessed in this research, it would appear that all but one of the women had some level of knowledge of their pregnancy. Table 2.1 indicates the women's reported awareness of their pregnancies. It is important to note that this is 'reported' knowledge, as this information is gleaned from the transcripts, and, as outlined below, the knowledge of pregnancy is deployed as evidence in these cases.

A consequence of a concealed/denied pregnancy is that the expected symptoms and bodily changes of pregnancy can be misinterpreted, significantly reduced, or absent (Brezinka et al., 1994; Milstein & Milstein, 1983; Spielvogel & Hohener, 1995), as can the signs and pains of labour (Spinelli, 2003; Miller, 2003). Two studies report cases of women whose pregnancies were at six or more months of gestation, who had no signs or symptoms of pregnancy, such as growth in breasts, weight gain, swelling of the abdomen, or detection of foetal movements. However, after the women received psychiatric treatment and acknowledged their positive pregnancy status, they suddenly and rapidly developed such signs and symptoms (Bascom, 1977; Sandoz, 2011).

Many studies have noted that those around pregnant women, including parents and sexual partners residing in the same home, are also involved in the concealment/denial, with the nature of their subjective knowledge also being uncertain (Amon et al., 2012; Beyer et al., 2008; Meyer & Oberman, 2001; Vellut et al., 2012). This is a factor in a number of the cases, as outlined in Table 2.1, with a number of partners and family members who lived with the women reporting that they had no knowledge or awareness of the pregnancy. In some instances, men would have been sharing beds with their pregnant partner and, potentially, having sex with them during the late stages of the pregnancy, reportedly without knowing about the existence of the pregnancy.

Much of the academic literature has focussed on attempts to identify women who conceal/deny pregnancies, to determine risk factors associated with such an experience, but with limited success. Studies have found that women who conceal/deny pregnancy come from all social classes and are not determined by age or marital status (Friedman et al., 2007; Wessel et al., 2007). Psychological distress, fear, stigma, and isolation have been noted as factors (Conlon, 2006; Thynne et al., 2012), as has being a victim of rape, incest, or domestic violence and

Table 2.1.   Reported Awareness of Pregnancy.

Alice	Aware she was pregnant – concealed from those around her, including professionals.
	Not indicated if people around her were aware of the pregnancy.
Bethany	Knowledge of pregnancy contended as evidence in the murder trial – prosecution presented evidence of internet searches about pregnancy.
	Partner indicated he was informed of the pregnancy by Bethany a month before she gave birth, but told that she had only just conceived.
Elizabeth	Knowledge of pregnancy contended as evidence in the murder trial – prosecution presented evidence of internet searches about pregnancy; the computer was used by multiple people including Elizabeth's pregnant sister.
	Friends suspected she was pregnant, and Elizabeth's sister asked, which Elizabeth denied.
Fiona	No evidence of any knowledge of the pregnancy.
	Fiona's parents were unaware she was pregnant.
Gwen	Family asked if she was pregnant, which she denied. Gwen told the father of the baby, and his aunt, about the pregnancy.
	Described as ignoring the pregnancy after a positive pregnancy test.
Hannah	Aware she was pregnant – concealed from family and friends.
	Family, whom she lived with, unaware of the pregnancy.
Hayley	Aware she was pregnant – concealed from her family. Initially told the man who impregnated her but then advised him that there was no baby. Attempted to obtain an abortion but denied as over 24 weeks' gestation and so referred to her doctors. Disengaged from medical care and took steps to end the pregnancy.
	Hayley's husband unaware she was pregnant.
Imogen	Described as keeping the pregnancy a secret. Pregnancy confirmed by her doctor and referred for a termination. Did not attempt the termination until after 24 weeks pregnant, which was refused.
	Imogen's partner unaware she was pregnant.
Jessica	Knowledge of pregnancy is contended as evidence in the murder trial – prosecution presented evidence of internet searches about pregnancy.
	Jessica's family, whom she lives with, unaware she was pregnant.
Lily	Described as keeping the pregnancy a secret from her abusive partner. Attempted to access an abortion but prevented attending by her partner.
	The partner claims he did not know she was pregnant. Other people reported that Lily was visibly pregnant.

Nicole	Aware she was pregnant – told the man who impregnated her but no one else.
	Nicole's partner unaware she was pregnant.
Olivia & Michael	Olivia stated she had no idea she was pregnant until about a month before she gave birth.
	Her family, whom she lived with, unaware she was pregnant. Michael reported not knowing about the pregnancy at all until after the birth.
Sally	Described as concealing her pregnancies from those around her.
	Not indicated if people around her were aware of the pregnancies.
Sophie	Acknowledged that she had an awareness of her pregnancy as she ordered abortion medication. Disputed if she knew she was over 24 weeks' gestation.
	Her partner was unaware she was pregnant.
Tanya	Following the death of the baby, Tanya acknowledged that she had blocked any thoughts that she might be pregnant.
	Family believed she was pregnant, which she denied.

abuse, including emotional abuse (Friedman et al., 2007; Porter & Gavin, 2010; Spielvogel & Hohener, 1995; Spinelli, 2001). However, other scholars have disputed some or all of these suggestions, noting that a denial/concealment could occur in any well-adjusted woman if the right external pressure and psychological conflict occurs (Jenkins et al., 2011; Wessel et al., 2007).

A motivator for developing a profile of women who experience concealed/denied pregnancies has been the perceived risk of these experiences of pregnancy for both the woman and the foetus/baby. For example, Sylvia Murphy Tighe and Joan G. Lalor (2016) note that a woman may experience psychological stress and childbirth complications, such as postpartum haemorrhage or death, while the foetus/child may have delayed diagnosis in foetal abnormalities that could be treated, such as low birth weight, prematurity, birth injuries, or face abandonment or death. Fears of such harm are not without their merit, but it must be noted that concern over the welfare of the foetus/child from concealed/denied pregnancies is largely due to the belief that there is a connection between concealed/denied pregnancies and the killing of newborn children.

Many studies which focus on neonaticide have concluded that a concealed/denied pregnancy is a risk factor for these homicides (Beier et al., 2006; Beyer et al., 2008; Craig, 2004; Jenkins et al., 2011; Meyer & Oberman, 2001; Porter & Gavin, 2010). However, as Margaret G. Spinelli (2010) argues, newborn child killing is an unusual outcome of denied pregnancy and may be due to other types of psychopathology. Similarly, Natacha Vellut et al. (2012) argue that we cannot determine the extent to which concealment/denial of pregnancy results in the killing of the baby, as studies of occurrences of neonaticide draw on different sources to those studying concealment/denial, preventing any form of meaningful comparison. Statistical evidence further supports the argument that concealed/denied pregnancy is not a risk factor for neonaticide. Jens Wessel et al. (2002) argue that, in Germany, 1 in every 2,455 pregnancies is denied for the whole term and results in an unexpected birth of a viable newborn. Colette Pierronne et al. (2002; cited in Gonçalves et al., 2014) argue that the rate in France is 1 in 1,000. In Wales, it is estimated by D. Nirmal et al. (2006) that concealed pregnancies occur 1 in 2,500 deliveries. In England and Wales, 642,892 babies were live and stillborn in 2019 (Office for National Statistics, 2020). Using the calculation from Nirmal et al. (2006), approximately 257 concealed/denied pregnancies would have occurred in England and Wales in 2019. While we do not know the exact instances of suspicious perinatal death that occur each year, as discussed in Chapter 1, the estimated figure is far lower than 257 (believed to possibly be between 27 and 63). Thus, it is reasonable to conclude that while the suspicious death of a later-term foetus or newborn child often occurs after a concealed/denied pregnancy, a concealed/denied pregnancy does not clearly indicate the risk of that pregnancy ending in the death of that later-term foetus/baby. Consequently, the arguments made by a number of scholars, that increased surveillance of all women of childbearing age is an appropriate tool to prevent concealed/denied pregnancies and so newborn child death – including regular administration of pregnancy tests (Jenkins et al., 2011; Kaplan & Grotowski, 1996), are an unacceptable and unwarranted response. Furthermore, such a proposed response reflects challenging approaches to women's bodies in relation to sex, pregnancy, and motherhood, which will be examined further in Chapter 4. Instead of viewing concealed/denied pregnancies in the context of surveilling all women for a potential 'reproductive dysfunction', we need to reconceptualise concealed/denied pregnancies and, in connection, women suspected of killing newborn children, which I turn to next.

Crisis Pregnancy

Concealed/denied pregnancies are, by their very nature, abnormal. To say they are abnormal is not to encourage or support a pathologisation of women who experience a concealed/denied pregnancy. Instead, it is to recognise how infrequently a woman responds to pregnancy in such a way, where she has limited or no cognitive awareness of, or engagement with, her pregnancy. The typical response is for a woman to observe and register the usual symptoms of pregnancy, of which most women experience some or all at various points in gestational development: the cessation of menstruation, nausea and/or sickness, an increase in the size of her breasts and their level of tenderness to touch, weight gain and the increased dimensions of the abdomen, and the feeling of the foetus moving. Suspicions (or fears) of pregnancy lead most to complete a pregnancy test, or if the thought of pregnancy has not occurred to the woman, to seek medical advice to determine a reason for the symptoms experience. Upon recognition, if it is unwanted, then there are steps that can be taken to address the pregnancy. If below 24 gestational weeks and wishing for an abortion, then this is one option that can be provided legally.[2] Alternatively, while potentially a more challenging approach if the woman wants to hide her pregnancy from those around her, adoption of the child after the baby is born is a further option.

---

[2]Although see the discussion in Chapter 6 about challenges accessing abortion.

While I am not suggesting that either of these responses to an unwanted pregnancy are 'easy', as women will have different thoughts and reactions towards both,[3] most people would perceive that they are easier options than 'deciding' to keep the pregnancy a secret from the world, to later be surprised by the birth.

Even more abnormal is the pregnancy ending with the woman giving birth alone, resulting in the death of the child around the time of birth. Of those women who experience a concealed/denied pregnancy whereby the concealment/denial continues until the woman goes into labour, it is likely that only a very small number of those women will experience an 'easy'-enough labour that means they will not determine that they need to seek medical assistance for the symptoms experienced.[4] Therefore, only a handful of women come to a situation where they labour and deliver alone, which results in the death of the foetus/baby. One of the few large-scale studies we have on the outcome of concealed/denied pregnancy supports this hypothesis. In their study of the frequency of denied pregnancy in Berlin over a one-year period, Jens Wessel et al. (2002, p. 1026) determined that the rate at which women who delivered a viable foetus without any presumption of being pregnant prior to birth is 1:2,455. The rate at which those women deliver at home rather than in a medical setting was far higher, 1:9,821. It should be noted that Wessel et al. make a distinction between concealed and denied pregnancies, and these numbers are based on women 'without any sign of or even a weak subjective presumption of the existing pregnancy', which will impact the numbers. Nevertheless, the data indicate that when labour begins, most women seek medical support due to the symptoms of giving birth.

As with concealment/denial studies, the neonaticide[5] literature has also attempted to profile 'perpetrators'; however, this research presents a fractured picture of the characteristics of the women who kill newborn children. This lack of consistency can be partly explained by the nature of individual studies. For example, Kristen Beyer et al. (2008) argue that psychiatric studies often include older women, whereas criminological literature tends to identify younger women. Similarly, the sources of data that a study utilises can also impact the conclusions drawn. Lillian De Bortoli et al. (2013), for example, reviewed studies conducted in prisons, psychiatric units, and in the general population, finding that higher rates of mental disturbance were reported in studies conducted in psychiatric units. Nevertheless, even with this caveat, key findings can be drawn from the literature.[6]

---

[3]For research on abortion stigma, see Kumar et al. (2009); Hoggart (2017); and Bommaraju et al. (2016). For discussion of responses to women who decide to have their child adopted following birth, see Marshall (2012).

[4]With thanks to Professor Elselijn Kingma for this point.

[5]I use this term here as it is the term employed in the literature.

[6]Due to the social, cultural, and religious contexts of newborn child killing, the literature reviewed is focused on Australia, Europe, New Zealand, and North America. Thus, literature that has focused on the killing of baby girls in countries such as India and China, due to female children being perceived to have less value than males, has not been included. This is a very different form of newborn child killing, which is beyond the scope of this study. There is limited evidence to suggest that newborn child killing in the context examined here has any form of sex-based bias in relation to the infant.

Neonaticide is almost exclusively a female crime: almost all research identifies only female perpetrators.[7] Much of the literature constructs a stereotype of the neonaticidal woman: she is young, often a teenager, single, lives with her parents, comes from a low socio-economic background, and has few economic, social, and emotional resources to deal with the pregnancy (see Alder & Baker, 1997; Camperio Ciani & Fontanesi, 2012; Craig, 2004; d'Orbán, 1979; Friedman et al., 2012; Porter & Gavin, 2010; Resnick, 1969, 1970). Many of the women are also described as 'passive', not taking active steps to address the pregnancy (Amon et al., 2012; Beyer et al., 2008; Brozovsky & Falit, 1971; Spinelli, 2001). Nevertheless, cases of non-stereotypical neonaticidal women have been presented in other studies, including this one. For example, perpetrators older than teenagers have been identified in numerous studies (Beyer et al., 2008; Friedman et al., 2005; Meyer & Oberman, 2001; Vellut et al., 2012). A review by Sabine Amon et al. (2012), of coroners' reports and death certificates in Finland and Austria, concluded that the perpetrators' average age was 28. There is also dispute in the literature about perpetrators' socio-economic background. For example, Kristen Beyer et al. (2008), in their review of law enforcement case files in the United States, concluded that the majority of the offenders were middle class, with only 5 out of 37 women identified as working class. Also, a review of French judicial files by Natacha Vellut et al. (2012) concluded that no distinctive socio-demographic profile could be identified. A review of cases in the United States using newspaper reports, conducted by Cheryl L. Meyer and Michelle Oberman (2001), found that the women came from diverse socio-economic backgrounds and across ethnic groups. Many studies reported that perpetrators are not always single, childless and living with their parents. Sabine Amon et al. (2012) noted that 16 of 28 perpetrators were married or living with a partner, and all 16 reported having sex during the pregnancy, while Kristen Beyer et al. (2008) found that 15 of 40 perpetrators had experienced previous pregnancies, with 11 women having living biological children. Therefore, a review of the literature supports a key finding of this study: there is no 'typical' woman who commits neonaticide.

As a consequence, we need to conceptualise concealed/denied pregnancies that end in the death of the foetus/baby in social context, rather than through individual characteristics. In contrast to seeing the pregnancy as a reproductive dysfunction experienced by a particular 'type' of woman, we need to understand the situation as a product of the environment in which the woman lives and becomes pregnant. This analysis is supported both by the cases presented in this research and also by academic literature that has focussed on the wider social circumstances of the lives of women who conceal/deny pregnancy, and give birth alone, resulting in a dead baby.

'Crisis pregnancy' is the term I use to conceptualise the pregnancies experienced by the women in the cases analysed here (Milne, 2019). Crisis pregnancy refers to an instance where a woman feels unable to determine how to approach her pregnancy and what decisions to make about the future of the pregnancy/

---

[7] I have identified two studies that include male perpetrators, both studies draw their findings from criminal justice sources (Beyer et al., 2008; Makhlouf & Rambaud, 2014).

foetus/child, causing her a crisis. An unwanted pregnancy is not necessarily a crisis pregnancy so long as services are available to support the woman to terminate that pregnancy if she so wishes. Similarly, while a crisis pregnancy may be an unwanted pregnancy, this is not always the case, as argued by Natacha Vellut et al. (2012).

One of the factors that connects women who experience crisis pregnancies is the high level of vulnerability they experience (Fineman, 2008) and a substantial level of stress and distress caused by the context of the pregnancy. Previous studies have highlighted the shame and fear that surround the women who experience crisis pregnancies that result in the death of the late-term foetus/baby. In their review of law enforcement files in the United States, Kristen Beyer et al. (2008) conclude that women are often motivated by fear, associated with shame and guilt of being pregnant, and concern about the reaction of parents, partners, and others if the pregnancy is discovered. Similarly, a review of cases from the United States by Cheryl L. Meyer and Michelle Oberman (2001) led them to conclude that overwhelming fear and shame of pregnancy explains women's behaviour. In many of the cases in their sample, women were living with other sources of stress, such as religious or social values governing sexuality, insecure immigration status, financial hardship, and domestic violence and abuse. Further studies have also reported women's feelings of fear of rejection or abandonment by their social circle if the pregnancy is discovered, leading to the concealment/denial of the pregnancy and resulting in the woman birthing alone, often shocked by the experience she is facing (Alder & Baker, 1997; Amon et al., 2012; Wheelwright, 2002). Similar vulnerabilities and situational stresses and crises are apparent in the cases analysed in this book, as outlined in Table 2.2. As with Table 2.1, this is 'reported' data taken from the transcripts, so cannot be assumed to provide a full account of the women's lives, and information should be assumed to be partial. For example, in sentencing Alice, in relation to claims that Alice survived intimate partner violence and abuse, the judge stated,

> I have heard no evidence about it, nor do I think that it is either necessary or appropriate to do so. I make no findings in relation to those allegations.

Table 2.2.   Context of Pregnancies.

Alice	'Difficult upbringing' (judge sentencing).
	Relationship with her partner ended, leaving her to solo parent three children aged under five and then discovering she was pregnant: 'the defendant was suffering from postnatal depression following the birth of her third child… and when her partner left things clearly began to spiral out of control' (judge sentencing).
	Believed if the fourth pregnancy was discovered all four children would be removed from her care.

Table 2.2.   (*Continued*)

Bethany	History of mental health concerns, including reports of paranoid hallucinations.
	Reports of intimate partner violence and abuse.
Elizabeth	Intellectual disability.
	History of crisis pregnancies.
	Living with two children 'in very cramped conditions without a partner in a foreign country, unable to speak English and without the immediate prospect of a job' (judge sentencing).
Fiona	No evidence she was aware of her pregnancy.
	No further background information provided.
Gwen	Described as having a 'miserable life' (judge sentencing).
	Survivor of intimate partner violence and abuse.
	History of crisis pregnancies.
	Felt unable to tell her mother about the pregnancy. 'Her intention was always to address the issue with her family which she found extremely difficult, particularly with her mother' (defence mitigation).
	Feared having her other children removed from her care.
Hannah	Strict family rules and customs.
	Believed could not have a child outside of marriage and feared family reaction to her pregnancy, so kept the pregnancy secret from them.
	Her family disapproved of her partner.
Hayley	History of crisis pregnancies.
	Became pregnant in the context of an affair.
Imogen	Psychiatrist concluded that she concealed the pregnancy as a consequence of a 'several psychological defence mechanisms' (defence mitigation).
Jessica	History of crisis pregnancies.
Lily	Living in a violent and abusive relationship.
Nicole	Described by the defence as socially and emotionally isolated.
	Relationship with her partner, who she was co-habiting with, had broken down.
	Became pregnant in the context of an affair.
	Her father died a few weeks before the child was born.
Olivia and Michael	Both described by the police involved in the case as 'very vulnerable people… in the sense of their backgrounds, their chaos' (Olivia defence mitigation).
	Olivia previously told by her Grandfather, whom she was raised by and lived with after the death of her parents, that if she ever got pregnant she would lose her home.

Table 2.2.   (*Continued*)

Sally	Impoverished, raising three children alone.
	Alcohol and drug abuse.
	Survivor of intimate partner violence and abuse.
Sophie	History of crisis pregnancies.
	Suffered from depressive episodes and mental ill health.
	'Suffering from mild depression, anxiety and panic symptoms whilst pregnant' (judge sentencing).
Tanya	Became pregnant as a result of unwanted sex, which she felt forced to participate in (defined as not rape by the court).
	Experienced post-traumatic stress disorder as a consequence of the sexual attack, resulting in flashbacks to the attack every time she thought about the pregnancy. Acted to silence the child as the noises it made post-birth trigger flashbacks to the attack.

Crisis Pregnancy Leading to a Suspected Homicide

One of the key debates in the neonaticide literature is the extent to which women are in control of their actions at the time they cause or allow the death of the baby, including their state of mind. Scholars argue widely that neonaticidal women are not psychotic and that psychopathology is rare (Amon et al., 2012; Beyer et al., 2008; Craig, 2004; d'Orbán, 1979). After reviewing the literature, Theresa Porter and Helen Gavin (2010) conclude that women's 'actions of concealing the pregnancy, labour, and corpse strongly suggest they are able to function in their own best interest' (p. 108). Indeed, many scholars appear to consider the actions of the women to be for the purpose of personal gain or self-preservation in ridding themselves of an unwanted child (Camperio Ciani & Fontanesi, 2012; Friedman et al., 2012; Makhlouf & Rambaud, 2014). Studies of this nature provide limited context to the lives of women suspected of perinatal homicide, failing not only to take into consideration the vulnerabilities of women who experience a crisis pregnancy, as argued above, but also the impact of the fear and anxiety surrounding the pregnancy.

Cheryl L. Meyer and Michelle Oberman (2001) conclude that the death of the child happens as a consequence of the active fear and cognitive denial of pregnancy experienced by the women. This leads them to postpone any decision about the pregnancy until it is too late and they are giving birth alone: the birth comes as a shock to the woman. They argue that the motivation for killing comes from the fear and panic, rather than anger. It is common for women not to remember the birth, and some women, with a more profound denial, will not recall the pregnancy. Spinelli (2003) draws similar conclusions after conducting psychiatric interviews with 17 women in the United States who were accused of killing their newborn children. The aim of the interviews was to determine the mental status of the women at the time of the offence in order to assist the courts with the cases. Spinelli categorised the women as having unassisted births associated with dissociative psychosis in 10 cases, dissociative hallucinations in 14 cases, and intermittent amnesia at delivery in 14 cases. All the women in her study described 'watching' themselves during the birth. Twelve experienced dissociative hallucinations ranging from an internal commentary to critical and argumentative voices, 14 experienced brief amnesia, and 9 described associated psychotic symptoms at the sight of the infant. Following the dissociation hallucination and amnesia, the women awoke to find a dead newborn child whose presence they could not explain. The women lived in a context of social isolation, emotional neglect, leading chaotic lives, and with 'bizarre' and strained relations with their parents. Two psychiatric case studies presented by Morris Brozovsky and Harvey Falit (1971) provide similar accounts. Both women in the case studies denied knowledge of their pregnancies and Brozovsky and Falit conclude that, in these situations, the birth of the child is a shock to the woman. Denial continued through labour and only ended when the babies began to cry. Brozovsky and Falit hypothesise that it is the end of the denial, accompanied by the overwhelming fear of abandonment by family which prompted the initial denial, that leads women to kill the child.

Similar psychological responses, as a consequence of the context of the pregnancy and the women's wider lives, are reported in a number of the cases examined here. For example, in Gwen's case, a psychiatrist concluded:

> [...] the defendant left the baby because she was overwhelmed by auditory hallucinations, panic and fear of losing her other [children] if she was unable to cope with the new baby and your Honour may be able to understand that to a certain extent – that fear to a certain extent – given the history of two previous children being taken into care, one taken into care at birth and that has clearly traumatised her to a significant extent and that fear plays on her mind significantly and so there was a real fear here that she may lose her other children. (Gwen, defence mitigation)

Similarly, Bethany's report to the police:

> She was recounting in detail what had happened and about clearing up: 'I cleaned up the bathroom as best I felt able and I wasn't feeling well physically or emotionally. Emotionally my head was all over the place with what had happened. The whole situation right from the start with the pain really affected me, affected my emotional state and my mental state massively. I felt a complete mixture of emotions. I've no idea why I didn't phone an ambulance when I wasn't in the right state to be dealing with it myself. I've absolutely no idea why I bagged the foetus up and put it in the bin in the kitchen because that behaviour is completely out of character for me. It completely goes against the way I would act on a normal basis and I feel like I was just on autopilot, if you will, just doing things without even thinking, without consideration. I wasn't acting in a way I would on a normal day because my mind was all over the place'. (Bethany, defence summing up)

A psychiatrist's conclusions about Fiona:

> [...] Fiona appeared to have been genuinely unaware of her pregnancy and [the psychiatrist] found no evidence of any real criminal intent. Her actions appear to have been driven by panic and the effects of both mental and physical shock. He further says, and I quote from him, 'I am clear that these effects of physical shock are apparent in her account and that these had almost certainly temporarily adversely affected her levels of judgment and decision making'. (Fiona, prosecution opening)

And the psychiatrist's retelling of the account provided by Tanya:

> Her waters broke at 4 a.m. on ... and she had abdominal cramps. She knew when her waters broke that she must be pregnant and was about to have a baby. She wanted to scream but something was stopping her. She was overwhelmed by the urge to push. She had absolutely no pain. She felt outside herself, staring down at herself. Everything felt unreal and strange. She felt very confused and felt she could not turn for help. Her body felt extremely numb. At the time she had flashbacks of the incident when she was raped. She felt very abnormal, a sense of climbing out of her body and staring down at herself. She gave birth. She cut the cord with scissors. There was a great deal of blood. She panicked. She used makeup wipes to mop up the blood from inside her legs. She heard the baby gurgling. She pushed a wipe down the baby's throat. She was panicked by hearing him trying to make breathing and gurgling noises. She wanted the noises to stop. She put the tissues deep into his throat and kept them there until she thought he had stopped breathing but wasn't sure as it all happened in a daze. (Tanya, prosecution opening)

The conclusion from the cases, as supported by the literature, is that the context of a woman's life before she becomes pregnant, and how that pregnancy is experienced as a consequence, has a significant impact on her engagement with her pregnancy – her concealment/denial and thus a crisis pregnancy – as well as her behaviour around the time of the birth, and so the death or near-death of the baby. Michelle Oberman (2003) has come to a similar conclusion, arguing that maternal filicide is deeply embedded in and responsive to the societies in which it occurs. Similarly, Natacha Vellut et al. (2012, p. 563) argue that the context for neonaticide is formed in relation to the characteristics of the woman, the lack of social existence granted to the foetus by both the woman and the people around her, and the nature of the woman's relationships with those around her, 'leading to situations of secrecy and isolation'.

Crisis Pregnancy in the Dock

I have advocated that cases of suspicious perinatal death need to be understood and explained in the social context in which they occur, with an appreciation of the experience of pregnancy and the woman's subsequent actions or inactions, rather than through an individualised narrative of pregnancy dysfunction. When analysing court transcripts of the cases presented here, two points become clear: the courts generally do not appreciate and consider the context of crisis pregnancy, and that this lack of understanding results in and facilitates a construction of the women as acting intentionally and deliberately to kill or harm their foetuses/newborn children.

The Norm of Pregnancy

One feature of many of the cases that illustrates the lack of appreciation or understanding of crisis pregnancy is the extent to which pregnancy is presented as something normal that women experience, and that women should engage with and respond to easily. For example, a consultant obstetrician and gynaecologist who gave evidence about Jessica's time in hospital after she had killed her baby, gave an overview of 'the physical changes that a woman undergoes in pregnancy', such as:

> Late 28 weeks [i]nto [pregnancy] he said the woman, mother would definitely be feeling movement in the uterus .... He went on to say that these matters do not necessarily apply in every pregnancy, it varies from pregnancy to pregnancy. (Jessica, judge summing up)

However, no evidence was presented that, for women who experience a crisis pregnancy, symptoms may be dulled, if not absent (Brezinka et al., 1994; Milstein & Milstein, 1983; Spielvogel & Hohener, 1995).

A further example of pregnancies being seen as 'normal', and so not considered a challenge for a woman to address, is presented in Imogen's case. The suggestion being made is that, after discovering she was pregnant, it should have been a simple process of ending an unwanted pregnancy:

JUDGE: So the situation, looking back historically at this, making no moral judgment at all because that's no purpose of the court whatever, as of January, had she taken up the recommendation of her General Practitioner to go to the Marie Stopes clinic, forthwith basically, she could have had, for her own reasons, and probably quite discreetly if she had have wished, a termination.

PROSECUTION: Yes.

JUDGE: And that would have been the end of it.

PROSECUTION: It would.

JUDGE: And no unlawfulness would have occurred. But for her own reasons, and I would welcome some explanation as to this in due course, she delayed and delayed to a point when it is no longer lawful, or it was no longer lawful for the termination to take place, and thus she had to see it through.

PROSECUTION: She buried her head firmly in the sand and took no action or made no provision whatsoever ... (Imogen, prosecution opening)

In Sophie's case, it is presumed that if she knew she was pregnant then she must have known the developmental stage of her pregnancy:

PROSECUTION: ... the defendant knew that this pregnancy was sufficiently advanced for her to know that she was aborting a foetus that was otherwise capable of being born alive.

...

JUDGE: ... How – if you accept the defendant may not have known how far advanced this pregnancy was, how does, why does it follow that she knew that this was a viable foetus?

...

PROSECUTION: We accept that because this defendant had not sought any medical assistance, because she hadn't had any of her, the normal antenatal treatment, she would not have known with that sort of pinpoint accuracy. But the point at which she started to search the internet for articles in relation to, for example, the baby born at 24 weeks, which would have been when her foetus would have been about 24 weeks, is indicative of the fact that she knew that albeit she may not have known it was 32 to 34 weeks, she would have known that it wasn't far off that figure, and she had been pregnant before.

JUDGE: But of course a fully rational person would work it all out from some certain basic biological facts.

PROSECUTION: Yes.

JUDGE: Yes. We are not quite there, are we?

PROSECUTION: Yes, well, I accept that, but also she had experienced a previous pregnancy. (Sophie, prosecution responding to defence mitigation)

The judge's comment about a 'rational' person knowing the developmental stage of pregnancy focusses crisis pregnancy back on an individual woman experiencing a 'reproductive dysfunction'. Similarly, the prosecution's final comment about Sophie having prior experience of pregnancy is made with full knowledge that her first pregnancy was 'concealed' and resulted in her giving birth to a live born child, negating not only the current circumstances of a crisis pregnancy but also Sophie's history of such an experience.

The negation of women's experiences of previous crisis pregnancies is a reoccurring factor in the cases. For example, in Hayley's case, the judge appears to suggest that intellect and education level will impact the likeliness of a crisis pregnancy occurring. He then goes on to equate her previous pregnancy experiences as a reason why she should not have acted as she did, as if previous pregnancies would negate a crisis:

> You are a woman who obtained sufficient A Levels to attend ... University ... You have experience of childbirth, of abortion, and indeed of adoption, and you must have full knowledge of the developmental stages of the child in the womb as well as the lawful limits on abortion of which you were expressly told. (Hayley, judge sentencing)

Later, during her sentencing appeal, a more nuanced perspective of Hayley's reproductive history is presented as part of the hearing that resulted in a dramatic reduction of her prison sentence:

> Hayley is a married woman with two young children and an obstetric history which on any view would alert the reader to the potential for difficulty ... aged 21, she presented at hospital at 23 weeks' gestation. She did not return again until full term and she delivered a child immediately surrendered for adoption. [the next year] she presented at hospital at 23 to 25 weeks' pregnant and had a termination. [two years after] she presented at hospital seeking a termination. Her pregnancy had hitherto been concealed. The scan showed it was too far advanced. She gave birth to one of her children on [date]. [two years later] ... she presented at hospital in labour. Once again, the pregnancy had been concealed. Without going any further, we venture to suggest that it is a history which throws out the potential for disturbance, personal misery and entrenched problems. (Hayley, sentencing appeal)

Similarly, during Jessica's trial, her first crisis pregnancy was used as evidence by the prosecution that she should have known how to respond when she experienced her second crisis pregnancy:

> She was at home at about 11:00 in the evening and gave birth into a toilet.

...

First of all, you heard [evidence from Jessica's Mother]. Her daughter was screaming she had had a baby and she did not know she was expecting. She was on the toilet and screaming. You can hear on the recording that [Jessica's Mother] is saying to Jessica, 'Get off the toilet', saying that her husband was holding the baby and then she handed the phone over to [Jessica's Father] ... He gave details of the mother [Jessica], not knowing she was pregnant.

...

[Jessica giving evidence] The 999 call [about the birth of her living child] was put to her and it was suggested to her at the time that nobody was angry or violent and confused. She wasn't angry or violent and confused. And she said she was shocked and distressed at the time of [Jessica's living child]'s birth. But she was able to say that she was worried her mum might be angry. Yes, she said she was able to think clearly with [her living child]. She was asked what she would have done if no one else had been there with [her living child]. And she said, well, it wasn't what happened. She wouldn't have taken her to a waste ground. She couldn't answer. She said she wasn't the kind of person to hurt a fly. She wasn't refusing to answer the questions. She just couldn't answer something she couldn't remember. (Jessica, judge summing up)

Crisis Pregnancy as Evidence of Motive

The presumption in these cases, that pregnancy is a normal and easy experience for women to acknowledge and respond to, has an impact on how the women are presented, either in sentencing or as part of their trials. One of the key consequences of the lack of examination or consideration of the impact of a crisis pregnancy is that the women look deceitful for 'concealing' their pregnancies and keeping them secret from the people around them. For example, in Imogen's case, her perceived 'lies', which included hiding her pregnancy, added to her culpability in the eyes of the judge:

Thereafter, you sought to deceive everyone in a lattice work of lies. Your lies included the following. First, the deception of your parents and partner in several ways throughout this whole saga. Second, you lied to the Marie Stopes clinic about the date of conception in order to try to secure a termination when you knew it was too late. Third, you lied to the police from the outset, giving a wholly bogus account of having been raped by a taxi driver ... You told the police this pregnancy was a consequence of rape. That was a downright lie. Fourth, you lied to the police about when you became aware of the pregnancy and other details ...

...

> Many would describe your conduct as wicked. You wanted to
> conceal your pregnancy. You wanted to conceal the birth and the
> death of your son. Your conduct was truly deplorable. (Imogen,
> judge sentencing)

If viewing Imogen's action post-birth through the lens of a crisis pregnancy,
then we may ask what other options she may have felt she had: having concealed
her pregnancy from those around her, been surprised by the birth, found herself
with a dead child (one way or another), and therefore a body that needed to be
explained. Continuing the denial of the baby's existence is perhaps the most logical solution for a woman in such a situation. Considering what we know of crisis
pregnancies, a continuation of the concealment, through disposal of the body
out of panic, offers a more empathetic reading of Imogen's actions, rather than
that she acted purposefully and with planning, as indicated by the judge. Imogen
is the first woman since at least 2000 to have received a custodial sentence for the
offence of concealment of birth.[8]

The construction of women's crisis pregnancies as an intentional act of deceit
allows the prosecution to weave a narrative of motive to murder the infant, as was
the case in Bethany's trial:

> Now, you know that the evidence that Bethany gives to a number
> of other people, but, most importantly, gives you from the witness
> box is that she had no idea she was pregnant. She had not had a
> pregnancy test but when challenged by people about: 'Oh, what
> are you doing this for?' 'Well, I had this feeling, this instinct, this
> gut feeling that I was protecting more than myself' because by the
> time she is saying that – I interrupt myself and say – by the time
> she is making that up, ladies and gentlemen, she has got to explain
> why, despite believing herself not to be pregnant, she is making
> these [internet] searches.
>
> ...
>
> [...] and we are going forward now to [date], an important day
> because of the claim by Bethany that she just finds out that she
> is pregnant on this particular day. Will you look at number 310,
> please. 'Late miscarriage 20-ish weeks'. 'How many weeks' preg-
> nant did you think you were?' she was asked on more than one
> occasion. 'Handful of weeks'. Let us put it somewhere between
> three and maybe five or six. A Mums.net discussion that she has
> clicked on: 'Late miscarriage, 20-ish weeks'.
>
> ...

---

[8]Ministry of Justice, Freedom of Information Request 200908003. Two other people
were also imprisoned for the offence of concealment of birth in 2017. The nature of
the cases (or perhaps one case involving two defendants) is unknown.

> She decided all the way through this pregnancy to lie, to lie to her
> employers about how pregnant she was, to lie to everybody around
> her about how pregnant she was. (Bethany, prosecution closing)

In other cases, evidence of the women searching the internet for pregnancy-
related questions is used to illustrate that they knew they were pregnant. In each
instance, without denial of pregnancy being contextualised as being changeable,
and neither absolute nor total, such evidence creates a picture of deceit. When such
arguments are used as evidence to support a motive for murder, as in Bethany's
and Jessica's cases, a narrative can easily be constructed drawing on the principles
that no woman can be truly unaware she is pregnant, as illustrated in Jessica's trial:

> The prosecution cases that the defendant, with chilling clarity of
> purpose, deliberately and intentionally killed her baby. It was a
> cold-blooded killing intended to conceal the fact of pregnancy
> and the existence of the birth .... The prosecution case is that the
> defendant knew she was pregnant, she deliberately concealed her
> pregnancy despite having a loving family and parents who would
> have supported her. She knew it was no longer possible, upon her
> discovery of the pregnancy to have an abortion. She did not want
> another child, she made no plans for adoption or otherwise for
> the baby. She knew she was in labour when she went outside on
> the night in question. Before going outside, she considered how she
> might harm her baby by dropping it. She went outside so that
> she could give birth in secret. (Jessica, judge summing up)

In both cases, the women maintained that they did not know they were pregnant and so were surprised by the births. With the narrative of 'deceit' about
their pregnancies and the internet searches as evidence, it is not particularly surprising that both were convicted of murder, rather than manslaughter or infanticide. Lack of understanding of crisis pregnancy and assessment of the women's
actions alongside the 'normal' behaviour of pregnant women mean it is not difficult to construct a narrative that both women acted as they did in order to keep
the baby a secret and to facilitate their murderous actions post-birth.

These outcomes are in contrast to Elizabeth's case. Here the prosecution used
similar arguments to explain Elizabeth's experience of pregnancy, as the defence
summarised:

> Well, the way in which she was cross-examined and when the case
> was opened to you, you might have thought that the, the way in
> which it was put was this, that it was a cold blooded, planned in
> advance, murder ... the Prosecution put before you [evidence] to
> show that this was a woman who did not want this child, bore it
> for the full time, carried it within her for nine months and planned
> to execute it upon its birth. That, I'm sorry to be blunt, is what
> she's alleged to have done. That's why I ask you to stand back.
> (Elizabeth, defence closing)

To counter this narrative, the defence drew on the evidence of a forensic psychiatrist who concluded that, at the time of the child's death, Elizabeth was suffering from two recognised medical conditions: a mild intellectual disability and pathological denial of her pregnancy. In cross-examination, the doctor provided the following evidence about pregnancy denial:

> So it was suggested to him that there were two possibilities. One was a genuine pathological denial of pregnancy and the other was an awareness of pregnancy but a choice to deny it. He accepted that those were two possibilities, but he said they were not completely discrete. An awareness of pregnancy, he said, might settle into denial as a means of dealing with it. Dr [name] accepted that if the denial is unconscious and absolute, there is a need to see a psychiatrist, but, if the denial was merely for social convenience, it would not be a medical condition. He said that in the former case the birth will result in a great shock. There would not be such a shock if the person knew she was pregnant. He said that in the former case the person might panic and kill as a way of continuing the denial and that that would indicate an imbalance of the mind. It was suggested to him that if a person knows she is pregnant and kills, that is a different situation. He said that that is so but that is at one extreme end. (Elizabeth, judge summing up)

As can be seen by the judge's summing up of the evidence heard, the prosecution attempted to make the case that Elizabeth's denial of pregnancy was a choice, rather than a medical condition. Evidence of internet searches about pregnancy was used; however, this evidence could be disputed by the fact that Elizabeth was not the sole user of the computer; her sister, whom she lived with, was pregnant at the time, as was a friend who was experiencing problems with her pregnancy, which, argued the defence, explains why Elizabeth might have searched about pregnancy. Furthermore, to directly tackle the issue of people not believing that a woman could not know she is pregnant, the defence argued:

> Denial is the word that the medics use. It may in fact be the wrong word because in order to deny something you sort of know it to be or you might think you know it to be the case but you're denying. And you might, I don't know, and I'm certainly not asking, have struggled with that as a concept, even though one hears about it, one does hear infrequently of news stories where someone gives birth and says that they never knew, you might have struggled with that as a concept. But it's not a flight of fancy. It is a recognised medical condition and it is a state of mind known to the medics. (Elizabeth, defence closing)

Elizabeth was convicted of manslaughter by reason of diminished responsibility. This defence relies on the defendant proving on the balance of probabilities that at the time of the killing, they were suffering from an abnormality of mental function-ing which arose out of a recognised medical condition;[9] thus, the presentation of evidence of the denial of pregnancy as a medical condition was central to Elizabeth's successfully mounted defence. As the judge concluded in sentencing:

> The explanation for your conduct is that you suffered from an abnormality of mental functioning which substantially impaired your ability to form a rational judgment. That arose from a recog-nised medical condition, namely a condition known as a patholog-ical denial of pregnancy, which continued notwithstanding the act of giving birth and the obvious presence of a baby. The denial was not pervasive or absolute but partial. There were times when you suspected that you were pregnant, but those suspicions, to adopt the language of … the psychiatrist, settled into denial. Despite the symptoms of pregnancy, you did not believe or accept that you were pregnant. It is obviously an irrational condition.

> The giving of birth did not bring the denial to an end. On the con-trary, you continued to deny the pregnancy to family and medical personnel. In your irrational condition, the birth was a great shock and induced in you a state of panic. Your actions of killing the baby and then hiding the baby in a suitcase were a manifestation of your irrational condition. (Elizabeth, judge sentencing)

While this understanding of denial of pregnancy falls into the category of individualised reproductive dysfunction – a narrative of this experience of preg-nancy that I and others have argued against – the judge went on to highlight the significant vulnerabilities that Elizabeth was experiencing prior to and during her pregnancy:

> Quite why you developed a pathological denial of pregnancy is unclear, but it is likely to be because of the pressures of living with two of your children in very cramped conditions without a partner[,] in a foreign country, unable to speak English and with-out the immediate prospect of a job. Your intellectual disability, as assessed by two psychologists, probably contributed to your con-dition. (Elizabeth, judge sentencing)

The judge comes very close to indicating that it is the social conditions and context of Elizabeth's life – the poverty and hardship of motherhood – rather than individual psychological conditions, that could be considered the cause of her experience of pregnancy and, subsequently, her act of killing her infant following birth.

---

[9]Homicide Act 1957, s2, as amended by the Coroners and Justice Act 2009, s52(1). *Dunbar* [1958] 1 QB 1, [1957] 2 All ER 737.

Failure to Appreciate a Crisis Pregnancy

The experience of a concealed/denied pregnancy that ends in the death or near-death of the foetus/child is rare. On the face of it, the actions of the women who come to such a situation can be interpreted as the deliberate concealment of the knowledge of her pregnancy, to facilitate the killing of the child and escape from criminal justice sanctions, in order to be rid of an unwanted child. As we will see in Chapter 5, this narrative about women's pregnancies has a long history. To accept this narrative is to accept that women consciously and purposefully hide a pregnancy, plan when and where they will give birth to ensure it does not happen with witnesses present, and take the drastic steps of killing the child or leaving it to die, and then hiding the body – steps taken with clarity and purpose in the postpartum period.

There is now an overwhelming body of evidence that argues that clarity and purpose are not the mindsets of women who face a solo birth after a concealed/denied pregnancy. Instead, terms such as panic, fear, and shock are employed to define their actions or inactions that result in the death of the baby. As I and others have argued, this experience of pregnancy – a crisis pregnancy – needs to be understood in the wider social context of the women's lives. As is evident in the cases assessed here, the experience of a crisis pregnancy results in women acting in extreme ways because of their inability to respond to their pregnancy. As Natacha Vellut et al. (2012) argue, although the majority of the women whose cases they reviewed had some knowledge that they were pregnant, none of them anticipated or prepared for the labour or delivery, and they were unable to confide in a third party with their knowledge of pregnancy. Within this context, the only possible outcome was to give birth in secret, resulting in panic; consequently, the women became victims of their own deception, and the babies died.

What is apparent from the cases of suspicious perinatal death investigated in this study is that the English and Welsh criminal justice system appears to have limited ability to recognise the vulnerability of these women and their experiences of crisis pregnancies. As evidenced here, the lack of appreciation of the consequences of crisis pregnancy has substantial implications for how the actions of the women are understood and responded to in the application of criminal law. In the next chapter, I outline how such perceptions of crisis pregnancy are interwoven with the myths of motherhood, which dictate that all women are natural mothers and set the expectations for 'good' motherhood.

Chapter 3

Mothers in the Courtroom II: The Failure of the 'Mother'

> She died within two hours of her birth, and had you acted appropriately her life could have been saved. (Hannah, judge sentencing)

'Acted appropriately' ... an interesting turn of phrase used by the judge, as he sentenced Hannah after her guilty plea for child cruelty and concealment of birth. While not expanding on what he means by 'appropriate' action, it can be assumed that he was referring to her not taking steps to call for assistance after giving birth to her child; the lack of attention resulting in the child dying. However, it is the word 'appropriate' that is of interest here, rather than Hannah's specific actions. With this language, the judge is suggesting that there was a proper or correct way for Hannah to behave that would be 'natural' or the 'norm' considering the circumstances. However, as noted in Chapter 2, the nature of a crisis pregnancy would negate the principle of responding to the pregnancy by calling for assistance (medical, or from her family). Continuing the denial/concealment of the pregnancy and existence of the child is the logical next step for a woman in this situation, albeit an illegal and undesirable step in the eyes of wider society and the law. Calling for help to save the life of the child as a 'natural' or 'normal', and thus 'appropriate' response is connected to ideas that we hold in society around motherhood and pregnancy. It is these two notions that will be examined over the next two chapters: the ideals of motherhood in this chapter and the concept of the 'responsible' pregnant woman in Chapter 4.

Ideals of motherhood shape expectations for women in all areas of life, whether they have children, plan to have children, or want to have children. The concept of the 'good' mother, and what actions are required/assumed as part of this role and identity are woven through the fabric of society, which in turn impacts representations of women in the courtroom in cases of suspicious perinatal death. In this chapter, I will outline how the women's characters and actions are represented during their criminal hearings in the context of motherhood and mothering. These portrayals will be assessed within the context of feminist theories of the myths of motherhood. As will become clear through this chapter, an interesting aspect about these cases lies in how motherly behaviour and the woman as a 'mother' is assumed in almost all cases. Pregnancy appears to be seen as a signifier

Criminal Justice Responses to Maternal Filicide: Judging the Failed Mother, 51–72
Copyright © 2021 by Emma Milne
Published by Emerald Publishing under an Exclusive Licence
doi:10.1108/978-1-83909-620-420211005

of motherhood – to be pregnant is to be a mother; this connection is discussed in more detail in the next chapter. As outlined in Chapter 1, court hearings are sites where narratives are constructed to explain and contextualise the behaviour of the defendant. And so, in analysing how motherhood is portrayed in these cases, we can assess how motherhood is understood in relation to these women and in relation to women in general.

The Myths of Motherhood

As outlined in Chapter 2, it is well reported in feminist literature that representations of women in criminal hearings and media reporting, and consequently the presentation of her culpability, are closely connected to how neatly a woman's character and behaviour is perceived to align with gender norms (see, e.g., Carlen, 1983; Eaton, 1986; Lloyd, 1995; Worrall, 1990). For women defendants, this mostly means constructing women as the 'good' mother/caretaker, as illustrated by M. J. Gathings and Kylie Parrotta's (2013) research from North Carolina in the United States. They note that as a defendant's guilt is rarely contested, the defendant and attorney work as a 'performance team' to construct an impression of self that will elicit a lighter sentence by offering accounts that conform to the institutionalised 'symbol bank' recognised within the courtroom (Gathings & Parrotta, 2013, p. 682). Such a practice of presentation and/or representation of the defendant in line with motherhood ideologies can be witnessed in cases of suspicious perinatal death. Drawing upon and using tropes of 'good' motherhood is completed by each member of the court – the prosecution, defence, and judge, as well as witnesses, where they are heard and/or reported. To understand and explore the significance of these tropes, it is necessary to explore the myths of motherhood and how they work in wider society and so are drawn into courtroom narratives.

Feminist scholars have identified motherhood as a site of gender-based oppression for women (Caplan, 2013; Johnston & Swanson, 2006; Rich, 1986). Women who mother not only shoulder the burden and exploitation of the unpaid labour of caring for and raising children. They are also required to endure and navigate the messages and ideals that surround motherhood, which uphold and promote maternal care for children as the best and 'natural' care. These messages can be summarised in feminist literature as the 'myths of motherhood'.

Myths are defined as uncontested and unconscious assumptions that are so widely accepted that the cultural and historical origins are no longer remembered (Barthes, 1972). Thus, mothering is presented as 'natural' and 'instinctive', rather than cultural, political, economic, and historical (Hrdy, 2000). The myths hold merit due to the ideologies that shape popular thoughts and beliefs of mothering. The dominant ideology in a society represents that society's dominant group: the dominant group in Europe and North America is white, heterosexual, middle- and upper-class men. Within the patriarchal system that operates in these societies, the myths of motherhood facilitate locking women into biological reproduction, denying them identities and selfhood outside of mothering (Glenn, 1994). Thus, many feminists have identified the perpetuation of patriarchy as the underlying causes of these myths (Chodorow, 1978; Hays, 1996; Rich, 1986; Thurer, 1994).

The myths of motherhood maintain that to be a woman is to be a mother, and motherhood and mothering are natural, universal, and unchanging for all women. The myths draw on the perception that women are inherently caring, nurturing, and self-sacrificing, and such behaviours originate from biology and a woman's ability to birth children. As Ann Oakley (1974, p. 186) argues, the myths are based on three beliefs: 'that all women need to be mothers, that all mothers need their children, and that all children need their mothers'.

Feminist theorisation of motherhood does not lie in (and of) the fact that most women have the capacity to conceive a child, gestate, give birth, and lactate, but that some women choose to partake in the nurturing and raising of children. As Arendell (2000, p. 1193) argues, the issue for consideration is 'How these biological activities are culturally organised and given meaning'. As a consequence, the myths insist that:

> no woman is truly complete or fulfilled unless she has kids, that women remain the best primary caretakers of children, and that to be a remotely decent mother, a woman has to devote her entire physical, psychological, emotional, and intellectual being, 24/7, to her children. (Douglas & Michaels, 2005, pp. 3–4)

Inevitably, the myths set unachievable standards of perfection for women who are mothers, while also constructing and maintaining a popular belief that all women should want to be mothers and motherhood is the true destiny for women to fulfil. The myths saturate society and social and cultural interaction (Dally, 1982; Gillis, 1997; Johnston & Swanson, 2003; Kaplan, 1992).

Through the myths, the notion of the 'good' mother is constructed – a woman who conforms to the myths – in contrast to the 'bad' mother. Today, the 'good' mother is the intensive mother, defined by Sharon Hays (1996, p. 8) as a method of child-rearing 'constructed as child-centred, expert-guided, emotionally absorbing, labour-intensive, and financially expensive'. In contrast, the 'bad' mother is identifiable by her 'deviant' caregiving practices and failure to conform to the ideal. The line between 'good' and 'bad' mothering is neither fixed nor stable, rather it is blurred and shifts over time and space (Smart, 1996; Thurer, 1993). Such an example can be seen in guidance around leaving a baby to cry and 'self-settle'; previously seen as the practice of a 'good' mother so as not to fuss over a baby, now characterised as the neglectful treatment of an infant by a 'bad' mother.

While the nature of myths is that they are presented as if from nowhere and no one, they are perceived to be applicable everywhere and to everyone. This aspect of the myths of motherhood is specifically problematic as the myths are rooted in class and race, as well as gender. The ideal 'good' mother is based upon the white, middle-class, married, heterosexual, able-bodied woman who has the exclusive responsibility for mothering her biological children, focussing her time and activities solely on their care and well-being (Glenn, 1994; Sanger, 1992). The further away a woman's identity and lived reality sit from this ideal, and the fewer advantages and greater vulnerabilities she has in life (Fineman, 2008), the harder it is for her to adhere to the myths and so adopt the role of the 'good' mother.

An example of the discriminatory nature of the myths is presented by Solinger (1994) in her review of the historical responses to illegitimacy in the United States – white single mothers were considered 'trouble' but 'redeemable', whereas black single mothers were labelled 'deviant' by the dominant culture.

The power and strength of the myths are evident in the perpetuation of such ideologies despite substantial evidence to the contrary. Much feminist work has been centred around disputing that women's roles as mothers and actions connected to mothering are not 'natural' and do not originate from women's biology, but rather motherhood and mothering is socio-cultural and is a learnt behaviour (see Chodorow, 1978; Ruddick, 1989, as examples of this early feminist work). This work is not without its limitations, particularly as it assumes a universal notion of womanhood, rather than considering the intersecting characteristics that make up individuals' lives. For example, see Patricia Hill Collins (1994, 2000) who argues that much feminist theorising about motherhood has projected white, middle-class women's concerns as universal to all women, whereas for women from black or minoritised communities the subjective experience of motherhood is inextricably linked to socio-cultural concerns of the racial ethnic community. Nevertheless, a key principle of feminist theorisation of motherhood is that it is not natural and inherent to women, as is evident in the fact that not all women mother, and the nurture and care of children is not inevitably or exclusively completed by women (Forcey, 1994; Rothman, 1994; Schantz, 1994).

The ideologies of motherhood also have specific historical and social contexts. As Carol Smart (1996, p. 48) argues, motherhood is a 'highly contrived and historically specific condition', with the ideal image being drawn from 'a class-specific, historically located ideal of what a mother should be' (p. 45). Although ideals are not accepted unquestioningly by all women, Smart argues that alternative ways of mothering are difficult to maintain when they oppose the dominant ideal, particularly when perceived to lack legitimacy. However, 'there is nothing natural in these manifestations of supposedly instinctual behaviour' (Smart, 1996, p. 47; see also Bassin et al., 1994; Glenn et al., 1994; Hays, 1996). Focussing on the historic, social, cultural, and political influences that shape the myths of motherhood allows us to challenge the principles of the 'naturalness' of motherhood and the notion of mothering behaviour as an instinctive element of being a woman.

The impacts of the myths of motherhood are far-reaching for women who are mothers, as they influence their behaviour and decisions. However, they also impact women who are not mothers, women who mother children who are not biological offspring, and men who care for children. Evelyn Nakano Glenn (1994) argues the impact of the myths is to conflate 'woman' with 'mother': making women appear as if they are undifferentiated and unchanging, as opposed to men who appear with historic specificity in a variety of roles and contexts. Thus, the myths conflate actors and activities, recognising only women, and specifically birth-mothers, as nurturers and caregivers. Consequently, people who are not birth-mothers are excused from the responsibilities of raising children, recognition is denied to those who provide nurturance and care but are not birth-mothers, and nurturance and care are assumed to only flow in one direction. Furthermore, Glenn argues that the myths conflate mothers and children, assuming they are one entity with one set of needs, denying personhood and agency to both, and failing to acknowledge that mothers' and children's interests may conflict. Lack of recognition of distinct subjects with different needs is also significant in relation to the interaction between the pregnant woman and the foetus, explored in Chapter 4. The impact of these conflations, described by Glenn, hinders women from achieving beyond the role of mother and places pressure on those women who are not mothers to take up the role. However, it also impedes all individuals who parent outside the 'norms' of white, middle-class motherhood constructed by the myths of motherhood, such as people of colour (Dill, 1988; Roberts, 1995); lesbian, gay, and bisexual people (Hequembourg & Farrell, 1999; Pollack, 1990); individuals who do not live within the gender binary (Halberstam, 2010); single parents (Dowd, 1997); young parents (Phoenix, 1991); poor parents (Fineman, 1995a); adoptive parents (Letherby, 1994); disabled parents (Frederick, 2015), and numerous others. The list is extensive as the majority cannot live up to the myths and norms of parenting as constructed through heteronormative, white, capitalist patriarchy.

The inability to live up to the myths and the construction of individual women as either 'good' or 'bad' has led scholars to theorise a particular form of gender oppression referred to as mother-blame (Caplan, 1998; Caplan & Hall-McCorquodale, 1985; Garey & Arendell, 2001; Jackson & Mannix, 2004). Children with problems, or children as problems, are often linked to the social situations of their mothers (poor, unmarried, divorced, unemployed) rather than to the social and economic forces that affect the lives of individuals (Arendell, 2000; Garey, 1999; Smith, 1988). Similarly, the feelings of unhappiness or dissatisfaction women may feel as mothers are attributed to the failings of the individual mother, rather than the system: a good mother is a happy mother. As with other factors connected to the cases assessed here, the individualisation of 'problems' remains a focus; identifying the individual woman who 'fails' to conform to the myths as the problem, rather than social, economic, and cultural structures inherent in heteronormative, white, capitalist, patriarchal societies (which is pretty much all of them). The consequence of failure, while felt by most women, notably with feelings of guilt and inadequacy (see Sutherland, 2010), is experienced most keenly by the most vulnerable. It is poorer women, single women, young women, and women from black or minoritised communities who are policed most aggressively and who face greater sanctions for their appearance of failure when compared to the myths (Smart, 1996). This policing is not necessarily completed by the police or even criminal justice authorities, but other institutions of the state, such as child protection services and medical professionals, explored further in Chapter 4 in relation to medical control of pregnancy and pregnant women.

The aim of feminist critiques of the myths of motherhood is to make apparent the structural oppression that exists within the dominant ideology of mothering. It does not aim to be deterministic, nor does it suggest that all women experience motherhood in the same way, even if the myths are consistent (Johnston & Swanson, 2006). Feminists have been keen to stress the distinction, first outlined by Adrienne Rich (1986), between motherhood as a relationship between a woman and her children, and the institution of motherhood, noting that the relationship can and does bring many women satisfaction and joy. By identifying and critiquing the myths of motherhood, feminists are highlighting the impact it has on how women experience mothering and how society responds and acts towards mothers and all women. Their aim is to demonstrate that the myths perpetuate inequalities and hardships for women. However, it is important not to see 'women' as a homogeneous group but to consider the vulnerabilities and struggles individuals and social groups experience due to their intersecting identities.

Suspected Mothers in the Courtroom

In reading the transcripts of the criminal proceedings against women suspected of killing their foetus/infant, one factor that becomes apparent is the ever-present expectation of motherhood, which reflects the myths of motherhood outlined above. The persistence of this narrative seems, on the face of it, jarring, when juxtaposed with the actions or inactions the women are suspected of – causing, or nearly causing, the death of their foetus/newborn baby and thus rejecting motherhood and their role as a mother to that 'child'.

The representations of women next to ideals of motherhood are completed by different parties in the courtroom – the prosecution, the defence, the judge, as well as witnesses – in reporting of their evidence. Each party uses the narratives of the myths of motherhood, and the woman's proximity to the narrative, to assist in crafting their representation of her behaviour and, connected to this, her culpability. Consequently, the woman's behaviour is represented as that of a 'real' mother, or in opposition to that of a 'real' mother. The motherhood ideals that play a central part in the myths of motherhood are apparent within the cases, presented as natural and inherent to the women. Three key points can be discerned from the narratives constructed in the cases: first, that the existence of the pregnancy is the basis of the motherhood narratives and expectations of motherly behaviour by the women: to be pregnant is to be a mother. Second, at no point does anyone question whether the women should be required to be mothers, it is simply assumed she will be. Finally, it is assumed that there is a correct way to behave as a 'mother' and limited scope to deviate from this 'correct' conduct.

The two exceptions to this motherly narrative can be seen in the cases of Fiona and Tanya: during their hearings, motherly responses are not mentioned, hinted at, nor, apparently, considered. Both women were 16 at the time they killed their newborn children. No mention is made by either the prosecution or defence about their role as mothers or even that their responses to their babies were unmotherly. The social 'crisis' that surrounds teenagers as mothers or 'children raising children' is well documented and critiqued within feminist literature (e.g., see Ayres, 2007, 2014; Phoenix, 1991). Nevertheless, social concern over the appropriate minimum age at which it is considered legitimate for a woman to adopt the role of mother continues to dominate in wider society, as evident in media coverage of the 'teen pregnancy rate' (BBC News, 2016) and as will be discussed later in this book. The perception that pregnancy at a young age is a social crisis could potentially offer one explanation as to why neither Tanya nor Fiona's actions and behaviour are presented alongside narratives of motherhood or motherly behaviour. If a perception exists that both women were too young to be mothers, then their actions of rejecting motherhood may be perceived as legitimate, even if the violent nature of the rejection is not.

A Real Mother

One clear example of how the myths of motherhood are used in representations of the women during their court hearings is the portrayals of them as good mothers in general, and that this works as a 'saving grace' for some of the accused women. For a number of the defendants, their good character is discussed in relation to their role as a good and doting mother to existing children. For example, in Lily's case, her offending is attributed to her violent and abusive relationship with the man with whom she co-offended. In contrast, the narrative of her life after surviving the abuse and leaving the relationship is framed around her role as a mother to her other children:

> [...] she went on to have two children, who your Honour will see from those letters she clearly presents as a good mother, she is involved in their lives and in the school life and is somebody who is thought well of by people within that local community. (Lily, defence mitigation)

The defence goes on to note that social services have no concerns with her caregiving despite her offending. Similar arguments are made in Hayley's case, where the defence portrays Hayley as a good mother, with the judge confirming:

> There is no suggestion that she is not anything other than a caring mother for her two children. (Hayley, judge during defence mitigation)

The defence also uses Hayley's role as a mother and the needs of her children as the basis of requesting mercy from a custodial sentence:

> Above all, my Lord, and as an element of mercy, ask that my Lord in passing whatever term is to be passed, be mindful to that again which I have referred, the testament that speaks to her good parenthood of [child 1] and [child 2], that is reflected in, it is not just self-reporting, but in the independent reports from the schools … They are the focus of her life, she loves them unconditionally. (Hayley, defence mitigation)

Such narratives around the women's character are similar to those reported in other research, as discussed (Carlen, 1983; Eaton, 1986; Gathings & Parrotta, 2013; Milne & Turton, 2018; Worrall, 1990).

In contrast to representations of the women's behaviour, in spite of their role as good mothers, Alice's actions of abandoning her child are presented by the judge as occurring as a result of her attempting to be a good mother to her other children. While her decision to conceal her pregnancy and to abandon the baby was perceived negatively by the judge, due to the risk to the newborn child's life, her actions were presented as an understandable motherly response to her situation in relation to her other children. In sentencing, the judge summarised Alice's behaviour as an act of desperation and love for her existing children:

> When she realised she was pregnant, she feared her children would be removed. That, regrettably but understandably, was reinforced by some observations made by members of the family, and thus she decided to conceal her pregnancy. Although the family suspected she was pregnant, she denied it, and on [date] the baby was born and, in panic and desperation, she acted as she did. (Alice, judge sentencing)

The judge accepted that Alice did not want her child to be hurt and that she left the baby in a place where it would soon be found.

Further evidence of Alice's motherly behaviour is drawn from the long-term plans held by social services to reunite Alice with all her children, including the child she abandoned. Therefore, while Alice's act of abandonment of her child is considered to contradict the role of a mother and the accepted understanding of motherly behaviour, it can be interpreted that she maintained the position of a mother, and thereby conformed to the myths, as she was acting in a manner that she felt was best for her other children. She has not rejected the principles of motherly behaviour, nor the expected norms by which to act as a mother. Instead, she fails to achieve success within the boundaries of the dominant discourse – to be a good-enough and competent-enough mother who cares for her children to the required standard. Arguably, therefore, she is presented as the 'bad' mother, but a mother nonetheless. However, an element of motherhood that is assumed in this case is that Alice will extend her motherly behaviour to all of her children, including the foetus she concealed and then abandoned post-birth. Thus, the final child is seen to be requiring her protection and motherly care purely through its existence, on equal terms as her living children: a theme that is reflected in other cases.

In a number of the cases, the woman's identity as a good mother is contested by the prosecution and defence. The contest is clear in Elizabeth's case. The prosecution drew on the fact that she was a mother prior to the pregnancy that she concealed/denied resulting in the death of the baby, and that she is reported to be a good mother by witnesses who gave evidence in the case. They use these points to argue that as she knows how to be a good mother, then her actions around the time of the birth of the child must signify her intent to kill:

> Secondly, why no call for help? Why, if you [*sic.*] baby is stillborn in the circumstances that she still maintains, not ask anybody for

help? Nobody would do that, would they? An experienced mother who's given birth on many occasions in the past gives birth to a baby. (Elizabeth, prosecution closing)

In contrast, the defence use the evidence that Elizabeth is a good mother as the basis for why she would not have intended to kill the child:

> Are we sure this baby was born alive, and, if we are, are we sure that this mother, described by one of her friends, [name], as the best mother in the world, turned or perhaps had planned to be and to become a baby killer? Why? Because the bedroom was a bit cramped and because her life might have been imperfect in another way. (Elizabeth, defence closing)

In both instances, the prosecution and the defence are drawing on motherhood as a natural phenomenon, which has connected instinctive behaviour, and that to intend to kill the baby is to go against such an instinct: the prosecution maintained she went against it to kill, while the defence argue she would not kill her child because of her instincts as a good mother.

A further example of the contestation of good motherhood is apparent in Hannah's case, with the prosecution and defence barristers sparred over her portrayal as a mother. The prosecution's case was built upon the notion that Hannah did not want the child and so rejected motherhood, supported by evidence of her failed attempts to have an abortion and her decision to conceal her pregnancy from her family. The prosecution barrister pointed to Hannah's response following the death of the child as further evidence of her wrongdoing and lack of motherly behaviour, exclaiming, 'And of course the defendant then simply returned immediately to her normal life and sought to keep her secret, it would appear, forever' (Hannah, prosecution opening). Hannah's behaviour of resuming her day-to-day life was remarked upon several times by the prosecution, implying that this was an abnormal response to the situation of a dead child and, therefore, demonstrated her unmotherly behaviour and nature.

In her defence, Hannah's barrister argued that the behaviour that the prosecution construed as unmotherly, namely carrying on with daily life, was in fact evidence of Hannah's motherly behaviour:

> But lest there be any misinterpretation about her behaviour, this is not, I would submit, before you a callous, hard-hearted individual who simply swept this aside and carried on as normal, because she is, after all, a grieving mother, this was her child and within two hours or so of giving birth her child had died. (Hannah, defence mitigation)

The suggestion here is that she was deeply affected by the death of the child because she is a mother and is motherly, which is why her behaviour is so 'odd' for a mother.

It is unclear from the transcript whether either side was successful in its portrayals of Hannah in line with ideals of motherhood, but the judge's comment, quoted at the start of this chapter, about the 'appropriateness' of her behaviour may suggest not. Nevertheless, it is significant that this is one of the standards by which her behaviour and character were judged. As with Alice's case, the narratives are based upon the assumption that the existence of the pregnancy will naturally lead to the exhibiting of motherly behaviour by Hannah. Such an expectation exists in spite of the complex and difficult circumstances that resulted in Hannah perceiving the pregnancy as a crisis, and that Hannah's behaviour would suggest that she did not believe she could be a mother to this child, if, indeed, she wanted or wants to be a mother at all.

Real Mothers Wouldn't Do This

An alternative way that the women are represented in these cases is as not being motherly, thus divorcing their behaviour and character from the natural and inherent role of motherhood experienced by women. In a number of cases a representation of a rejection of motherhood is made plain by the prosecution, used to illustrate the accused women had a motive to cause harm or death to the foetus/child. Much like presenting the concealment of pregnancy as a motive, as explored in Chapter 2, presenting the women as not wanting children or further children is used as an indication of a motive. However, the suggestion that the women did not want to be mothers is connected to a much more fundamental notion of what it means to be a woman and thus the 'inappropriateness' of their actions in not responding as is expected of a woman who is pregnant. For example, in Imogen's case, the argument is made that she did not want a child because she was focussed on her career:

> [Imogen's mother to the police] described her daughter as this, 'Career minded and did not want children at that time', and that may give your Honour a glimpse of some important background to what then transpired. (Imogen, prosecution opening)

The prosecution goes on to outline that it was her lack of desire for the child that led her to reject the pregnancy/child and to not prepare for the birth:

> When pressed on what arrangements were made for post birth, she stated it was her intention to take the baby to a nearby hospital and arrange for adoption to commence at that point, and at that point only
>
> …
>
> She finally accepts in this final interview that the pregnancy was not a result of her alleged sexual assault. She simply did not want to deal with having a child at that time. (Imogen, prosecution opening)

In sentencing, the judge continues with the narrative that Imogen acted as she did due to her focus on her career:

> It is clear to me that you are a young woman with a sense of purpose. You were very career minded. You had a university education. You sought and obtained good employment. There is absolutely nothing wrong with being career minded. In many respects it is very creditable. (Imogen, judge sentencing)

Later, the judge describes the pregnancy as 'inconvenient' to Imogen. An aspect of Imogen's conviction that needs to be borne in mind is that the offence she was charged with and pleaded guilty to – concealment of birth – relates to how a person disposes of the body of a baby and has nothing to do with conduct during pregnancy or desire to be a mother. However, as I have argued elsewhere (Milne, 2019) and as discussed in Chapters 5 and 6, offences such as concealment of birth appear to be used as means to criminalise women's lack of motherly behaviour. The focus on Imogen, apparently placing her career before her 'child', illustrates, once again, the narrative of pregnancy and motherhood being synonymous, and the existence of the pregnancy as a basis for expected maternal behaviour. By juxtaposing her actions with her focus on her career, the suggestion is that a rejection of motherhood for the reasons of non-motherly activity – paid labour outside the home – is both unnatural and indicates motive to harm the 'baby'.

Similar arguments are made by the prosecution in Jessica's case, that she did not want another child:

> It was put to her she didn't want another baby. She said I've never said that … Did you want another child, she was asked. And she then said, if I had one, I would want one in proper relationship. (Jessica, judge summing up)

However, further evidence was provided to build a narrative of her being unmotherly for reasons beyond her declaration of not wanting another child. First, due to her initial lack of bonding with her existing child:

> [Public health nurse] said that her impression of the defendant was that the defendant was very closed, it was difficult to form a relationship with her. It was not a two-way engagement, but perhaps the defendant was a private person. [Public health nurse] told you that she appeared to her the defendant did struggle to bond with [Jessica's living child] in the early stages, but there were no concerns about the care of [Jessica's living child] or the fact that the defendant was capable of meeting [Jessica's living child]'s basic needs. (Jessica, judge summing up)

Second, through evidence of Jessica's emotional reactions after she had killed the baby:

[Social worker] said the defendant showed no emotion. She was not crying or even tearful throughout. She only cried when discussing seeing [Jessica's living child]. [Social worker] thought this was unusual given the loss of a child. With the other concealed pregnancies she would expect upset and crying. [She] felt the defendant was blank and emotionless, which she found, as I say, unusual. There was no focus, she said, on the loss of the baby. All the defendant wanted to do was to talk about seeing [Jessica's living child]. She said she enjoyed being a parent to [Jessica's living child] and was very positive about that. She wasn't showing any signs of shock or emotional connection to what had happened. (Jessica, judge sentencing)

The suggestion here is that there is a natural, motherly response to children, and specifically the loss of a child regardless of the circumstances of the death, and that Jessica is lacking it. The notion of an 'appropriate' emotional response by a woman after her 'baby' has died, and so, that these women have 'unnatural' responses, is presented in other cases:

About ten minutes later another paramedic ... arrived. She also described Sophie as calm and relaxed and [not] distressed in any way

...

Again he [responding police officer] was to observe that she appeared calm and unemotional, but she did become briefly upset when describing the baby being in the toilet, and she said, 'I'm panicking that you're going to come and put me in jail'. (Sophie, prosecution opening)

And to counter the prosecution's narrative of Sophie's emotional response being abnormal, unnatural, the defence argued, not against the notion of a 'normal', 'appropriate', 'motherly' response, but that she acted as she did due to not being able to feel the emotion of the situation at that time:

[...] her actions initially, when speaking to paramedics and initially at the hospital, were those of somebody who at least appeared to a great extent to be in shock. I know that the paramedic in her statement talks about Sophie having no tears, but then goes on to say that she appeared blank, like nothing had happened, then later on it was as if she was in total denial about what had happened. (Sophie, defence mitigation)

Perhaps, the clearest example of an argument that women suspected of peri-natal killing are unmotherly, and that their behaviour is an unnatural response to a pregnancy compared to 'normal' women, can be seen in the arguments put forward by Bethany's defence barrister. In an attempt to convince the jury that hers is not a case of murder, but of manslaughter by reason of diminished responsibility, the defence barrister describes evidence given by the midwife who first treated Bethany upon her attendance in hospital:

> 'And you've passed a baby, haven't you?' was what the nurse said to her, that she said: 'Well, I have. I've managed it, I've sorted it. It weren't alive when it was born'. [midwife] has come across no doubt many women who have lost their babies in circumstances not dissimilar to these but it was the contrast in how that was conveyed to her by Bethany that was the most striking element of that conversation and one which caused the upset. It was the complete lack of emotion, it was the empty, vacant look as she recounted those terrible events. It must have been something to have affected that experienced nurse so much. It was a theme and remains the theme that was repeated across and by a range of both health professionals and police officers in the course of the hours and the days after Bethany's arrival in hospital .... (Bethany, defence summing up)

The barrister goes on to state that, as Bethany's behaviour is strange, as it is not the normal behaviour of a mother or woman, then she must be mentally unwell:

> It is one of the many things that simply cries for an explanation in this case. Why was it like that when you might expect the complete opposite, when a woman had given birth on her own in her own bathroom, the baby had died, why was the presentation by that woman so markedly different? It cries out for an explanation from the health professionals, from the doctors and two psychiatrists say that Bethany's reaction and her demeanour were part of an ongoing mental health problem affecting her at the time and had been doing so for some time previously, an emotional blunting effect and one symptom from the condition she was suffering from at the time. (Bethany, defence summing up)

This presentation of evidence by Bethany's barrister not only draws on the notion that there is a normal and natural way for a mother to behave after her child has died but also that if a woman does not behave like this, then she must be mentally unwell or unstable. The implication is clear – the naturalness of motherhood is so strong and so overwhelming, that women who do not behave accordingly must be ill. Again, the assumptions and beliefs are that the existence of a pregnancy will lead to a 'normal' motherly reaction; it is biologically driven and inherent to women, unless they are sick.

Aside from specific arguments that the women have rejected motherhood and so are culpable for the death or are unnatural in their actions, smaller pieces of information are provided by prosecutors that indicate the women are not acting in a motherly way. For example, information that suggests unmotherly behaviour is sprinkled throughout the prosecution's opening of Hannah's hearing, later to be contested by the defence in their attempt to maintain the image that she is act-ing as a mother. While not specifically labouring the point that these facts of the case indicate non-motherly behaviour, the prosecution's decision to include them is significant. As discussed in Chapter 1, decisions around what to include and discuss – what information will be used to tell the story about the case – are a key element of the construction of narratives about the events and the defendant. For example, how the baby's body was left:

> The paramedics arrived and noticed that the birth fluids had not been washed off the child's body. It was lying, as I have indicated, near the wall, its head was lying on flagstones.

and Hannah's communication about the baby:

> The defendant was taken to … Hospital for examination … she was asked about the birth and she gave some details, but at no stage asked after the child or indeed referred to it at all. (Hannah, prosecution opening)

The indication from the inclusion of both pieces of evidence is to imply further examples of bad-motherly or unmotherly behaviour. Real mothers, women who are motherly, would wash/clean a child post-birth, would take the time to lay out the child's body and not abandon it, with its head on a flagstone, would ask after her child at the first opportunity. The defence attempted to counter Hannah not asking about the child, not by stating that she would have known the baby was dead prior to her arrest and so why would she ask after the well-being of a dead child, but rather by focussing on the fact that:

> physical and emotional trauma that any woman undergoes in childbirth is multiplied to an extent which we can't begin to imag-ine when that happens in isolation, in secret. (Hannah, defence mitigation)

In other words, the defence argue that Hannah would have acted like a 'real' mother, a 'good' mother and asked after the baby but for the trauma experienced by the birth; so, like Bethany and Sophie, she is unmotherly due to being unwell and in shock. Motherly is the norm: the natural response.

A further small, but significant, example of unmotherly behaviour that is pre-sented by prosecution barristers is how the women refer to the child/foetus, with particular attention focussed on references to the baby as an 'it':

> She decided to deal with 'it' and the use of that pronoun is hers, ladies and gentlemen, not mine, that is how she described her baby daughter for some considerable time, certainly until she went into custody. (Bethany, prosecution summing up)

> In [a nurse's] police statement she had said that the defendant had told her that on the Tuesday, the defendant had passed something into the toilet that was larger than a tennis ball. She described it as 'a thing'
>
> ...
>
> It was Nurse [name] who said that the defendant never referred to the sex of the baby, always referring to the baby as 'It'. (Jessica, judge summing up)

Again, the decision to include this information is a subtle suggestion that a real mother would not refer to their child in this way, would not dehumanise the baby.

A connected, and interesting, note here lies in the preparation of the transcripts of these cases. When enquiring of one of the transcription companies how they transcribed the content of the court hearings, the response was 'pretty much verbatim'. In some of the transcripts, when the women refer to the child as 'it', the 'it' is placed in inverted commas, as with Bethany's case above, and here in Tanya's case:

> She was in shock and was scared. She pushed the baby out at 8.30 onto an old blue hoody. She saw 'it' wasn't moving. The cord was around the baby's neck. She said, 'It wasn't moving. So I had to get rid of it'. She cut the cord with scissors from a drawer in her bedroom. She said, 'The whole thing was blue. Lips were purple, blue'. She wrapped 'it' in the jumper. She used a tissue to clean herself up then put the tissue and 'it' in a River Island bag and left it near the bedside table. She then went to the toilet and the placenta came out. She caught it and put it in the bin. She told her mother she had her period. She said to the police, 'it is an "it", still nothing more'. She said she didn't want to see 'it'. (Tanya, prosecution opening)

The decisions about highlighting the women's reference to the foetuses/infants as 'it' would appear to have been made by the transcribers with their use of the inverted commas. It is perhaps the case that the punctuation was included in the transcription to reflect the added emphasis of those words as spoken by the barrister; a challenge of the nature of this source of material is that this is unknown. Either way, a clear emphasis of the women's reference to 'it' is being made, again suggesting that this is unusual behaviour for women in these circumstances.

A final example can be seen in how the women who attempted to access abortions are presented. Out of the 15 women, 4 attempted to access legal abortions for the pregnancy around which the criminal proceedings centre, and a number obtained abortions prior to this pregnancy. The decision to access an abortion and reasoning for this is discussed specifically in Jessica's and Lily's cases. For Jessica, the discussion focussed on her recollection of the termination of a previous pregnancy:

> [...] this is the interview [by police] where she is asked about [a previous] pregnancy and her answer was that she had forgotten about that one. She thought that she had the termination at about nine weeks. She knew that she had been pregnant. She had been in a serious relationship and then he turned vile. She was asked how she could forget about having an abortion, and she said, 'I don't know. It's not something you really talk about'. (Jessica, judge summing up)

Inclusion of this evidence and the suggestion that no woman should forget about a pregnancy or the termination of that pregnancy again points towards a suggestion that she is not a 'real' mother; a woman who is a real mother would always remember a 'child' or potential 'child' and/or the 'trauma' of ending a pregnancy.[1]

In Lily's case, the discussion of her attempts to access an abortion of the pregnancy that would, by Lily's uncontested account, eventually end with the birth of a stillborn child, focusses on the dispute between the prosecution and the defence as to why Lily wanted an abortion. As the prosecution stated:

> [...] the defendant discovered that she was pregnant. She told her GP that she did not want another child as she already had three boys with her ex-husband, and in particular she did not want another male child. She arranged to have the pregnancy terminated. (Lily, prosecution opening)

Later, the defence disputed this suggested reason for her wanting an abortion, stating she did not know the sex of the baby at the time of seeking the abortion and, therefore, could not have been requesting an abortion on the basis of not wanting another boy.

> The defendant does indicate that in this [police] interview that she had expressed that she did not want any more boys because she already had three, but at the time that she went for the termination in this case, she does not indicate that at all. She did not know the sex of the baby. (Lily, defence mitigation)

Afterwards, the prosecution barrister offered an apology for misspeaking, confirming that Lily had told her doctor that she did not want another child, which was why she was seeking an abortion. The misspeak is not in and of itself the concern here, rather it is the determination with which the defence disputed the error and pushed for it to be corrected. Similarly, the judge challenged the prosecution barrister on this point three times during the sentencing hearing, highlighting the inconsistency in the facts presented in the opening speech. The significance lies in the symbolism of the reason given for Lily wishing to access an abortion – not wanting a boy child – and what this reasoning is seen to indicate about her

---

[1] See Bommaraju et al. (2016), Hoggart (2017), and Kumar et al. (2009) for research on abortion stigma.

character and her behaviour. Representations of women accessing abortions have historically been, and today are still, laced with motherhood ideals, entrenched with the myths of motherhood and the notion of worthy and unworthy reasons for an abortion (Amery, 2020; Sheldon, 1997). The level of discussion as to why Lily wanted to end her pregnancy, and the reasoning she gave, would suggest that ideas about 'worthy' and 'unworthy' motivations for terminating a pregnancy remain and are closely connected to the notion of a woman displaying motherly behaviour.

The Sin of the Mother

A final element of how motherhood is presented in the court case hearings of these women relates to the wider harm it is perceived has been caused by the women to people other than the foetus/baby – including to themselves – and how this is connected to being motherly. For example, the defence highlight that Gwen's actions of abandoning her baby caused harm to her wider family:

> Your Honour, this is a sad and unusual case. Sad not least because a young family has been torn apart and of all of the consequences that have flowed and that may flow from the defendant's actions. (Gwen, defence mitigation)

The suggestion here is that the role of the mother is to safeguard the well-being of the family, which Gwen has failed to do through her actions; thus, one of her failures is to not put the needs of her family first, a theme that is prominent in the next chapter.

A similar point that is made by members of the court relates to the harm the women have done to themselves through their actions. For example, Olivia's barrister argued:

> She says that there is not a day that goes by that she doesn't think about that baby and in some ways she's had to live with that on her own, in silence, for a very long time because I think it's almost two years before it came to light. Now, that's of course one might say entirely of her own making but it must be a very difficult thing. (Olivia and Michael, defence mitigation for Olivia)

There is a similar argument of the trauma of losing a child in such a way highlighted by the judge in Sally's case:

> In mitigation ... You have had the trauma of suffering four still-born deaths and have had to live with the consequences of those deaths and the concealment which must have caused you many anxious and distressing moments. With those remains being with you as close as your own bedroom there can't have been any closure for you in relation to any of those young children, and this is a matter which has gone and on for many, many years. (Sally, judge sentencing)

The implication being given in both examples is that the loss of a child is an experience of such significance for a mother that it will live with them for the rest of their lives, as is 'natural' for a woman.

The perceived importance of losing a child is also highlighted in Gwen's case, as her barrister argued:

> [...] your Honour may accept that that separation for her [from her children] is by far the greatest punishment.
>
> ...
>
> It is of course tragic that her actions in abandoning the baby have in fact led to her worst fears being realised because now all three children have been removed from her care and your Honour will have seen in the documentation received that whilst no final decision has been made, certainly the view of all of the doctors is that her mental health needs to be resolved before care might be resumed. (Gwen, defence mitigation)

It is interesting that this point is made: the notion that separation from her children is the greatest punishment, a greater punishment than the public sanction of being convicted of, and punished for, criminal offending. Again, this feeds into the idea that the experience of motherhood is natural to women and consequently the loss of her children will be the worst possible outcome: an unimaginable outcome for any woman as per the myths of motherhood. In making this argument, I am not disputing the potential of the sorrow experienced by Gwen, or by Sally or Olivia, but commenting on how, in the aftermath of the events, it is assumed this was the experience of these women.

Finally, and perhaps, most telling of the way that motherhood is understood and represented in the criminal hearings in these cases is the idea that what the women have done in hurting their children has gone against 'nature':

> The case is unusual in that thankfully a mother's instinct is not commonly defeated in this way. (Gwen, defence mitigation)
>
> The powerful instinct of any parent is to protect and to nurture their offspring. What you did went entirely against that. (Gwen, judge sentencing)
>
> The unlawful homicide of anyone is a tragedy, especially is that the case when the victim is so young. Even more so that is the case when the child dies at the hands of her mother. (Nicole, judge sentencing)

The suggestion being made in each instance, focussing around the 'naturalness' and 'normalness' of motherhood, and the extent to which it is instinctive for a woman to be a mother and act in a motherly way, comes straight from the myths of motherhood – the direct connection of motherly behaviour to women's bodies and reproductive function; the focus on the individual nature of the women and their own failings against what is considered to be a 'natural' response of a proper mother and woman.

Individualising Maternal Failure

When considering how the women who are suspected of causing the death of their foetus or newborn child are discussed and presented during their criminal hearings, the myths of motherhood are ever-present for the women who were over the age of majority at the time of their pregnancy and birth. The perception of motherhood as a natural and universal experience that is inherent to all women surrounds and embodies these cases. The women's actions are measured against the principle that they, as women, should have acted as mothers to their foetus/ child. This expectation of their behaviour is in spite of two facts: first, that on the face of it, each woman has acted in a way that is in opposition to mother- hood and to motherly behaviour by rejecting the child/foetus, often violently; and second, that the context of the women's lives and crisis pregnancies means that the existence of the pregnancy and their role as 'mother' to this 'child' appears to have been a substantial threat to them and their lives, safety, and well-being. Neither point is contemplated, nor considered by the courts in their assessment of the women, their behaviour, and their actions towards the child. Instead, the fact that the women were pregnant is the basis upon which their role as a mother is assumed, and consequently, their motherly behaviour is expected and therefore used as a measure to judge them against.

The ideology of natural and inherent mothering and motherhood is assumed unquestioningly. At no point is it considered whether or why these women would want to be mothers, specifically to the 'child' that they have perceived as a threat. At no point does a defence barrister or judge point out that not all women want to be mothers or to mother, nor that there is substantial evidence that mothering as experienced in heteronormative, white, capitalist patriarchy is a social, cultural, and political construct, and not a 'natural' role of a woman, as argued in the femi- nist literature outlined above. Instead, the prosecution argue that the women have failed to be motherly and so to act as appropriate women. In response to this, to attempt to mitigate the damage of such a representation of character, the defence contend that the women were, in fact, acting in a motherly way or have indicated that their lack of motherly behaviour is due to a mental health condition or shock and trauma connected to the birth and death of the child. Such representations draw on the trope of 'natural' motherhood outlined above and so replicate the gender-based oppression that feminists have rallied against in their critical assess- ment of motherhood as an institution structured by heteronormative, white, capitalist patriarchy. These cases provide evidence that women continue to be reduced to their bodily functions; that behaviour and activities are assumed to flow as normal, natural, and inherent due to the expected reproductive capacity of a woman; and that she will be judged both within and outside a legal context next to such misogynistic expectations. As Martha Albertson Fineman (1995b, p. xii) argues, 'social constructions and legal ramifications [of motherhood] tend to operate independently of individual circumstances': it is the women's social and biological category as 'women' that leads to their assumed role of mother, not their individual circumstances and their behaviour.

The argument that women who offend are judged next to gender norms and expectations of motherhood, one of the findings from this research, is not new for either feminist socio-legal or criminological research or research focussed on violent or filicidal women. As already outlined, feminist researchers have repeatedly found that women are judged next to gender norms and ideals (Carlen, 1983; Milne & Turton, 2018; Morris & Wilczynski, 1993; Morrissey, 2003; Worrall, 1990). The findings from this chapter add to this body of research, outlining the extent to which the mere existence of a pregnancy leads to an expectation of motherhood and how these expectations play out in the courtroom: the presupposition of conformity to gender norms is so strong that it is present in spite of the women's attempts to keep the existence of the pregnancy/child a secret, and of their, at times violent, rejection of their foetus/child.

The findings also show how powerful and omnipresent gendered expectations of motherhood continue to be, despite decades of feminist campaigning and women's widening participation in society outside of the home and child-rearing roles and responsibilities. Conforming to gender norms of domesticity, caring responsibilities, and motherhood continue to dominate narratives for women. As M. J. Gathings and Kylie Parrotta (2013) argue, defence attorneys' attempts to construct identities of defendants that are considered worthy of leniency by judges create an incentive for defendants to cooperate with these gender performances, embracing gender norms. Inevitably, there are consequences: firstly, the courts are providing formal social control in response to deviant behaviour – harsher sentences for those who do not conform to the expected gender performance; and secondly, the courts are 'engag[ing] in the practice of gender policing where "doing gender" in conventional ways potentially results in the tangible reward of leniency' (Gathings & Parrotta, 2013, p. 682; citing West & Zimmerman, 1987).

Furthermore, as a number of feminists have argued, using gender norms as a basis for explaining women's offending has the impact of mitigating, nullifying, and explaining away the behaviour of women who offend. As Siobhan Weare (2016) argues, women who kill their infants challenge a fundamental feature of womanhood – the principle of the 'good' mother. The impact of challenges to that narrative is great and dangerous to social norms, and so the easiest way to approach this is to individualise the behaviour and explain it as a factor of the defendant's individual deficiency due to her 'badness', 'madness', or, in the case of a conviction for infanticide, her 'sadness'. Consequently, the wider social factors that lead women to acts of violence are negated, and so there is no need for the law, criminal justice, nor society to consider or address underlying causes of the violence that result from the oppressiveness of heteronormative, white, capitalist patriarchy (Ballinger, 2007; Brennan, 2018a, 2018b; Morrissey, 2003).

The negation of wider social circumstances that contextualise women's violence can certainly be seen in the cases assessed here. In Chapter 2, I outlined how the women's experiences of a crisis pregnancy are not recognised as contextualising factors of their actions or inactions during their pregnancy, labour and delivery, or in the postpartum period. Furthermore, the social factors that lead women to hide pregnancies, resulting in the death or near/death of the foetus/baby are also not addressed in the courtroom. Instead, as outlined in this chapter, we can see that exploration of the women's characters provides a means by which to 'explain' their actions. Such explanations are based on how motherly they are perceived to be in relation to their pregnancy and so are individualised: the narratives are based on their 'naturalness' as a woman. Their motherly nature is assumed to occur as a direct consequence of being pregnant. The further ways in which this natural-ness of motherly behaviour is assumed and presented in the criminal hearings of these cases will be explored in Chapter 4 through an analysis of expectations of pregnancy and how this is connected to motherhood ideals and perceptions of risk management by 'responsible' pregnant women.

One further point to consider in relation to feminist critiques of the use of gender norms in court hearings relates to the concept of agency. Feminists such as Anette Ballinger (2007) have argued that falling back on gendered expecta-tions and narratives constructed to explain away women's offending removes their agency as offenders, specifically for those women who have acted violently. Ball-inger's argument is that by explaining away women's decision to kill as a result of their 'madness' or 'evilness', the narratives reinforce the idea that such behaviour is not normal for women. Violence is not female, and so the woman is not acting rationally or as a moral agent in control of her actions but as a consequence of her deficit femininity, which is out of her control. She did it because she was mad or evil, or because she is not motherly, not because she chose to.

Let us ignore the question as to whether or not women who kill newborn chil-dren are in fact in control of their behaviour in the postpartum period[2]; as stated in Chapter 2, this is not the focus of this book. Instead, let us consider the con-cept of agency of women who offend. Karen Brennan (2018a) has challenged the analysis of Anette Ballinger and others on two counts. First, Brennan argues that the removal of gender stereotypes from narratives about women who kill infants during court cases could potentially result in women no longer receiving leniency in response to their offending. By no longer employing the traditional tropes of gender roles and norms that have facilitated leniency – that is, she did it because she could not cope (the 'sad' narrative), or because she was 'out of her mind' (the 'mad' narrative) – there is the potential that women will face more stringent punishments as their 'get-out-of-jail-free' card, which hinges on the adherence to gender roles, ceases to work. Laureen Snider (2003) has made a similar argument about women who offend in general, underscoring the negative consequences of feminist scholarship highlighting the rationality and agency of women who com-mit illegal acts. By restoring women's 'agency' and decision-making to offend, feminist criminologists have been complicit in the construction of narratives

---

[2]See my discussion of the work of psychiatrists and psychologists, such as Spinelli (2003), in Chapter 2.

about the responsibilisation of women who offend. The consequence has been that punishments of women have increased in severity both within and outside criminal justice institutions.

Second, Karen Brennan (2018a) argues that criminal law and justice do not recognise wider socio-political aspects of any offender; law, as an institution of control and regulation, and justice, are based on holding individuals to account regardless of wider socio-cultural factors that might have impacted the behaviour, including race, ethnicity, class, sex, and gender. Furthermore, as Brennan argues, to recognise wider socio-cultural political elements of life as influencing factors in a person's offending would undermine a foundational principle of criminal law – the behaviour of individuals as rational and thus being responsible for their actions – unless specific and personal mitigation can be proven to support a defence. Brennan's argument is well made and outlines the fundamental points of how criminal law and justice work today. It is this factor of the principle of criminal law and how the law is applied which needs to be unpacked and challenged in cases of suspected perinatal homicide and will be explored in the remainder of this book.

In the next chapter, I outline how the perceived risk posed by the pregnant woman to the foetus has been conceptualised and is used as a lens through which to understand the conduct of the women in these cases. In so doing, I outline the significance of gender in constructing such concepts of risk.

Chapter 4

Mothers in the Courtroom III: Criminalising the Irresponsible Mother

> [...] your chaotic lifestyle choices, including alcohol abuse and promiscuity at the time of your pregnancies was such as to put the good health of any unborn child at risk. (Sally, judge sentencing)

One of the key changes that can be seen to have occurred over the twentieth century is the nature of the conceptualisation of pregnancy, including how the foetus and pregnant women are perceived in terms of the roles they play in the process of pregnancy. The latter half of the twentieth century and the twenty-first century can be characterised as a period in which the foetus is recognised and perceived as a subject – a being that is independent of the pregnant woman. Foetal subjectivity is reflected and seen very clearly in cultural practices: think, for example, of the cover story of *Life Magazine* in 1965, 'Drama of Life Before Birth', featuring images of the foetus, represented as being outside the body of a pregnant woman (portrayed as if floating in space). Such a depiction suggests foetuses and pregnant women are separate entities, independent, and thus subjects in their own right. The independence of the foetus can also be seen in medicine, with, for example, developments in foetal medicine, where the foetus is the patient.

Similarly, in some legal jurisdictions, such as most states in the United States, the foetus has become a legal subject with varying levels of legal protection (Milne, 2020; Murphy, 2014; National Conference of State Legislatures, 2018). As outlined in Chapter 1 and explored in detail in Chapters 5 and 6, in England and Wales, the foetus is not a legal subject and has limited legal protection, including as a victim of crime, due to the born alive rule. While abortion[1] continues to be illegal, the only offence that can be committed against the foetus is child destruction: the destruction of a child capable of being born alive through a wilful act.[2] The role of criminal law in protecting foetuses will be explored later in this book.

In this chapter, the focus is upon examining the expectations of pregnant women in relation to their foetus which fall outside of the law, and how these expectations

---

[1]Offences Against the Person Act 1861, s58, offence of procuring a miscarriage.
[2]Infant Life (Preservation) Act 1929, s1.

Criminal Justice Responses to Maternal Filicide: Judging the Failed Mother, 73–99
Copyright © 2021 by Emma Milne
Published by Emerald Publishing under an Exclusive Licence
doi:10.1108/978-1-83909-620-420211006

are discussed and communicated in the criminal hearings of women who have been convicted of offences related to a suspicious perinatal death. Such expectations are very closely connected to the myths of motherhood and expectations of 'good' mothering and motherly behaviour. As outlined in Chapter 3, such expectations are pervasive in the hearings, woven throughout the discussion of the women and their actions, and used to construct their character and the narrative around what they did or did not do. As will be illustrated in this chapter, motherhood ideologies, and belief of the 'naturalness' of mothering, stem from the existence of a pregnancy. Such expectations are deeply enmeshed with the perception of the 'responsible' pregnant woman – the woman who manages any risk towards the foetus. These expectations can be encapsulated in the general belief that the women will prioritise the needs of the foetus – which I term the 'foetus-first mentality' (Milne, 2020). An example of such expectations can be seen in Sally's case, in the quote at the top of this chapter. While her conviction for concealment of birth has nothing to do with her behaviour while pregnant, the judge deemed it important to comment on the perceived increased risk experienced by her 'unborn child' due to her actions and inactions.

Much feminist scholarship has been critical of the changing conceptualisation of the foetus, and subsequent behaviour towards pregnant women, focussing on the substantial impact of foetal subjectivity on the rights of the women in all areas of life. Risk mentality and risk prevention are key areas of theorisation; as Rachelle Joy Chadwick and Don Foster (2014) argue, nowhere is the pervasiveness of risk as apparent as it is in pregnancy and childbirth (Smith et al., 2012). Therefore, the court transcripts will be analysed through the lens of this academic work. In so doing, it will become apparent that in the process of the criminal hearing, the women are framed not only as the failed mother, as explored in Chapter 3, but also as failing in their role as the 'responsible pregnant woman' and failing to put the foetus first. Finally, I will consider how narratives of risk could be adapted to take into consideration women's experiences of crisis pregnancy. Rather than always seeing the pregnant woman as the risk, I consider how perceptions of criminality change if we see a pregnancy as a risk to a woman.

Foetus-first Mentality

The changing conceptualisation of pregnancy, the pregnant woman, and the foetus is embedded in the process of the medicalisation of pregnancy. Pregnancy, labour, and delivery have developed from being, generally, a private experience that centres around the woman who is pregnant (Gowing, 1997), to becoming a medicalised, public activity that centres around the foetus which requires medical management and intervention to ensure its safety and well-being. The notion that the foetus should be put before the pregnant woman, in terms of both health and welfare, is one that can only exist if the foetus is conceptualised as a specific entity in need of protection and care. Historically, understanding and knowledge of the mechanics of pregnancy were limited. Awareness of pregnancy might be indicated by 'quickening' (the point at which a woman first feels the foetus move: typically, 15–17 gestational weeks), but otherwise unconfirmable until the final stages of labour. Similarly, the health of the foetus was unknowable until after delivery.

As Ann Oakley (1984) argued in her study of the history of the obstetric care of women, no body of knowledge or set of techniques to manage pregnancy existed; consequently, there was no rationale for medical supervision. In the lead up to, and during the twentieth century, the conceptualisation of pregnancy changed. Medical knowledge developed and pregnancy was pathologised – becoming an occasion for medical surveillance and treatment (Oakley, 1993). Tests to 'diagnose' pregnancy were developed; for example, the hormonal pregnancy test became available for use by doctors in the 1930s (Oakley, 1984). Pregnancy and childbirth moved from being female-led and community-based to an institution-based medical 'condition', managed predominantly by professionals who were mostly male (see Ehrenreich & English, 2010; Leavitt, 1986; Wertz & Wertz, 1989).

Medicalisation has led to two key consequences in the conceptualisation of pregnancy. First, a change in how pregnancy, labour, and delivery are understood and approached as a medical condition requiring treatment. Ann Oakley (1984) argues that medicalisation resulted in childbearing being divided between the 'normal' and 'abnormal', rather than simply a state of being that is experienced by women. When antenatal care first operated, the task was to screen the population in search of the few women who were at risk of disease or death. By the 1980s, screening is conducted in the 'population suffering from the pathology of pregnancy for the few women who are normal enough to give birth with the minimum of midwifery attention' (Oakley, 1984, p. 213). The change in perception happened rapidly – 70% of childbirths were thought 'normal' enough to be delivered at home by a midwife in the 1930s. However, by the 1950s, 70% of all births were considered sufficiently 'abnormal' to be delivered in hospital (Oakley, 1984, p. 142). Today, just 1 in 50 women give birth at home (National Health Service, 2018d).

Risk now defines women's experiences of pregnancy and childbirth (Helén, 2004), as they are seen as requiring expert management by medical professionals, drawing on evidence-based knowledge, prediction, and control (Lupton, 1999a). As Lealle Ruhl (1999) argues, medical professionals' involvement in pregnancy has had a dual impact: the creation of risk through testing, monitoring, and research, as well as the alleviation of that risk through treatment and medical management. To minimise risk, childbirth and pregnancy must be 'managed by experts, constantly monitored and [be] subject to a series of investigations in order to probe dysfunction and abnormality' (Chadwick & Foster, 2014, p. 70).

Second, and as a direct result of the medicalisation, the development and solidification of the idea that pregnancy involves two patients – the pregnant woman and the foetus – both of whom need medical surveillance and potentially treatment. Lorna Weir (2006) notes that the construction of the perinatal threshold was a key element in the development of current responses to pregnancy. She argues that the birth threshold, the point at which the foetus becomes a living subject and enters the social world, was disrupted in the early twentieth century. In attempts to lower rates of infant mortality and to optimise infant health, medical intervention moved into the new perinatal threshold. Deaths around birth – before, during, and after – were perceived as bearing similarities, and the foetus in later gestation in the womb was considered to be, in essence, the same as the newborn baby: different only by geography – inside or outside the woman. Consequently, physicians developed new targets and measures to prevent foetal and neonatal mortality – perinatal death. Weir concludes that this development reduced both the significance of birth and the nature of the treatment of pregnancy. As a consequence, the perception that 'mother' and 'baby' are distinct subjects moved from the end of labour (after the baby was born) to during pregnancy. This shift in perception assisted in the construction of the foetus as a subject. Rather than pregnancy being understood as a situation whereby one person (the pregnant woman) needs care to produce a new human life, pregnancy has been constructed as a situation where two distinct humans need care. Weir argues that the changing concept of the life/birth threshold, developed in the 1950s, signifies the start of the application of risk techniques towards pregnancy.

The medicalisation of pregnancy and, in relation to this, the construction of the foetus as a patient has received substantial criticism from feminists and feminist midwifery groups. Arguments have been made that the treatment of pregnancy as a medical condition has resulted in male control over women's reproduction, requiring women to consult medical experts for what is 'naturally' a woman's domain, thus disempowering women and pathologising the experience (Davis-Floyd, 1992; Ehrenreich & English, 2010; Leavitt, 1986; Lupton, 2012a; Martin, 1987; Oakley, 1984; Rothman, 1989, 1993). The aim of this critique is not to argue that all medical intervention and knowledge is inherently negative. Medical advancements have many benefits for women; for example, medical understanding of pre-eclampsia has resulted in the development of successful treatments for what was previously a fatal condition for women and their foetuses. Instead, the critique lies in the harmful consequences of the technocratic model promoted by medical professionals (Davis-Floyd, 2001). However, as Sarah Jane Brubaker and Heather E. Dillaway (2009) argue, there is no clear definition of the concept of medicalisation within sociological literature, nor is the concept of a 'natural' birth fixed or determined, particularly in the minds of many women or medical professionals. Instead, they argue, hospital births have become so common place that they may seem 'natural'. Furthermore, as Bonnie Fox and Diana Worts (1999) have argued, medicalisation developed with the endorsement and encouragement of communities of women, many of whom take great comfort in the support provided by medical institutions during pregnancy and labour and delivery. Nevertheless, critique of over-technical medical intervention remains strong as can be seen by campaigns in the United States, where most births are obstetrician led, such as *Our Bodies, Ourselves*, and the movement advocating midwifery-led care in the United Kingdom (Boston Women's Health Book Collective, 2008, 2011; National Institute for Health and Care Excellence, 2014; Strong, 2000; Wagner, 2006).

Feminist critiques of medical care have also focussed on the impact of the construction of the foetus as a patient. Feminists argue that it is now the foetus who is the focus as the patient, while the pregnant woman has been defined as no more than the foetal carrier or container and gestational environment (Bordo, 2003; Chavkin, 1992; Halliday, 2016; Longhurst, 2001; Lupton, 1999b; Martin, 1987; Phelan, 1991; Young, 1990). Further development of foetal imaging techniques (Petchesky, 1987) and foetal surgery to directly treat the foetus (Fletcher, 1981; Knopoff, 1991; Williams, 2006) have reinforced this critique. Feminists argue that such technologies and medical developments have framed the foetus as an independent entity, marginalising the woman (MacKinnon, 1991).

Medicalisation and the foetus as a subject have changed how the behaviour of pregnant women is perceived. Risk management and prevention are centred around protecting the unborn as the vulnerable subject, susceptible to danger. As the foetus exists within the pregnant woman, foetal protection requires management of her behaviour: protection of the subject through the maternal abdominal wall, as Phelan (1991) puts it. Consequently, the predominant focus is not upon averting maternal risk but reducing possible risk to the foetus that may be caused by maternal behaviour (Helén, 2004; Lupton, 2012b; Ruhl, 1999; Weir, 1996). These risk management techniques operate beyond women's interactions with medical professionals and are now a normal element of public discourses and advice surrounding pregnancy, for example, advice and guidance provided to women regarding:

- consumption of certain foods (Foodsafety.gov, 2019; National Health Service, 2020c, 2020d),
- drinking alcohol (Centers for Disease Control and Prevention, 2020a; National Health Service, 2020b),
- smoking cigarettes (Centers for Disease Control and Prevention, 2020f; National Health Service, 2019b),
- using controlled substances (Centers for Disease Control and Prevention, 2020g; National Health Service, 2019a),
- rates of obesity (National Health Service, 2020e; Office on Women's Health, 2018b),
- levels of stress (Burns et al., 2015; Public Health England, 2019),
- certain pre-existing medical conditions (Centers for Disease Control and Prevention, 2020c, 2020d, 2020e; National Health Service, 2018a, 2018b, 2018c; National Institute of Diabetes and Digestive and Kidney Diseases, 2018; Office on Women's Health, 2018a),
- how they wear a seat belt (Children's Hospital of Philadelphia, n.d.; Ford, 2018), and
- the level of pollution in the air they breathe (Carrington, 2019).

The advice and guidance given are focussed on women adapting and changing their behaviour for the benefit of the unborn, rather than for their own health.

The majority of these regulations of risk are achieved through, what Lealle Ruhl (1999) defines as, the 'liberal governance of pregnancy', which enlists the co-operation of the 'responsible' pregnant woman. This theorisation falls within the broad area of governmentality, which concerns itself with analysis of how the state attempts to direct the conduct of the population to remedy or improve perceived problems.[3] Rather than using force and coercion, the state manages the

---

[3] For discussion of the broader theories of governmentality and how they impact on wider areas of life, see Rose (1993, 1996a, 1996b, 2000), O'Malley (1992, 2000, 2004), and Simon (1988), who developed Foucault's (1991 [1977], 1992 [1985]) principles of governmentality.

For discussions of how governmentality, risk, and gender interact, see Hannah-Moffat and O'Malley (2007).

population through guidance that is regulated by experts. The ideal neoliberal subject embodies principles of prudence and self-regulation, managing risk and absorbing the cost of risk, as opposed to burdening society by requiring social support. Risk comprises language, practice, and modes of knowledge (Beck, 1992). The more attempts that are made to categorise risk, the more risks will be found. Hence, it is an unfulfilled process: no one can escape the fear of risk or its impact. Furthermore, while risk is often seen as value-free, with the use of scientific knowledge that is presented as objective, it is value-laden and, specifically for this research, is gendered (Chan & Rigakos, 2002; Hannah-Moffat & O'Malley, 2007; Stanko, 1997; Walklate, 1997).

The liberal governance of pregnancy is an individualised risk model, rather than a collective risk model, meaning the pregnant woman absorbs the burden of the risk. It is her behaviour and the context of her life that is perceived to have the most impact on the health and well-being of the foetus, rather than wider societal factors (Ruhl, 1999; see also Bordo, 2003; Chavkin, 1992; Lane, 2008; Lazarus, 1994). For example, public health messages now advise that women should be a 'healthy' weight prior to becoming pregnant, and that 'if you are overweight, the best way to protect your health and your baby's wellbeing is to lose weight before you become pregnant' (National Health Service, 2020e). The message is individualised – the problem identified is the weight of the woman: her body. As a result, the focus is on her food choices and exercise levels, rather than, for example, upon the structural pressures placed on individual's lives as a consequence of white, patriarchal, capitalist society. A woman may struggle to afford fresh fruit and vegetables, and a gym membership, and/or she may have limited time to cook from scratch, or exercise due to the need to work two jobs to afford to pay her rent. Nevertheless, the messaging is around her 'choices' to not exercise and to eat 'junk' food. Furthermore, wider social 'problems' that have an impact on the health of a foetus, but that are beyond the control of women, such as pollution in the air and chemicals in water and food, are excluded from the lists of potential risks to the foetus. It is the risks that attract social commentary that are borne by the foetus, such as 'fat' mothers, and the responsibility for these risks falls to the pregnant woman, regardless of the fact that many are beyond her control (Ruhl, 1999).

The concept of upholding health as an act of responsible citizenship within neoliberal society is not solely experienced by pregnant women. However, as Deborah Lupton (1999b) argues, greater pressure is exerted on pregnant women as they are expected to uphold not only their own health but also the health of their foetus. Consequently, the individualised risk model constructs the pregnant woman as her foetus' most ardent protector but also its greatest threat (Ruhl, 1999). This construction of the pregnant woman as a potential threat opens up the role of foetal protectors to professionals who may intercede on the foetus' behalf to ensure its well-being and security. In medical settings, it is healthcare professionals who 'safeguard' the health of the foetus (Halliday, 2016; Phelan, 1991). For example, they 'protect' the foetus by applying for a court order to conduct a caesarean section against the will and consent of the pregnant woman, as it is in the best interest of the 'baby' (Kingma & Porter, 2020; Michalowski, 1999;

Rhoden, 1986; Wells, 1998). However, other professionals such as social workers[4] can and do take such action, and, as explored in this book, criminal law and criminal justice are able to do the same.

One of the key critiques of the individual risk model of pregnancy is that it is inappropriate, as women do not 'control' their pregnancies as the risk model suggests, and the definition of 'responsibility' in pregnancy is often moral and scientific (Ruhl, 1999; see also Weir, 1996, 2006). Furthermore, the demands on pregnant women to adapt their behaviour are extensive and rarely acknowledged. The model of risk concludes that a woman is complicit in any birth defects regardless of whether she could have prevented them. Such a perception overlooks women's lack of control over their foetus' development. The 'prudential model of pregnancy' makes demands on women that are simply unrealistic, requiring 'that pregnant women be on their guard, every second of their pregnancy, for something, anything, which might prove to be the slightest bit harmful to their foetus' (Ruhl, 1999, p. 110).

Risk discourses are now also targeting women who are trying to conceive a pregnancy (Centers for Disease Control and Prevention, 2020b; National Health Service, 2020f) and even women who may unintentionally become pregnant. The Centers for Disease Control and Prevention (2016) released a public health campaign arguing that, as approximately half of all pregnancies in the United States are unplanned, women not using a long-active reversible contraceptive should refrain from drinking alcohol as the damage to the foetus caused by alcohol could occur before the woman even knows she is pregnant. Similarly, in the United Kingdom, the National Health Service of Greater Glasgow and Clyde, Scotland, published guidance to support medical professionals working with women of childbearing age to increase foetal health (Sher, 2016). The report advocates that, at any time said group of women come into contact with medical professionals, the professional should ask if there is a reasonable chance the woman will start a pregnancy that year – note, not if she wants to become pregnant, but if there is a *chance* she will. The guidance advised that in instances where women answered 'yes', health professionals should encourage women to abstain from harmful substances, such as alcohol, smoking, and drugs; lose weight; leave violent and abusive partners; and avoid exposure to radiation and illnesses such as HIV, diabetes, rubella, and the Zika virus. This health advice is targeted at making women 'healthy' not for themselves but for the 'child' who is yet to be conceived. The implication of such a message is that women who are having sex need to adapt their lives significantly, just in case they become pregnant. Considering the rate

---

[4]However, in England and Wales, it is not possible to make a foetus a ward of the court as the foetus has no independent existence from the pregnant woman and so the court could not exercise the rights, powers, and duties of a parent over the foetus without controlling the mother's actions, *In Re F (In Utero)* [1988] Fam. 122. However, in states in the United States, it is possible to detain pregnant women on the basis that they may do harm to the foetus, see the National Advocates for Pregnant Women (2018) campaign against Wisconsin's 'Unborn Child Protection Act'.

at which women are raped,[5] and that even long-active reversible contraception cannot guarantee a pregnancy will not be started, this advice can be interpreted to apply to all women of reproductive age: approximately 13–50.

The perniciousness of the liberal governance of pregnancy lies in how it is connected to motherhood ideals and so to the notion of the 'good' mother, informed by the myths of motherhood, as outlined in Chapter 3. Lealle Ruhl (1999) argues that responsibility for risk management by pregnant women is equated with rationality and the principle of adopting behaviour that will ensure the greatest benefit with the least risk. Thus, this risk discourse is moralistic, as it is premised on the idea that any 'rational' woman would take these steps to protect her unborn 'child'. As outlined in the previous chapter, the myths of motherhood conflate mother and child, assuming they are one entity with the same needs and desires. The same conflation is exhibited with pregnant women and foetuses: the 'responsible' pregnant woman, who manages risk appropriately, is expected to put the needs of her foetus before her own, while the pregnant woman who puts her own needs and desires first is deemed 'irresponsible' (Ruhl, 1999). Such judgements of pregnant women's behaviour go beyond perceptions of responsibility, connecting specifically with the myths of motherhood. The responsible pregnant woman is the 'good' mother, while the pregnant woman who does not put the needs of the foetus before her own needs and desires is the 'bad' mother (Gregg, 1995; Lupton, 2011).

Studies focussed on women's experiences of pregnancy report that women feel pressured to conform to the messages of risk discourse, monitoring and disciplining themselves, and surveilling and being surveilled by others (Harper & Rail, 2012; Lupton, 2011; van Mulken et al., 2016). The myths of motherhood, as they operate on pregnant women, promote and legitimise the foetus-first mentality. The myths construct expectations of what it means to be a responsible pregnant woman who places the foetus' welfare before the welfare and needs of herself. Furthermore, women's self-regulation and sacrifice are deemed symbols of love and her role as a 'good' mother (Brooks-Gardner, 2003). In line with the myths of motherhood, few questions are raised as to whether a woman should sacrifice herself for her child and by extension her foetus. The construction of this expected maternal sacrifice legitimises and normalises the hierarchy of foetal and maternal health and well-being and, thus, the idea that the pregnant woman will act as the foetus' most ardent protector (Bessett, 2010). By extension, if she does not, then she is constructed as the 'bad' mother, as the 'good' mother would never be in conflict with her foetus (Roth, 2000). Thus, mother-blaming now starts at conception, rather than birth (van Mulken et al., 2016). If conflict does exist, then others can and must intervene to protect the foetus from its 'irresponsible', 'bad' mother. Consequently, pregnant women have become public figures; their bodies have become a display for others to monitor, touch, and comment upon in ways that

---

[5]Official estimates are that one in five women will experience some type of sexual assault at least once in her lifetime (Office for National Statistics, 2018).

would not be considered appropriate for other adult bodies (Lupton, 2012b; Stormer, 2000). As with the control and regulation of mothers, the policing of pregnancy is not conducted equally, with the most vulnerable women, and those situated furthest from the ideology of the 'good' mother – the white, middle-class, married, able-bodied, heterosexual woman – being most heavily monitored and most likely to experience intervention from state agencies (Flavin, 2009; Lupton, 2011; Ruhl, 1999).

Failure to Put the Foetus First

As detailed above, there is now substantial evidence that, as 'good' mothers, women are expected to put the needs of the foetus before their own needs, welfare, and desires – the foetus-first mentality, and so this is an accepted part of the day-to-day reality of women. What becomes clear from reading the court transcripts in cases of suspicious perinatal death is that such expectations are also reflected in the criminal hearings of suspected women. These expectations are presented despite the limited scope of the law, to compel women to prioritise the needs of the foetus, as discussed in Chapters 5 and 6.

In a number of the cases, the idea is presented that as a consequence of being pregnant, the women should have acted to prioritise the needs of their foetus, regardless of the circumstances of the pregnancy. This can be seen clearly in Hannah's case, as the prosecution argued:

> The Crown's case is that she had made it plain she didn't want the child and that she could not have a child out of wedlock. She told no one for those reasons. She sought no assistance with the birth as she sought to keep it a secret. She sought no assistance for the newborn child and it died without any attempt, it would appear, by the defendant to give it the care the child required. The child remained unwashed and died without expert or experienced assistance which may have prevented its early death. (Hannah, prosecution opening)

The suggestion being made here is that Hannah acted in her own best interests – keeping the pregnancy a secret and delivering alone, rather than doing what would be best for the 'baby' by telling people she was pregnant. The prosecution is directly connecting her behaviour prior to the birth of the child, and the outcome that occurred following the birth, with Hannah's role as risk manager for her foetus/child. While not directly spelt out, the conclusion of this position is clear: if Hannah had been a responsible pregnant woman, and so a 'good' mother, then she would have taken steps to ensure the protection and safeguarding of the foetus/child through antenatal treatment and ensuring she delivered in a location to facilitate medical care for the child following birth. Hannah maintains that she passed out after the birth and the baby had died upon her regaining consciousness; not an unlikely occurrence, as collapsing from exhaustion post-birth is documented in the neonaticide literature (Oberman, 1996).

In presenting Hannah's behaviour in this manner, the prosecution is directly linking her conduct in pregnancy to her culpability for the death of the child. The focus is upon her decision to place her need to not be pregnant, because she believes she could not have a child in her situation, above the needs of her 'child'. The consequence is that Hannah's actions look purposeful, and she appears culpable for the death of the child after birth precisely due to her behaviour while pregnant – for allowing herself to end up in a position whereby others were not there to monitor and prevent risk to her 'baby' during and after the birth. As already noted in Chapter 2, Hannah's response to her pregnancy needs to be understood as a response to a crisis pregnancy, a point that is negated by the court, and arguably by wider criminal justice, in their assessments of her actions. More than this, the assumption that underpins the prosecution's narrative that Hannah is an irresponsible pregnant woman is that to be pregnant is to be a woman who puts the needs of the foetus first, regardless of the personal consequences or sacrifices of that situation. Hannah's apparent fears of how her family would react if they discovered her pregnancy are not factored into expectations of her conduct following her own discovery of her pregnancy. The foetus-first mentality is considered to be a far greater influence on women's behaviour and thought processes, so much so that it will supersede any concerns a woman may have about herself, and the impact of her pregnancy on her life and well-being.

In her defence, Hannah's barrister does not challenge the idea that she should have put the needs of her foetus first. Instead, the barrister argues that Hannah was mistaken in both her conduct and her beliefs about her pregnancy:

> There were other options. The defendant didn't avail herself of them. The defendant didn't avail herself of them. She ought to have done .... And so I suppose it begs the question as to why it was that this young woman made such a bad and a wrong decision that she did in the circumstances that she did in the early hours and thereafter of [date], why she failed to seek the prompt medical attention really being the gravamen [*sic.*] of the offence to which she has pleaded guilty. (Hannah, defence mitigation)

The suggestion from the words of the defence is that it was not just her behaviour post-birth when Hannah's neglect of the infant became a matter for criminal law that was 'bad and wrong', but that it was also her actions leading her to birth in these circumstances. The defence also describes the loss of the child's life as 'needless', stating that Hannah was wrong to not trust her family, who declared after the death of the child that they would have stood by and supported Hannah if she had told them about the pregnancy. Hence, her actions in relation to the pregnancy are presented as misguided; that she should have put the foetus first, and that she failed to do this due to her mistaken belief that she could not tell her family about the pregnancy.

Similar arguments can be seen in Hayley's case. Central to the discussion is the belief that she should have put the foetus first, regardless of her needs or desires, or the consequences she perceives for herself or her family of being pregnant:

> Despite marrying your long-term partner in [date], it seems, on your own say so, that you conducted an on-off seven year affair with a work colleague before becoming pregnant. You clearly decided, or you clearly thought, I should say, that the child was his because you told him, but not your husband, of the pregnancy in [date]. He offered to leave his wife to start a family with you, but you declined. You broke off the relationship with him … saying that there was no child and it was none of his business. You told the Probation Officer, however, that it was not until [date] that you decided you wanted to remain with your husband and to have an abortion. (Hayley, judge sentencing)

Again, we can see here the idea that Hayley is perceived to be putting her relationships with her husband and lover before the needs and well-being of the foetus, which is presented as unacceptable behaviour for a pregnant woman. A similar position is presented in Nicole's case, where the prosecution noted that the only person who knew about the pregnancy was the 'father of the baby'; that she did not know why she strangled the baby, and 'she had decided to stay with [her partner] and not leave to be with the baby's father' (Nicole, prosecution opening, presenting evidence from Nicole's assessment by a psychiatrist). Without directly stating it, the implication here is that her actions were those of a woman thinking of her own needs and not those of the 'baby'. Similarly, in Imogen's case, the narrative is constructed as her not wanting a child due to being career-minded, the pregnancy being an 'inconvenience' to her, and so she did not act to put the needs of the foetus first.

It is cases where the prosecution attempt to prove murder that the implications of the foetus-first mentality are most clearly outlined and are actively connected to motive and culpability. As already argued in Chapters 2 and 3, by not contextualising the pregnancies as crisis pregnancies, and by constructing the women as unmotherly, women such as Bethany and Jessica are easily presented as cold-blooded killers who intentionally kept the pregnancy a secret as they wanted to kill the child. The foetus-first mentality provides further fuel for such a fire:

> The defendant, says the prosecution, is somebody who is profoundly self-centred.
>
> …
>
> It was suggested to [Jessica when on the stand] that she had no concern for her baby's welfare. She took no steps to ensure that it was well, to see a doctor or a midwife, or to make any arrangements. And she said she was burying her head in the sand or she didn't know what she was thinking. It wasn't because she had no concern for the baby's welfare and it wasn't the case that her focus was on ensuring how the baby would not survive. She didn't know why she said nothing to the family when her waters broke.

> She wished she had. She didn't know why she didn't seek help. She
> nearly died she said. Why was it so important to justify this risk?
> She didn't know. (Jessica, judge summing up)

An implication of such lines of argument is that it is 'natural' to put the welfare
and needs of a foetus first: to be pregnant is to be a mother, and to be a mother
is to put the foetus first. In Jessica's case, the prosecution construct the narrative
that as she did not have the foetus' well-being at the centre of her thoughts and
actions, she must have intended and planned to murder the baby after birth. Lack
of understanding of a crisis pregnancy, accompanied by the widely accepted
foetus-first mentality, allows for women in cases of suspected perinatal killing to
easily be constructed as intentional killers who reject their 'natural' role as mothers and foetal protectors.

Putting the Foetus/child at Risk

Connected to expectations expressed in court of women putting the foetus
first, the idea of risk management of the foetus/child's health, and the role
the women play in that process, also features heavily in the cases. Three key
areas of risk management are identifiable. First, that the woman's behaviour
towards the foetus/baby was inherently risky; this was mostly expressed in relation to the women who abandoned their babies ending with the survival of
the children – Alice and Gwen. This sentiment was also expressed in relation
to Imogen, as her behaviour in the final stages of her pregnancy was deemed
to put not only the foetus at risk but also herself and people around her. Such
a position reflects the notion that pregnancy is inherently risky and that risks
need to be managed:

> This defendant kept a pregnancy a secret throughout the term of
> said pregnancy, placing herself in a perilous position, and pre-
> carious position throughout. She did not seek medical assistance
> following an attempt to abort the pregnancy, and I will return to
> that in a moment if I may, but almost incredulously she took a
> flight with her now husband to Turkey and landed probably whilst
> in labour, and your Honour made the observations that not only
> was she placing herself and the child in a precarious and danger-
> ous position, but also passengers on that flight and the crew. Her
> actions at the very best could have been described as reckless.
> (Imogen, prosecution opening)

A second identified key element is that the women should have averted the
risk they posed to their foetus/child by asking for help while they were pregnant, so allowing others to manage the foetus' risk. The notion that the women
should have safeguarded their foetuses by telling someone about the pregnancy
is reflected in a number of cases. For example, in Sophie's sentencing hearing,
the judge stated:

It is an aggravating factor of this offence that you took time to plan and prepare for it in the form of the internet researches and purchase as I have mentioned. To the extent that you were suffering from personal and psychiatric problems at the time, you could and should have turned for professional help. (Sophie, judge sentencing)

The defence relied heavily on psychiatric reports to mitigate her behaviour of illegally terminating her pregnancy, describing Sophie as 'clearly a young woman who is troubled' (Sophie, defence mitigation). The suggestion intimated by the defence and, seemingly accepted by the judge, is that Sophie would not have acted to illegally end her pregnancy if she had not been experiencing psychiatric 'problems ... I fully accept that you were suffering from mild depression, anxiety and panic symptoms whilst pregnant on this occasion' (Sophie, judge sentencing). However, the judge then indicates that Sophie should have acted to mitigate the risk she posed to the foetus by obtaining professional 'help'.

A similar position is expressed by the judge in Tanya's case:

It is quite clear that by the time the baby was due, you were in complete denial and so in the early hours of that morning you delivered the baby yourself in your bedroom at home, alone. You didn't cry out. You asked for no help. You were at home in your household. Right next door to you were members of your family who could have and would have helped you but you couldn't see that. You were not rational.

...

I accept that you hadn't planned to kill him and at some stages during the pregnancy, you checked on whether certain things might harm a developing foetus. At those times you were obviously rational and you will live with the knowledge that, had you been able to confide in someone during your pregnancy, all of this could have been avoided. (Tanya, judge sentencing)

Again, the suggestion being presented is that Tanya, like Sophie, should have alerted someone to the existence of her pregnancy in order to allow others to safeguard the well-being of the foetus. The expression of such sentiments during the women's criminal hearings suggests that the foetus-first mentality is both prolific and widely accepted. The expectation is that the women will put the needs of their foetus first, and if they cannot, then they should make room for people who can, by informing third parties about their pregnancy – other professionals who will safeguard the well-being of the foetus through the maternal abdominal wall. Such suggestions are made in spite of evidence that the women were not in a position to do this, due to their ability to accept the pregnancy, and/or their perception of the pregnancy as a threat to their well-being.

In Hayley's case, there is evidence that medical and child protection services attempted to manage the risk of the foetus:

> My Lord, as a result of the scans in mid-March, the health authorities were made aware of her pregnancy, and they awaited contact from [Hayley] with regard to antenatal care, and no such contact was made by her, and so it was that in mid-May the midwifery department at .... Hospital initiated some contact by telephone, and during a conversation on the 17th May the defendant indicated that she had attended at the Marie Stopes Clinic ... and had a termination on the 15th March, and this was an account that she was to maintain to those in authority for some considerable time.
>
> ...
>
> [...] on the 11th June a General Practitioner from the practice that she was registered at attended at her home address and she again gave this same account as to having had a termination at the Marie Stopes Clinic.
>
> On the 14th June, she had a telephone conversation with the designated nurse from the Safeguarding Children's Services and again gave the same account. (Hayley, defence mitigation)

Hayley's actions of ordering the misoprostol via the internet only came to the awareness of criminal justice authorities after professionals alerted the police that Hayley would not have been able to access a legal abortion, and that no baby had been registered following her due date. In England and Wales, duties to promote the welfare of children, and so safeguard them from harm, are given to specific organisations, agencies, and individuals under section 11 of the Children's Act 2004. These include members of Local Authorities, including children's social care; National Health Service organisations, including general practitioners as primary healthcare providers; and the police. Thus, a missing child that is expected to have been born but has not been presented to professionals would raise safeguarding concerns, which professionals have a duty to investigate under statutory guidance in *Working Together to Safeguard Children* (Department for Education, 2019; this is the most recent iteration of the policy).

However, as per the born alive rule, safeguarding requirements are not in place for a foetus and only come into practice after the child is born. Thus, the concerns raised by professionals must, officially at least, have related to the absence of a born child, not to the welfare of a foetus. In Hayley's case, the first recorded call occurred around the time when Hayley was expected to have reached full term; so arguably, the call by medical professionals in May related to the risk management of the child following birth, thus falling under statutory duty of child protection. However, a 'qualified person' has 42 days after the birth of a child to register the birth or stillbirth.[6] Thus, the concern for the well-being of the child could not be due to the realisation that a 'child' was missing, as the 42 days would not have passed until approximately the end of June or early July. Consequently, the safeguarding checks must have related to concerns that Hayley had not engaged with prenatal care and so was perceived to be putting her foetus at risk by not allowing the medical community to manage her pregnancy.[7] As Hayley's case highlights, and as will be discussed later in this book, the 'invisible line of birth' that changes the nature of the law and child protection policies is complex and appears to no longer be fixed and resolute.

Finally, concerns were raised during the court hearings of the risk that the women were considered to pose to other children in light of their conviction. Most of the women are automatically barred from working with children and vulnerable adults under the government Disclosure and Barring Service (n.d.). However, concerns are also raised in a number of cases about the women's ability to care for their own living children in light of their convictions. For example, both Alice and Gwen had their children removed from their care following their arrest. However, the indication given during the hearing is that the removal of custody was due to wider personal circumstances of the women's lives, suggesting there were other child protection concerns. The abandonment of the newly born infants occurred in these contexts, and it is expressed during both women's hearings that they concealed their pregnancies as they feared knowledge of the pregnancy by third parties would result in the removal of all their children from their care. In Alice's case, it is indicated that she is able to spend time with her children and that, at the time of the hearing, attempts were being made to reunite the family. Hope for a similar outcome was expressed during Gwen's hearing.

Child protection services were also involved in Elizabeth's and Hayley's cases at the time of the sentencing hearing. In Elizabeth's case, following her acquittal for murder and conviction of manslaughter by reason of diminished responsibility, but prior to the sentencing hearing, children's social services were in touch with Elizabeth's sister to indicate their concern for the welfare of that sister's children if Elizabeth were to return to live with the family. Elizabeth's barrister explained during the sentencing hearing:

---

[6]Births and Deaths Registration Act 1953, ss1-2. Qualified people include the mother and father of the child; the occupier of the house in which the child was, to the knowledge of that occupier, born; any person present at the birth; any person having charge of the child; in the case of a stillborn child found exposed, the person who found the child.

[7]Similar concerns have been expressed by health professionals and child protection services in relation to women who have chosen to not engage with antenatal services, often referred to as 'freebirthers'. There is currently very little research into this, see McKenzie et al. (2020). Those interested in women's experiences of freebirthing, including attempts to regulate and control women's behaviour by health and child protection professionals, should look out for work by Gemma McKenzie, who is currently completing a PhD on the topic.

DEFENCE: But as My Lord knows, [Elizabeth's sister] has
                  children who live with her, including two par-
                  ticularly young children and [an] infant ... And
                  we understand that Social Services, as they're
                  described in the [sentencing] report, would con-
                  sider taking draconian steps if this Defendant
                  were to be living with her sister, an arrangement
                  both would wish to take place, as I understand
                  it. That is why, as I understand it ...

JUDGE: Whose word, whose word is: 'Draconian'?

DEFENCE: Mine. What I mean is they would consider tak-
                  ing proceedings if my client, that Elizabeth, were
                  to live with her sister, because of concerns, no
                  doubt, about what they describe as risk. I say
                  that because these circumstances are, are partic-
                  ular to this case, and that which the Jury found
                  took place occurred at a time when this Defend-
                  ant was labouring under a condition which she
                  no longer labours under. Things have changed,
                  and changed materially, since [the delivery and
                  death of the child]. I don't use that word in a crit-
                  ical sense and I'm not being critical, I make clear,
                  of Social Services. It's not my place to be and I
                  am not being. But draconian means harsh in the
                  circumstances where one has two loving sisters,
                  one of whom has been convicted of the offence
                  of manslaughter but at a time when her respon-
                  sibility was substantially impaired through no
                  fault of her own, and those circumstances have
                  changed. (Elizabeth, prosecution mitigation)

The situation was resolved through Elizabeth's family paying for her to live in a
hotel while permanent accommodation could be sourced. It is noted though that
this is not the best outcome for Elizabeth:

> My Lord, then one would venture to suggest on her behalf that what
> this woman actually needs is an opportunity to start her life or con-
> tinue the life in which she had led it before, without criticism or blame
> or fault, until she fell under that condition which caused her to behave
> in a way which otherwise she would not have done so. My Lord may
> well have had in mind what [psychiatrist] said in his report, his sub-
> stantive report prepared at the beginning of March, that she is a vul-
> nerable woman and likely to remain. (Elizabeth, defence mitigation)

The support of her family is considered an essential element of her recovery from
this experience of pregnancy and involvement with criminal justice.

A similar discussion about child welfare occurs in Hayley's case:

DEFENCE: Social Services, as you will be aware, are involved in the sense that because of her appearance before the Court, there are parallel child protection hearings. There have been no issues raised at that.

JUDGE: Well, it seems to have been unnecessarily cautious, if l may say so, in relation to the other two children.

DEFENCE: But understandably.

JUDGE: Absolutely.

DEFENCE: It is not said in any way critically. So they are awaiting the sentence of the Court today. (Hayley, defence mitigation)

Hayley was sentenced to an immediate custodial sentence, so, one assumes, the children remained in the family home with their father. It is unknown whether or not social services became involved with the family following Hayley's release from prison.

At no point in my research have I come across any evidence to suggest that a woman who kills a newborn child or aborts a foetus, legally or illegally, and at any stage of gestation, poses a risk to other living children due to her actions of causing the death of the foetus/newborn baby. The only instance whereby she may pose a risk to other children is in those such as Alice's and Gwen's cases, where there are wider circumstances of their lives that raise child protection concerns. In cases such as Elizabeth's and Hayley's, where there are no wider concerns about their ability to parent and maintain the well-being of their living children, the death of a foetus/ child following a crisis pregnancy does not indicate a risk to older children (as noted in Chapter 2, both women have a history of multiple crisis pregnancies). Therefore, I would agree with Elizabeth's barrister, and the judge in Hayley's sentencing hearing, that the intervention of children's services is both 'draconian' and 'unnecessarily cautious'. However, as has been argued by Stephen A. Webb (2009), social work has been reconfigured through forms of governmentality, using risk calculation techniques based on the principles of actuarialism – the ability to calculate the probability of risk and operate accordingly. While the extent to which actuarial calculations play a role in risk decisions is disputed, as Mark Hardy (2017) argues, social workers make decisions about child protection in an environment where the fear of blame if they do not act and a child is harmed is palpable:[8] the culture of

---

[8]See Rose (1998) for a discussion of the impact of actuarial practice and the role of assessment, prediction, and management of risk as central to the logic of 'community psychiatry'. Rose concludes that the changing approach to understanding the risk of psychiatric patients is that mental health professionals operate to seek strategies to minimise the aggregate levels of risk posed by 'risky' individuals, thus working in a culture of

blame undoubtedly has an impact on how child protection professionals assess the possibility of risk.

Further concerns are expressed in terms of the risk that the women may pose to future foetuses. In Sally's case, the judge states, 'In mitigation, you are now a lady [in her fifties] and at your age there is no risk of any future similar activity' (Sally, judge sentencing); thus, indicating that her level of risk to future 'children' is averted due to her no longer being able to conceive. Similarly, in Hayley's case, the judge makes a point while sentencing that other foetuses will be at risk of her illegally aborting them, justifying the sentence that would later be described by the Court of Appeal as 'manifestly excessive':

> As a matter of public policy, and bearing in mind the need for deter-
> rence, a long determinative sentence is required. There is no reason
> to believe that you would not act in the same way if the same cir-
> cumstances arose, but fortunately the chances of that are so small
> that I do not consider it necessary further to consider the danger-
> ousness provisions of the 2003 Act. (Hayley, judge sentencing)

Here, the judge is referring to Part Twelve, Chapter Five of the Criminal Justice Act 2003. This Chapter of the Act allows for a defendant to be sentenced to life imprisonment if the offence is serious (punishable by either life imprisonment or for a determinate period of 10 years or more [s224(2)(b)]), and if the offender is considered dangerous (if the court considers there to be 'a significant risk to members of the public of serious harm occasioned by the commission by him [*sic*.] of further such offences' [s229(1)(b)]).[9] The judge is implying that the only aspect of the case that means Hayley is not an offender who poses 'a significant risk to members of the public of serious harm occasioned by the commission by him [*sic*.] of further such offences' is that the chance of her becoming pregnant again is small. However, the judge is also implying that he considers her to be a significant danger to any foetus she may carry. The judge's position here is alarming for a number of reasons, but specifically, because he is considering a not-yet-conceived foetus to be a 'member of the public'. The logical next steps of such a view are that it would be reasonable and acceptable to imprison a woman, presumably to prevent her from becoming pregnant, in order to safeguard a foetus that may be conceived if she is not imprisoned. Such a position not only negates the born alive rule but also poses a significant dan-ger to women's rights of bodily autonomy and equality under the law, as will be discussed in Chapter 6.

---

risk management where the focus is less about averting danger and more about illustrat-ing that the risk assessment and approach was appropriate. See also Feeley and Simon (1992, 1994), Garland (2000, 2001), and O'Malley (1992, 2000, 2004) for their discus-sions of risk mentality and actuarialism in criminal justice policy and practice.
[9]See Crown Prosecution Service (2019) for an overview of sentencing guidance for dangerous offenders under this provision.

Legitimate Risk

As has been presented here, the women's behaviour is considered and discussed in line with the principles of maternal management of risks towards the foetus. The expectation is that the women will put the needs and welfare of the foetus before their own and so avert risk to the foetus. As outlined in the academic literature, this expectation is directly connected to ideals of motherhood and motherly behaviour: to be the 'good' mother is to be the 'responsible' pregnant woman (Lupton, 2011; Ruhl, 1999). In Chapter 3, I outlined that, during the criminal hearings, there is an expectation voiced that the women will act as mothers to their foetuses purely due to the existence of the pregnancy. Coupling that conclusion with the findings presented in this chapter, it is clear that the women are expected to do everything to be the 'good' mother and so being the 'responsible' pregnant woman who will protect her 'child'. For the women to achieve this status as the 'good' mother, they would need to have revealed their pregnancies to third parties, in order to receive medical treatment and then medical assistance in labour and delivery, so allowing professionals to assess and mitigate the risks the women pose to the foetus. In not disclosing the pregnancy, the women are conceptualised as failing as individual mothers, with suggestions during these hearings that these failings are part of the reason why they require criminalisation and punishment.

However, as outlined in Chapter 2, criminal justice fails to understand the experience of a crisis pregnancy and the impact that this will have on the women's ability to assimilate the 'good' mother and 'responsible' pregnant woman. Consequently, the actions or inactions of the women are easily portrayed and interpreted as intentional and perhaps even as a motive to kill the foetus/child. If we understand a crisis pregnancy in line with the main thrust of the literature on concealed/denied pregnancy and neonaticide as a reproductive dysfunction (Beier et al., 2006), then an argument can be made that the women had little ability to mitigate the risk they posed to the foetus, due to their inability to fully acknowledge and respond to their pregnancy. Such an approach leads to the women's actions being dismissed along the lines of the 'mad', 'bad', 'sad' narratives. As outlined in Chapter 3, these narratives have been opposed by feminist scholars as they remove the concept of women's agency as offenders and so individualises their actions (Ballinger, 2007; Morris & Wilczynski, 1993; Weare, 2016). If, however, we conceptualise a crisis pregnancy as I advocated in Chapter 2, and as argued by others (Oberman, 2003; Vellut et al., 2012), as a product of society and a result of the complex personal situations faced by exceedingly vulnerable women, then there is scope to view the actions and/or inactions of the women in a holistic and socially contextualised manner. Viewing their behaviour during pregnancy, labour and delivery, and following the birth, as relational to wider social structures that both facilitate and result in a crisis pregnancy, gives us the ability to understand what has occurred as more than simply an individual response deserving individualised criminalisation and punishment. The focus is no longer upon personal failure to act as pregnant women and mothers 'should', as presented in the court hearings, nor on explaining away the women's actions and thus removing any form of agency by the women, as critiqued by feminists.

To allow for this contextualised view of the women's actions/inactions, it is necessary for us to reconstruct the concept of risk in cases of suspicious perinatal death. At the moment, perceptions of risk and risk management strategies flow in one direction – the foetus at risk from its 'mother'. This normalised flow of risk is not just evident in the cases assessed here, but in most pregnancies, as outlined in the literature at the top of this chapter.[10] However, if we conceptualise the woman as at risk from the foetus, this challenges the interpretations of the women's actions/inactions that are presented as the norm in the criminal hearings analysed here. For example, in Hayley's case, the understanding here is that she failed to put her foetus first because she did not want her husband to discover that she was pregnant following an affair. If we reconstruct the narrative of events with Hayley as the subject of risk, then it could look something like this: Hayley, who has a history of experiencing her pregnancies as risks to her sense of self and her well-being, became pregnant, which she did not want to be. This pregnancy threatened her living children, her relationship with her husband, and with her lover. If this pregnancy was accepted, and later if this child was born, it would have potentially caused a breakdown in Hayley's personal relationships, thus destroying her life as she knows it, and so is a fundamental risk to her well-being.

Similarly, Hannah's story can be reframed to prioritise her account of her fears about her family's reaction to her pregnancy. Rather than being portrayed as making 'bad and wrong decisions' about her relationship with her partner, we can interpret her decisions about her emotional and sexual relationship in a woman-focussed, sex-positive way: a woman, over the age of consent, choosing to have a relationship with a man she desires. Rather than seeing her decision to keep her pregnancy from her family as being a 'mistaken' belief that her family would not accept the pregnancy, and so would reject her, we can reconceptualise the foetus as a risk to Hannah's sense of safety and acceptance by her family. We can see Hannah's relationship with her family, and her sense of security as a woman who believes she cannot legitimately become pregnant out of marriage, as her being at threat from a foetus, and subsequent child. Each of the cases can be reframed in this way, to centralise and prioritise the well-being and safety of the woman over the foetus.

One of the potential challenges to reconstructing these cases, to conceptualise the foetus as a risky entity with the potential to cause harm to the woman, is that

---

[10]The one exception to this may occur whereby the woman has a medical condition that means a pregnancy would be a risk to her health – for example, cancer requiring chemotherapy or radiotherapy. However, even in this situation, it is most likely that the foetus will not be considered the cause of the risk; instead, it is the cancer that is the risk to the woman's health, with the possibility of the foetus being seen as also at risk due to the woman needing treatment for her cancer. See, for example, *In re AC*, 573 A.2d 1235 (DC 1990): Angela Carder was forced to undergo a life-threatening, court-ordered caesarean section against her wishes (and the wishes of her family and her doctors) in an unsuccessful attempt to save the life of her foetus, due to Angela requiring treatment for cancer and wishing to terminate the pregnancy to facilitate that treatment. Angela and the baby died soon after the caesarean section.

this is not how our society (read: heteronormative, white, capitalist patriarchy) conceptualises children. As outlined in the literature presented above, foetuses are now widely considered to be unborn 'children' in public discourses, health approaches, child protection policies and services, and, as presented here, in criminal hearings. Children, including foetuses, are conceptualised as 'innocent', 'vulnerable', 'precious', and in need of care and protection (Ariès, 1965; Zelizer, 1994). Therefore, how can a category of humans, who are, quite literally helpless, in that they cannot help themselves and so are in need of protection, be conceptualised as a risk to adult women who have the ability to protect themselves. As Robin West (1988, p. 69) argues, 'the fetus is not one of Hobbes' "relatively equal" natural men against whom we[women] have a right to protect ourselves' and thus is not conceptualised as such by men, nor in law, which is created by men to address the harms perceived by men. In order to square this circle, we again need to move away from the individualised model; rather than seeing the foetus/ newborn child as an individual threat, we need to conceptualise the threat caused by them to women in a wider social context – as a product of heteronormative, white, capitalist patriarchy. We also need to identify and acknowledge that the threats to women will differ depending on their intersecting characteristics: there is no singular women's experience (Harris, 1990).

Foetuses and pregnancies, as they are conceptualised and perceived by societies in the Western world, are, regularly, threats to women. The threat of a pregnancy is tied to how sexuality, family, and the importance and value attributed to women as members of society have been constructed and portrayed – today and historically. The historical elements will become clearer in Chapter 5, as the history of criminal offences connected to suspicious perinatal deaths is assessed. So, for now, let us consider the contemporary representation of women, sexuality, and family in the UK.

We have already seen one element of how pregnancy, childbirth, and child-rearing can pose inherent threats to women, in our review of feminists' critiques of motherhood and mothering in Chapter 3. Feminists are not united in their assessment of motherhood as either being inherently a negative aspect of life for women that needs to be overcome and transcended (Beauvoir, 1997 [1949]) or to be reclaimed as inherently positive outside of man's control and patriarchal structures (Rich, 1986). Nevertheless, the social, cultural, and political association of woman with mother, and motherhood as inherent to women's identities and role in society, has had, and continues to have, an impact on women's ability to operate outside of the role of 'mother', beyond the domestic labour of gestating, birthing, and then rearing children (Glenn et al., 1994). Ideologies of motherhood, and the norms that are constructed by and through those ideologies, reach into all areas of social life, shaping how women are able to interact with the world.

But, as outlined in Chapter 3, the myths of motherhood do not operate equally on all women and are impacted by elements of identity such as race, ethnicity, class, (dis)ability, immigration status, nationality, age, sexuality, marital status, educational level. Controls have always been placed on who should or should not 'breed', replenish/contribute to the population of the society and/or nation (Foucault, 1998 [1976]; Fyfe, 1991; Weeks, 1981). Such controls continue to operate today, although in less punitive forms than in previous centuries, as illustrated in Chapter 5. Examples of regulation of women's procreation can be seen in a policy change in the United Kingdom to limit the child element of child tax credit to the first two children a woman has, excluding all future children, brought in by the Conservative Government in 2017 (HM Revenue & Customs, 2020).[11] Such a policy has a very specific focus on poor women and their families – women who need to claim child tax credit to provide or supplement their income. The message of such measures is clear; if you cannot afford to support more children, then you should not have them, as the state will not be supporting them. Such regulations on family size are not placed on women who live with financial security and wealth and so do not rely on state support to survive and live. In this context, a pregnancy could be a threat to a woman's financial security and her ability to provide for herself and her existing and future children.

Similarly, in terms of age, the government guidance, *Teenage pregnancy prevention framework*, sends the message that society is hostile to women under 20 years of age reproducing (Public Health England, 2018). At the other end of the age spectrum is the representations of 'older' or 'geriatric' mums as being at 'risk [of] missing out on motherhood' if she has not had a baby before her mid-thirties (National Health Service, 2009), together with the ominous 'ticking' of a woman's biological clock (Weigel, 2016). Such representations of women's ageing bodies and motherhood operate in public discourse and health policy. Despite evidence that men's fertility also declines with age (Sample, 2017), it is women's bodies, age, and lifestyle that bear the brunt of social and cultural scrutiny. Whether too fat or too thin, too employed or too unemployed, too single, too poor or too rich ('too posh to push'; Rustin, 2016), too uneducated, too educated, too drunk, too disabled, too gay, too butch, too black – the list of conditions placed on women to regulate and censure the 'rightness' of her decision to reproduce is endless. These impact most women, falling hardest on the most vulnerable in terms of the involvement of child protection services, economic implications, criminal justice intervention, and public scorn.

In addition to policing who can have a baby, limits are also placed on women's decisions to end a pregnancy. Pressures are placed on a woman's ability to access an abortion, and whether the decision to terminate a pregnancy is considered 'valid' or 'appropriate'. As Sally Sheldon (1993, 1997) and Fran Amery (2020) argue, legal provision of abortion in Great Britain was not granted on the basis of allowing women reproductive freedom and bodily control to allow them to decide whether they continue a pregnancy. Instead, the Abortion Act 1967 was constructed to gatekeep access to abortions, ensuring that only women deemed worthy and who want to terminate a pregnancy for the 'right' reasons can access the medical procedure. Women's desires to control their bodies and prevent an unwanted pregnancy are not considered good-enough reasons for a termination to be legal. Abortion continues to be shrouded by stigma and notions of shame that a woman would end up in such a situation where an unwanted pregnancy

---

[11]With the exceptions of a further pregnancy resulting in a multiple birth or a child born as a result of 'non-consensual conception'.

needs to be ended (Bommaraju et al., 2016; Hoggart, 2017; Kumar et al., 2009). Society continues to resist seeing abortion as an element of reproductive health, part of a continuum for preventing unintended pregnancy that ranges from methods to prevent ovulation, barrier methods or hormones to create a hostile environment for sperm and so prevent fertilisation, emergency contraception to prevent implantation, and ending with abortion (Sheldon & Wellings, 2020a). Such resistance is evident in the uneasiness of accepting the artificial line between 'contraception' and 'abortion': developments of contraception that would work to end the pregnancy after implantation are illegal under the statutory framework for legal abortion in Great Britain (Sheldon, 2015).

Less researched are the stigma and social difficulties faced by women who continue their pregnancy but terminate their role as a mother to that child through adoption. As Marshall (2012) argues, women who decide to give up a child for adoption are often confronted with arguments by state actors that they will regret their choice, or that the choice is not 'natural'; their decision to conceal the pregnancy and relinquish their parental role towards the child is seen as inauthentic and therefore impermissible. In relation to this, state intervention to take children from women following birth, due to their role as a mother being seen as dangerous, unacceptable, and/or too risky towards or for the child, is the latest measure in a long history of what Pamela Cox (2012) terms 'governing intimate citizenship'; preceded and flanked by institutionalisation, sterilisation, and coercion to use long-acting, reversible contraception.

For those women who continue a pregnancy, whether wanted or not; and become mothers to that child, whether wanted or not; or who parent a child that they have not gestated and birthed, the hardships and labour of motherhood are, for many if not most, relentless and all-encompassing. Across societies, the vast majority of childcare responsibilities still fall to women, with a substantial gap between women and men in terms of the amount of unpaid work conducted. As Diva Dhar (2020) argues, women's unpaid care work has been unmeasured and undervalued for too long:

> Women perform 75 per cent of such work globally, dedicating, on average, four hours and 25 minutes daily to it – more than three times men's average of one hour and 23 minutes.

Often not perceived as work, and not valued as equal to paid employment, women bear most of the burden of caring for and raising children. The gap between men's and women's engagement in unpaid care has a dramatic impact on women's paid employment prospects post-birth, as outlined in the key findings of the UK household longitudinal study by Understanding Society (2019):

- Fewer than one-in-five of all new mothers, and 29% of first-time mothers, return to full-time work in the first three years after maternity leave. This falls to 15% after five years.
- 17% of women leave employment completely in the five years following childbirth, compared to 4% of men.

- In the year before birth, the man was the main earner in 54% of couples. This increases to 69% three years after birth.
- Mothers who leave employment completely are three times more likely to return to a lower-paid or lower-responsibility role than those who do not take a break.
- For new mothers – but not fathers – staying with the same employer is associated with a lower risk of downward occupational mobility but also with lower chances of progression.

Similarly, in their study, The Fawcett Society (2016) concluded that 29% of people think men are *more* committed to their jobs after having a baby, while 46% believe women are *less* committed to their jobs after having a baby. Also, women are more likely to take time off when the child is ill, rather than the father. Thus, the cost of having a child in terms of both lifestyle and employment prospects is substantial for women, compared to men.

The detrimental experiences of pregnancy and motherhood outlined here, and others I have not discussed, require a structural analysis so as to move away from the notion of individual responsibility. The concept of 'gendered harms' has been deployed by feminist legal scholars to acknowledge harms in society experienced by women due to their gender – not a product of their biological sex per se: 'biology is indeed destiny when we are unaware of the extent to which biology is narrowing out fate, but that *biology is destiny only to the extent of our ignorance*' (West, 1988, p. 71, her emphasis), as women do not need to be led by their biological destiny and would not be, with the destruction of the patriarchal order. As Joanne Conaghan (1996) argues, 'gendered harm' is based on the principle that harm has a gendered content, specifically that 'women suffer particular harm and injuries *as women*: their experiences of pain and injury are distinguishable, to a large extent, from the experiences of men' (Conaghan, 1996, p. 407, her emphasis; see also Fineman & Thomadsen, 1991; Graycar & Morgan, 2002; Howe, 1987; West, 1997). Here it is important to reiterate that women's experiences of harm, while distinct from men's, are not universally the same (Harris, 1990). For Conaghan, there are at least two dimensions to gendered harm: first, pregnancy and childbirth, and menstrual and/ or ovulation pains; and second, harms that are not exclusive to women in a biological sense but are risks that women are more likely to experience – risk of rape, incest, sexual harassment, intimate partner violence and abuse, and harmful medical intervention. Many feminists would argue we can add raising children and associated unpaid labour of care to this list, as I have noted above.

For feminist legal scholars, gendered harm is a tool of analysis, a prism through which to see how the Rule of Law (not just criminal law) fails to recognise, address, and protect against the harms experienced by women. In her analysis of legal outcomes of cases of newborn child killing in Ireland during the twentieth century, Karen Brennan (2018a) uses the concept of gendered harm to assess the structural dimensions that contribute to women killing their newborn children – lack of reproductive autonomy, including access to contraception and abortion; stigma over pregnancy outside of marriage; and lack of economic, cultural, and social support to raise children. For Brennan (2018a, p. 186):

patriarchal norms and values, which were embedded in various legal provisions and in the Irish state's approach to unmarried mothers, cause harm to women … it is possible to see that the harm caused to the baby by its mother was a consequence of the 'gendered harms' caused to her by patriarchy, and the state's adoption of patriarchal values in its laws and policies.

Brennan concludes that the state bears some responsibility for the crime of newborn infant homicide by mothers. Furthermore, the state causes more harm to these women, by holding them solely responsible for their actions and thus criminalising their behaviour, rather than contextualising their actions in wider social structures that lead to newborn child killing.

Using this conceptual framework, we can see pregnancy, reproduction, and child-rearing as a potential gendered harm, in that they are experienced exclusively or disproportionately (in regard to child-rearing) by women. As with all social harms, the pains of the harm are experienced most greatly by those who are most vulnerable (Fineman, 2008), thus it is not a universal experience, but one that is deeply entrenched in and shaped by intersections of identity and the disadvantages of life that are disproportionally experienced by some women due to race, class, and other aspects of identity. In the context of the arguments I make here, the gendered harm is a consequence of the lived experience of reproduction and mothering today, and the conditions under which women are expected to engage in both – in the context of heteronormative, white, capitalist, patriarchy. Accordingly, it is not women's fundamental ability to become pregnant that is the source of gendered harm – the 'invasion' of the body, as pregnancy is conceptualised by some radical feminists[12] – but the conditions under which women are expected to become pregnant, carry a foetus, labour and deliver that foetus, and then mother the child. Reproduction and mothering need to be 'released' from patriarchy: the institution that makes the acts compulsory and so constrains them (West, 1988, p. 47).

Despite considerable harms experienced by women due to pregnancies, foetuses, and children, these 'life experiences' continue to fail to be conceptualised and appreciated as legitimate risks to women's well-being and life, in law and criminal justice, as well as in health and wider society. As outlined by Wendy Chan and George S. Rigakos (2002), risk discourses and theoretical discussions of 'risk society' and governmentality have generally been perceived to be gender neutral, whereby risk theorists have made 'dubious claims about the death of class, gender and race' (p. 745). Risk taking and risk management have been assumed to be generally universal experiences of calculation and effect borne from instrumental science; thus race, gender, and class are perceived as but one more risk variable. However, as Chan and Rigakos argue, risk is not a neutral concept – it is political.

---

[12]Analysis of pregnancy, as an invasion that women need to be able to protect themselves from, is an argument that certainly could be made here. See West (1988) for her discussion of radical feminists' positions on pregnancy and heterosexual sex as the intrusion of women's bodies and, thus, oppression of her subjectivity.

Women perceive and experience risks very differently to men, shaping their lives accordingly (Stanko, 1997; Walklate, 1997): most women can tell you about the precautions they take when walking home alone at night, to counter the perceived risk of the stranger in the night, an experience either not lived or lived differently by most men.[13] The unpleasantness of this perception of risk, Chan and Rigakos (2002) argue, is that it works as a form of social control of women, pushing them into the private sphere, the home, and the 'protection' of the men they know intimately, who, many, many feminists have concluded, are of most danger to women (Hanmer & Saunders, 1984; Stanko, 1985).

But the gendered nature of risk goes beyond how risk is perceived and experienced. What and who counts as risky, and which situations are seen to not embody risk are also shaped by gender; as Chan and Rigakos (2002, p. 754) argue, risk is determined through 'unabashed male privilege in the formulation of official dangers'. Here they are referring to how patriarchy – the masculinity of the Rule of Law and institutions of social control – respond to the perceived danger posed by some women; for example, the danger perceived, and responded to, through the witch-hunts of the sixteenth and seventeenth centuries. In the context of suspicious perinatal deaths, it is the woman who does not embrace motherhood nor act as the responsible pregnant woman upon conceiving, who is seen as dangerous, and thus a risk that criminal justice and law responds to.

'Masculine privilege' also accounts for the lack of perceived risk in other situations; for example, refusal to acknowledge that men who commit intimate partner violence and abuse against women are a risk to the safety and lives of those women. In a number of instances where a woman kills her violent and/or abusive partner, if she waits for time to pass since he last beat her before she kills him, or kills him while he sleeps or is unconscious, or kills him with a weapon while he is unarmed, she is denied use of legal defences, such as provocation or self-defence to murder charges.[14] In these instances, women's perception of the risk to themselves (being killed or seriously harmed) and the appropriate and proportional steps they need to take to ameliorate that risk (kill their partner) are understood by law and criminal justice to be either unreasonable levels of fear or a desire for revenge, consequently delegitimising the risks that these women face (Chan and Rigakos, 2002).

The same logic can be applied to offences relating to suspected newborn child killing. The assumption is that the foetus/newborn child supersedes the woman who is pregnant/has given birth and so she is expected to manage any risks experienced by the foetus. Added to this is the widely held perception that the foetus

---

[13]The public discussion and protests following the murder of Sarah Everard in London in March 2021 highlight the risks experienced by women every day.

[14]In England and Wales, changes have been made to the defence of provocation, now known as loss of self-control (Coroners and Justice Act 2009, ss54-56), with the aim of making it easier for women to use the partial defence to murder in such circumstances. However, see Edwards (2016) for her discussion as to how and why the new defence is still likely to preclude women receiving leniency.

cannot pose a risk to the woman. The result is that any perception that the foetus/pregnancy is a risk to the woman is considered illegitimate. The concept of there being a risk to the woman is so foreign to discourse and understanding surrounding these cases, it is not even considered or mentioned in the court hearings. Instead, the perception is that the pregnant woman, as a mother, should put the foetus first. Her perception of risk is considered illegitimate, mistaken, foolish, wrong, unjustified, unnatural. This perception of her concept of risk delegitimises her choice to not respond to the pregnancy as anticipated, as expected. Thus, her actions are perceived as individual failings – the response of the 'bad' mother and 'irresponsible' pregnant woman. By individualising the failings, the social cultural factors that lead a woman to conceal/deny a pregnancy, and to give birth alone resulting in the death of the child, continue to be masked: the gendered harm continues to be obscured. It is she, and she alone, who is to blame.

As we will see in Chapters 5 and 6, this perception of the foetus/pregnancy as an illegitimate risk to a woman has significant consequences for how her actions or inactions in pregnancy and following the birth of a baby are perceived. Society sees her as a risk and a danger, and so criminal law and justice are deployed accordingly to manage that risk and to facilitate punishment of her deviant mothering. As part of this, I will explore how criminal law is utilised to facilitate the criminalisation of women in these cases, both historically and today. In theory, the born alive rule prevents a woman from being held criminally liable for being the 'irresponsible' pregnant woman. However, as will be explored, in practice, the law is applied in ways that effectively defeat the born alive rule. Consequently, the risk women are perceived to pose to the foetus when they fail as mothers can be, and is, captured as criminal offending. First, in Chapter 5, I will outline how the 'menu' of criminal offences came into existence and the historical context of the adoption of these laws.

Chapter 5

Mothers in Law I: Criminalising the 'Illegitimate' Mother

A woman, whose age might have promised more Chastity and prudence, being privately delivered of a Bastard-childe, made shift, by her wickedness, to deprive the poor Infant of that life she had contributed to by her wantonness. She pretended it came by its untimely end, by falling from her body on the floor whilst she unhumanely went from the bed towards the door; but she concealing it above a week under her Pillow, the Law justly Condemn'd her as a wilful Murtheress. (Old Bailey Proceedings Online, April 1677)

The criminal law and justice responses to suspicious perinatal deaths are not modern phenomena; they have a long history. The laws that are applied in the cases analysed in this book, and the attitudes held towards women who experience a crisis pregnancy resulting in the death of the foetus/child, are shaped by the past. Specifically analysed, are the menu of offences that are open to prosecutors to draw upon, to facilitate criminalisation of a woman's actions – child destruction, concealment of birth, infanticide, and procuring a miscarriage. Therefore, it is important for us to consider the current legal situation in the context of its history, or rather its herstory, as it is a story about the control and regulation of women.[1] The herstory of legal developments in this area reveals that there is a long and sustained concern over which women should be mothers, when they

---

[1] A desire to uncover herstory of suspected perinatal homicide needs to be tempered by the ability to perform such a task. The nature of the development of laws, the records that were created and then preserved, and whose voices were included versus those that were excluded, makes it challenging, if not impossible, to examine legal developments from a herstorical perspective – laws were created by men, for men, and were implemented by men and then that implementation was recorded by men. Furthermore, as the history of 'infanticide' has been of such interest to historians and legal scholars, most of whom have been men – and continue to be in the professorial ranks – the telling of legal, political, and social developments has mostly been by men, no doubt having an impact on the nature and content of the narratives that exist today.

Criminal Justice Responses to Maternal Filicide: Judging the Failed Mother, 101–125
Copyright © 2021 by Emma Milne
Published by Emerald Publishing under an Exclusive Licence
doi:10.1108/978-1-83909-620-420211007

should be mothers, and which man's child they should mother. As a consequence, significant concern has been raised over women's sexuality, ability to become pregnant, and what actions she may take to 'rectify' her transgression of socially and culturally unauthorised pregnancy. These concerns are reflected in law, politics, and societal attitudes. It is these perceptions and popular concerns that will be focussed upon in this chapter.

Public perceptions of the actions of, and state responses to, women suspected of perinatal killing, from the end of the sixteenth century through to the early twentieth century, have been assessed through the lens of perceptions of risk as legitimate/illegitimate. As in the twenty-first century, the notion of a pregnancy/ newborn child as a legitimate risk to the well-being of the woman who is pregnant is delegitimised and so socially controlled. Whereas the risk of a woman who is pregnant when she should not be (being unmarried) is perceived as a legitimate risk to men's integrity and so needs to be controlled, regulated, and punished: socially, culturally, economically, and legally. The consequence is that women who are pregnant when it is deemed they should not be are criminalised and so required to bear individual responsibility for their reaction to a situation of being pregnant (killing the foetus/baby), regardless of the fact that the situation is caused and constructed by society's discriminatory attitudes towards, and regulations of women. However, what we see over the period under review – the end of the sixteenth century to the early twentieth century – is a change in the way the criminalisation is processed and how individual women have been perceived, and thus their actions responded to through criminal law and justice. There is a clear movement over the time period from stringent punishment to a reluctance to punish. However, as I will argue, this change in the nature of the criminal law and justice response does not indicate a relaxing of the social control of women's sexuality and legitimate motherhood. Instead, it indicates a changing social perception in the palatability of punishing women's transgressions of patriarchal rules – killing illegitimate children to escape public ridicule of premarital sex and pregnancy. In all instances, the women's behaviour in response to their pregnancy – ending the pregnancy through abortion or killing the newborn child – is seen as action taken in response to a risk that is considered to be illegitimate.

The Murder of Bastard Children

The fear that women have the ability to hide their pregnancy, give birth to a child, and then kill the child following birth, meaning that no one knew she was pregnant, has existed for centuries. As outlined in Chapter 2, the perception that women can, and do behave like this, is reflected in the cases of Bethany and Jessica. In contemporary context, concern that women may demonstrate such behaviour reflects the perceived risks that may befall the foetus/child; as outlined in Chapter 2, there is a misconception that a concealed/denied pregnancy is a risk factor for neonaticide. In the late sixteenth century and during the seventeenth century, where our herstory begins, social, legal, and political concern over hidden pregnancy resulting in the death of an infant had a different focus; namely that the women were unmarried and that their actions of killing the baby after the hidden pregnancy were to hide their 'immoral' sexuality. As illustrated in the extract from the Old Bailey trial from 1677, quoted at the top of this chapter, specific focus was given during criminal hearings to the accused woman's 'chastity and prudence'.

During the early modern period (1500–1750), the sexuality of women was closely monitored and controlled in social, cultural (including religious), and legal contexts. As Sara Heller Mendelson and Patricia Crawford (1998) argue, women were defined by their relationships with men. The expectation was that a woman would refrain from sexual practices except for those she had with her husband:[2] 'the ideal state for a woman was marriage and motherhood, under the governance of a man' (Mendelson & Crawford, 1998, p. 67). The control of women's sexuality centres around, and originates in the management and trans-ference of private property from father to son, as women were (and continue to be?!) the vessels of reproduction of men's lineage and patrimony. Thus, control-ling whose seed is planted inside the 'fertile soil' of a woman's womb was of the utmost importance. If a woman was not a virgin upon marriage, then a man could not be certain any children born from her would be his. Similarly, if she did not remain chaste in marriage, then he could father another man's child, who then inherits his property. In this cultural and social context, tolerance for unmarried mothers was low, with women risking financial and social ruin if they became pregnant without a man to marry and to claim the child as his. Historians have concluded the mid-sixteenth century to the Civil War (approximately 1550–1642) was a particularly dangerous time for women, as society was focussed on disorder, and women who challenged accepted gender norms were perceived as a serious threat (see Mendelson & Crawford, 1998, pp. 69–70). During that period, more women were physically punished[3] or executed than at any other time in history.[4]

It is in this context that specific laws were introduced, targeting women who conceived children outside of marriage. During the Tudor period, following the Reformation, fears of the sexual immorality of the population, with the admin-istration of punishment for acts of 'debauchery', were slowly moved from the Ecclesiastical Courts to the Royal Council. This transference of jurisdiction resulted in a growing number of women being brought before the Magistrates' Courts on charges of fornication, bastardry, and other similar offences (Hoffer & Hull, 1981). As Joan Kent (1973) outlines in her review of laws relating to per-sonal conduct, eight Bills against 'bastardry' were heard in Parliament between 1576 and 1627. It was in 1576 that one of the many poor laws enacted over this period included a clause for the punishment of bastardry:

---

[2]Marriage was not formally regulated by the state at this time. Smart (1998) argues that the status of being married or not married was more fluid in the early modern period than in subsequent eras.

[3]The pillory, stocks, branding, flogging.

[4]This period is also marked by the large number of women who were murdered by state agents under the justification that they were witches.

> it was ordered that bastards should be supported by their putative
> fathers, though bastardy orders in the quarter sessions date from
> before this date. If the genitor could be found, then he was put
> under very great pressure to accept responsibility and to maintain
> the child. (Macfarlane, 1980, p. 75)

While the focus of the law is clearly moral in judgement, numerous commentators
have argued that economic implications of illegitimate children were also a significant consideration, to regulate the financial burden of the wandering poor who
were deemed to be 'defrauding' the parish of its ability to assist the 'true poor'
(Hoffer & Hull, 1981; Kilday, 2013; Sharpe, 1983). Hence, the legislation required
that all efforts be made to determine who fathered the illegitimate child so that he
may be forced to pay a weekly bond for the child, so removing the financial cost
from the community (Hoffer & Hull, 1981, p. 13; Kent, 1973; King, 2014). The
financial 'burden' of an illegitimate child also needs to be seen and understood as
a feature of discriminatory attitudes and regulations of women. To bear a child
outside of marriage was to face reputational and financial ruin, as women struggled to obtain employment and make a living for themselves, due to the perceived
'immorality' stemming from her engagement in premarital sex.

While the focus of the financial outcome – the payable bond to support the
child – targeted the man, the law had a specific impact upon community attitudes towards, and treatment of, unmarried women who were suspected of being
pregnant. Justices of the Peace were required to examine a woman accused of
'bastardry', with the case heard at the quarter session, where the woman would be
pressured to reveal the identity of the man who impregnated her, resulting in the
public disgrace of the woman (Hoffer & Hull, 1981). Another tactic to obtain a
name from the woman was for the midwife to ask her who fathered her child while
she was in labour. J. A. Sharpe (1983) states that, in order to *persuade* the mother
to reveal the identity of the father of the baby, members of the community would
surround a labouring woman and remind her that death was a possibility during
childbirth, and so she should be truthful before she dies. Sharpe also found evidence that the midwife might refuse to attend a woman in labour until she gave
up the name. Parents who did not conform to the requirements of the 1576 Act
would face corporal punishments and a jail term. Thus, we can see significant
social pressure and focus on the behaviour of women suspected to be pregnant
while not married.

Further legislation in 1609 focussed on illegitimacy (labelled bastardry) as the
burden of the community, a 'great dishonour' and 'great charge' to the nation.[5]
Mark Jackson (1996b) cites other legislation from the period with a similar
focus and message: 1610 legislation provided Justices of the Peace with the right
to send "'every lewd woman" bearing a chargeable bastard to the House of

---

[5]*An Act for the due execution of drivers Laws Statute heretofore made against rogues,*
vagabonds, sturdy beggars, and other lewd and idle persons; cited in Hoffer and Hull
(1981, p. 13).

Correction for one year' (p. 30); if she 're-offended', she could be committed until she made assurances she would not 'offend' again. Under these laws, the majority of people punished were women. While Jackson (1996b) does acknowledge that it was easier for the authorities to identify a mother of an illegitimate child due to her physical development during pregnancy, he concludes that the law acted to reaffirm societal prejudices towards women, interpreting it as 'a manifestation of a double standard that was applied to male and female sexual experience' (p. 30).

It is the enactment of the poor laws, identifying illegitimate children as a source of financial burden for the community, that Peter Charles Hoffer and N. E. H. Hull (1981) and Mark Jackson (1996b) attribute to the increase in unwed women killing their illegitimate newborn children. Their arguments are that the laws, and the public condemnation they fostered, encouraged unwed women to conceal their pregnancies and kill the child following birth, to avoid the shame associated with bearing an illegitimate child. Hoffer and Hull (1981) cite a 225% upsurge in the number of criminal indictments of women accused of killing their illegitimate newborn children after 1576 (p. 8). However, such a rise in prosecutions does not necessarily reflect an actual growth in the number of cases of women committing this form of homicide. The figures tell us that there was an increase in state investigation and application of the law, thus a rise in the prosecution statistics. This change in numbers may be attributed, at least in part, to greater public concern of the sexual behaviour of unwed women and the potential for an illegitimate child who would financially 'burden' the local community. Thus, the rise could signify greater surveillance of women and reporting of behaviour deemed suspicious, rather than an actual increase in the number of homicidal unmarried women. Hoffer and Hull argue that the Magistrates' Courts were actively prosecuting more women accused of newborn child murder after 1576, and that coroners and grand juries were more readily accepting evidence that a homicide had taken place in instances where infants died in suspicious circumstances. So, while the increased hostility to unwed mothers may have resulted in an actual rise in homicidal behaviour by women, together with the social pressures and possible criminal consequences if the community discovered she was pregnant, it needs to be remembered that this cannot be confirmed.

Regardless of whether the number of women murdering newborn children changed during the period, or simply the rate of prosecution, concern grew among the public and legal and political professionals that unmarried women were attempting to circumvent the requirements of the bastardry laws. The belief was that in order to avoid the punishments inflicted on unwed pregnant women and mothers under the poor laws, single women were purposefully concealing their pregnancies, giving birth alone, and killing the child, with the intention of concealing the fact that they were ever pregnant or gave birth (Beattie, 1986; Hoffer & Hull, 1981; Jackson, 1996b; Kilday, 2013). If the community did not know an unmarried woman was pregnant, and she killed the baby and hid the body, then she could not be punished for her immoral sexuality and for the financial implications she placed upon the state as a consequence – a fatherless baby. The belief that women were escaping punishment was intensified by the difficulty of securing a conviction under the common law of murder. As outlined in Chapter 1, under English and Welsh criminal law, a person must be fully born alive in order to be a victim of homicide. The outcome was that it was incredibly difficult to convict women of the murder of their infants due to a requirement of at least one witness who could testify that the child was born alive, rather than stillborn (Jackson, 1996b). Therefore, it was seen that unmarried women were getting away with two crimes: the first, her criminal sexuality and inflicting the financial burden of an illegitimate child on the community (punishable under the poor laws); and the second, her killing of the baby after birth due to lack of evidence of the child being born alive (punishable by death under the common law of murder).

To redress the belief that unmarried women were getting away with the crime of her sexuality, in 1624, Parliament passed *An Act to Prevent the Destroying and Murthering of Bastard Children* (hereafter 1624 Act), mandating that in instances where a 'lewd' woman:

> [...] be delivered of any issue of her Body Male or Female, which being born alive, should by the Lawe of this Realme be a Bastard, and that she endeavour privatelie either by drowning or secret bury thereof, or any other way, either by herself or the procuring of others, soe to conceale the Death thereof, as that it may not come to light, whether it were borne alive or not, but be concealed, in every such Case the Mother soe offending shall suffer Death as in case of Murther, except such Mother can make proof by one Witness at the least, that the Child (whose Death was by her soe intended to be concealed) was borne dead. (Parliament Papers, 1624 21 Jac 1 c27; cited in Kilday, 2013, pp. 17–18)

The legislation reversed the burden of proof of live birth: no longer was the Crown required to prove that the child was born alive; instead, the accused woman was required to prove that the baby was stillborn, and thus she had not killed it, by the testimony of at least one witness. Without production of proof of stillbirth, the woman could be convicted of murder, a capital offence. The 1624 Act only applied to unmarried women, while married women accused of newborn child murder were still afforded the privilege of the requirement of evidence of live birth, provided by the prosecution, to secure a conviction.

As a consequence of the 1624 Act, murder trials of unwed women accused of newborn child murder centred around who knew she was pregnant, and whether she had purposefully hidden herself away from witnesses to conceal the live birth of the baby, so allowing her the opportunity to kill the child post-birth, as is evident in this case from the Old Bailey Proceedings Online (April 1675):

> A woman was here also Indicted for the Murthering of her Bastard-child which she had hid in a Box, and was there discovered; it being questioned as the Law requires in such cases, whither the cryed out at the time of her Delivery, she affirmed she did, and that a Woman (one of the witnesses) at that time lay with her, but that she could not wake her; the said woman affirmed that she did

not acquaint her, nor did she suspect any thing of her condition, but that the other rose from her, and went into another Room, where it seems she was delivered, and the child afterwards found dead in the aforesaid box: The Jury brought her in guilty.

Thus, a woman's concealment of the pregnancy and subsequent labour became a key feature of these cases. As William Blackstone (1791, p. 198) explained in his exposé of the law, evidence of concealment of the birth and death of an illegitimate child provided 'almost conclusive evidence of the child's being murdered by its mother'.

The focus upon, and public and legal concern about unmarried women concealing their pregnancies, occurred in the context of it being very normal for women to keep knowledge of their pregnancies from their neighbours. Pregnancy was considered a private affair, and it was deemed immoral for a woman to clearly display her pregnancy bump in public. Privacy in pregnancy was a privilege not afforded to unmarried women, who were the subjects of communal scrutiny and surveillance and were the focus of suspicion in relation to their sexuality and pregnancy status (Gowing, 1997; Kilday, 2013). The influence of public suspicion and concern over unmarried women's sexuality is evident in records of women being prosecuted for newborn child murder, despite their claims they had never been pregnant and no body of an infant ever being discovered (Jackson, 1996b, p. 83). As Elizabeth Rapaport (2006) argues, while the killing of both legitimate and illegitimate newborn children persisted, unwed women were the focus of prosecutions, while married people were, mostly, afforded privacy to decide the size of their family, allowing unwanted children to die; a historical practice that was still tolerated, albeit conducted discreetly. Thus, the focus of criminal justice intervention in these cases cannot be said to be due to concerns over the welfare of infant life. Illegitimate children had little to no value, and death rates of infants meant that social enquiry into the death of a newly born child of wed parents would often be limited. Consequently, the 1624 Act, and pursuit of criminal convictions and the hanging of convicted women, needs to be seen as a mechanism to control and regulate women's sexuality, for financial reasons and perceptions of morality. As John M. Beattie (1986, p. 113) argues, the law 'sought to discourage fornication by making it more difficult for unmarried women to escape the results of their immorality'. While Mark Jackson (1996b) concludes that the law was designed to punish women, not directly for fornication but for their attempts at avoiding punishment for immoral sexual activity, by destroying the evidence their premarital sex created – the baby. Jackson argues that although relatively few women were prosecuted each year, it was enough to provide a warning to all other women: you cannot escape punishment for your premarital sex, so the best approach is to keep chaste.

It should be noted here that little concern was given to the nature of the sexual act that led to the conception of the child, and many of the women who faced a murder trial and the prospect, if not actuality, of a death sentence may well have been raped by family members, employers, or other members of their community. Sexual violence and exploitation are certainly seen as reasons for the rise in illegitimacy during the eighteenth century (Meteyard, 1980; Mitchison & Leneman, 1998); however, this claim is debated among historians (see Kilday, 2013 for her assessment of this debate).

From 'Lewd' Women to 'Disturbed' of Mind

Following the enactment of the 1624 law, there was an initial increase in the number of convictions of unwed women for newborn child murder; although the rise was not sustained. By the second half of the eighteenth century, unmarried women were more often tried under the general rules of common law murder, rather than under the 1624 Act. As in cases of a married woman accused of newborn child murder, the trial operated under the principles of the infant being presumed dead at birth, requiring the prosecution to provide evidence of live birth and murder in order to secure a conviction (Beattie, 1986; Jackson, 1996b). By the turn of the century, the 1624 Act had fallen out of favour within legal and political circles, seen as dissuading juries from convicting suspected women of murder due to the perceived harshness of the reversal of presumption of stillbirth (Jackson, 1996b). As Lord Ellenborough, the Lord Chief Justice, stated in his speech to Parliament while introducing a Bill to repeal the 1624 Act, '... to harsh was this law, as to oblige the Judges, in their construction of it, to admit proof of the child having been still-born'.[6] However, repeal of the 1624 Act should not be seen as evidence of relaxation of social attitudes towards women who became pregnant outside of marriage and were then suspected of killing the child following a secret pregnancy and birth. Ellenborough also introduced a new capital offence – concealment of birth:

> [...] if any Woman be delivered of any Issue of her Body, Male or Female, which being born alive, should by the Laws of this Realm be a Bastard, and that she endeavour ... to conceal the Death thereof ... in every such Case the said Mother shall suffer Death as in case of Murder.[7]

As I have argued elsewhere (Milne, 2019), the proposal of this new offence, with a punishment of death, suggests that the principles of the 1624 Act remained – the punishment of unmarried women for the 'crime' of having sex and becoming pregnant. The concealment of the birth of the child (and the pregnancy) was the focus under both laws, but the label of her 'criminal' behaviour was different.

---

[6]Reported in *The Times*, 29 March 1803, p. 2.

[7]House of Lords Sessional Papers (1714–1805). Full title: A Bill, Intituled, An Act for the further Prevention of malicious shooting, stabbing, cutting, wounding, and poisoning, and also the malicious setting Fire to Buildings; and also for repealing a certain Act, made in the First Year of the late King James the First, intituled, An Act to prevent the destroying and murthering of Bastard Children, and for substituting other Provisions in lieu of the same. v1. 3 December 1802 to 1 July 1803. 117–120.

The 1624 Act classified her crime as 'murder' (regardless of the lack of proof of live birth), whereas the offence of concealment of birth (hereafter concealment) specifically recognised her acts of concealing the birth and death as criminal: deemed so severe that only the punishment of death would suffice. For the offence of concealment, it did not matter if the child was born dead or alive, nor how it died if born alive; only that the unmarried woman had hidden the birth and the body of the child. Though the Bill did become law, and concealment of birth became a criminal offence,[8] the maximum sentence was reduced to two years' imprisonment, with or without hard labour. No records exist of discussions that led to the changes to the Bill; Mark Jackson (1996b) concludes that the precise origins of the final construction of the 1803 statute are unknown.

While humanist sentiments about the plight of unwed mothers began to emerge over the course of the seventeenth century (see Jackson (1996b) for discussion on this), understanding of the contextual factors leading a woman to hide her pregnancy and kill the child were not at the centre of the introduction of the offence of concealment. Instead, a focus on making the law workable and facilitating convictions to prevent women from 'escaping' justice were key drivers for Ellenborough. It was perceived that removal of the 1624 Act and the apparent harshness of this law would allow for more convictions, and, in instances where murder could not be proven, that concealment would facilitate an alternative conviction. As Angus McLaren (1984) argues, Ellenborough was a firm believer in using the law to instil terror and was motivated by the desire to penalise women, even if the punishment was minor, rather than have the courts appear to condone the actions of such women by the refusal to convict. The offence of concealment applied when a woman had been charged with murder, but a conviction could not be secured (potentially due to lack of evidence of live birth). In such an instance, the jury was free to determine a woman was not guilty of murder but was guilty of concealment. Accordingly, concealment had a practical function: a 'convenient stop-gap', as characterised by D. Seaborne Davies (1937, p. 213), allowing a form of punishment (a maximum of two years' imprisonment) when murder was suspected but could not be proven (Milne, 2019). Concealment was not a substantive offence until 1828, as a woman could only be convicted of concealment if she was charged with murder, and the jury returned a verdict of not guilty of murder but

---

[8]Popularly known as Lord Ellenborough's Act or as the Malicious Shooting or Stabbing Act 1803, the Act was an attempt by the Lord Chief Justice to consolidate and codify common law offences, including abortion. The long title is: An Act for the further Prevention of malicious Shooting, and attempting to discharge loaded Fire-Arms, stabbing, cutting, wounding, poisoning, and the malicious using of Means to procure the Miscarriage of Women; and also the malicious setting Fire to Buildings; and also for repealing a certain Act, made in England in the Twenty-First Year of the late King James the First, intituled, An Act to prevent the destroying and murthering of Bastard Children; and also an Act made in Ireland in the Sixth Year of the Reign of the late Queen Anne, also intituled, An Act to prevent the destroying and murthering of Bastard Children; and for making other Provisions in lieu thereof.

guilty of concealment.[9] In 1828, the law changed so that women could be charged with the offence of concealment, either for that offence alone or alongside a murder charge. A further change in the law, in 1828, meant that married women could also be charged and convicted of the offence. It was not until 1861 that men could also commit the offence, as the wording of the statute was changed to include 'every Person' who endeavours to conceal the birth of a child.[10]

While compassion, leniency, and mercy cannot be said to be at the heart of the 1803 Act, sympathies for the plight of unmarried women suspected of killing newborn children became increasingly important to the criminal law and justice responses to suspected offenders. As the nineteenth century developed, pity for the 'infanticidal' woman was expressed in public discourses, impacting both the outcome of murder trials and the judge and jury responses to women accused of killing newborn children. A growing reluctance to convict accused women of murder, and thus to see women hang for such acts, is now well documented in academic literature (Brennan, 2013; Brennan & Milne, forthcoming; Davies, 1937; Grey, 2014; Loughnan, 2012; Ward, 1999), despite overwhelming evidence of violent acts towards the infant in some cases (Higginbotham, 1989). In popular sentiment during the 1800s and early 1900s, the infanticidal woman was not solely to blame for her crime, as her situation of being pregnant outside of marriage, and thus her 'fallen' status, was seen, in part, to be due to the man who impregnated and then abandoned her (Wiener, 2004). Acting out of shame at being pregnant out of marriage was widely accepted as the motivation for the women's criminal intent (Brennan, 2013; Davies, 1937). Consequently, a divide existed between public perception – sympathy towards and a desire for leniency to be shown to accused women – and the letter of the law – a mandatory death sentence handed down to those convicted of murder. As D. Seaborne Davies (1937) argues:

> The widespread dislike of the application of the law of murder in all its severity to cases of infanticides by mothers led to such a divorce between law and public opinion that prisoners, witnesses, counsel, juries and even many of H.M.'s judges, conspired to defeat the law. (p. 203)

The onus to prove live birth continued to impact convictions as it had in previous centuries. Medical tests to demonstrate live birth were still considered unreliable (Graves, 2006; Kilday, 2013), and medical witnesses and jurors actively used these ambiguities to find a woman not guilty so as to spare her the gallows (Brennan, 2013). If a murder conviction was achieved then justice was still considered

---

[9]Offences Against the Person Act 1828.
[10]Offences Against the Person Act 1861, s60. It is under this legislation that the offence of concealment still operates today. However, it is no longer possible to be convicted of concealment following a not guilty verdict on an indictment of murder due to changes under the Criminal Law Act 1967, Schedule 2, s13(1)(a). A concealment conviction can only be obtained following indictment for that offence.

to have been evaded due to the unlikelihood that the mandatory death sentence would be carried out. The last execution of a woman for infant murder was in 1849, and the last execution of a woman for newborn child murder was in 1832 (Wiener, 2004, pp. 124–125). After this date, all other women found guilty of infant murder had their death sentences commuted by Home Secretaries. This pattern of condemning a woman to die, only to have the sentence reprieved, was dubbed the 'solemn mockery' by one judge providing evidence to the Royal Commission on Capital Punishment in 1866 (Davies, 1937). Similarly, Nigel Walker (1968) notes that the parliamentary debates on the various Bills submitted to Parliament in the latter half of the nineteenth century, to amend the law of homicide, frequently discussed the distress experienced by judges when sentencing women to death in such cases. By the end of 1800s, and in the early twentieth century, the law was deemed to have completely broken down: it neither prevented newborn deaths, as the punishment was never enacted and so did not offer a warning to other women, nor punished offenders, as the use of offences such as concealment as alternatives, while offering some punishment, did not provide the severity deemed suitable for homicide (Brennan, 2013). A consequence of this gap between public sentiment and the law meant that holding women criminally responsible for newborn child murder was essentially impossible.

It is within this context that the Infanticide Act 1922 came into law, allowing for women suspected of killing newborn children to be charged with infanticide or to be convicted of infanticide following a murder prosecution; so negating the mandatory death sentence for a murder conviction.[11] A superficial reading of the legislation would suggest that the offence is based on women's experiences of psychological illness due to giving birth, with the use of the phrase:

> at the time of the act or omission she has not been fully recovered
> from the effect of giving birth to such child, and by reason thereof
> the balance of her mind was disturbed ....

However, as Tony Ward (1999) outlines in his analysis of parliamentary papers about the Infanticide Act 1922, the language about accused women's mental state at the time of the killing, employed in discussion of the offence, embodied a lay understanding of 'madness', which was considered temporary and resulting as a consequence of the social circumstances surrounding the pregnancy (see also Brennan & Milne, forthcoming; Loughnan, 2012). The creation of the Infanticide Act 1922 allowed an end to the 'black-cap farce'[12] and offered 'an official mechanism for compassionate response' (Brennan, 2013, p. 800). So the Act, argues Ward (1999), facilitated punishment of women who killed newborn children,

---

[11]The 1922 Act was passed after numerous attempts to change the law in the preceding 60 years, see Brennan and Milne (forthcoming). The maximum sentence was life imprisonment.

[12]So named due to judges donning the black cap to hand down a death sentence to a defendant who was very likely to be commuted.

while, informally, recognising that becoming pregnant out of marriage had led them to this vulnerable position.

However, public sentiments of pity, and displays of leniency towards accused women by judges and juries, do not indicate that concern over women's 'deviant' sexuality and 'inappropriate' motherhood had disappeared. Unease that women could become mothers when they should not, through 'immoral' sex, continued to trouble politicians, legal professionals, and the general public in connection with women suspected of newborn child killing. This is evident from the speech to the House of Commons by the Home Secretary, Robert Peel, in 1828 (100 years before the enactment of the Infanticide Act) when proposing to extend the offence of concealment of birth to married women:

> [...] instances might occur in which married women might conceal the births of children, as where their husbands had been absent from the country for so long a time as to render the illegitimacy of the children a necessary consequence. A woman might thus be tempted to conceal the birth. The question was one of great difficulty. It appeared to be somewhat severe, that in cases where children were still-born, a woman should not be permitted to hide her shame; but the very operation of this feeling, and the great case with which a new-born infant could be put to death, might lead to the worst consequences. It was extremely inconvenient to leave the wilful concealment of birth without any penalty.[13]

Indeed, as Karen Brennan (2018a) has argued in her analysis of legal outcomes of cases of newborn child killing in Ireland during the twentieth century, compassionate legal responses to infanticidal women act to uphold the authority and legitimacy of criminal law as a mechanism of society's control and regulations. In instances where a harsh stance of criminal law – a mandatory death sentence – undermines the legitimacy of law, provision of mercy and leniency functions to preserve the legitimacy of the Rule of Law. In this sense, Brennan argues, leniency is not solely a benevolent expression, as it also serves to maintain the authority and control of the law, specifically as a function of maintaining patriarchal structures that mandate women be chaste and should only be having sex and becoming mothers in certain situations and contexts. Furthermore, she continues, compassion for defendants provided under infanticide legislation, and unofficially through not-guilty verdicts or a reprieve from a death sentence, allows for the socio-political structures to be maintained. In this sense, the infanticide law is paternalistic, as it allows some women to benefit from leniency, while refusing to relax controls and regulations of all women's sexual and reproductive rights and freedoms. As Brennan argues, women who kill their newborn children to escape the stigma, and social and cultural sanctions of 'unauthorised' pregnancy and motherhood, are a small number of women at the extreme end of patriarchal

---

[13]Hansard [HC Deb] 5 May 1828, Home Secretary, Sir Robert Peel. vol. 19, col. 353.

controls. Most women will either conform to the social norms by not having sex out of marriage (part of this 'conforming' will involve being 'lucky' that they do not become pregnant after being raped); find other ways to manage an unwanted pregnancy (see discussion below of abortion); or accept the consequences and hardship that comes from giving birth to and mothering an illegitimate child. These are hardships that may all be mitigated by wealth and connections held by the woman or her family, if they choose to support her.

For the small number of women who commit, or are suspected of committing, the murder of their newborn child, infanticide laws mitigate the harshness of the patriarchal system. In this sense, Brennan concludes, leniency facilitated by the law, or 'defeat' of the law by judges and juries in the period prior to the enactment of the Infanticide Act, maintains the status quo of patriarchal controls, as the display of mercy draws public attention away from the wider issues – women's rights and social controls and regulations of their sexualities and reproduction. Without this leniency, greater public attention, and potentially debate, about the circumstances that lead a woman to hide a pregnancy and kill the baby upon birth may result in calls for legal and cultural reform, thus disturbing the status quo.

If we take the criminal law and justice responses to unwed women suspected of killing newborn children across the period of the late sixteenth century to the early twentieth century as a whole, then we see a dramatic shift in the law and criminal justice responses – from implementation of the 1624 Act to facilitate a death sentence to the Infanticide Act 1922 to facilitate leniency. These two responses appear to be at opposite ends of a spectrum: harshness to compassion. However, using Brennan's analysis, along with the idea of the reversal of the flow of risk I developed in Chapter 4, we can assess these criminal law and criminal justice responses as two sides of the same coin.

Across the entire period, there are a number of constants. First, patriarchal control and regulation of women's sexuality and motherhood – marriage is the only place for a woman to legitimately engage in both. Second, when a woman becomes pregnant outside of marriage and, seeing the existence of the pregnancy and subsequent baby as a risk to her well-being and her life, kills the child and so remedies the risk, society, the state, and criminal law and justice (as a mechanism of state control) delegitimise her perception of the risk of the pregnancy to her well-being and safety. To see the risk a pregnancy poses to an unmarried woman as legitimate, and so respond accordingly, the state would need to decriminalise the actions of killing a newborn child or find a reasonable means of mitigation. To do so would be to accept that the social structures in place and the valuing of women's chastity result in women subjectively experiencing pregnancy out of marriage as a threat. Furthermore, it would involve acceptance of the legitimacy of the threat of an illegitimate child and so see the killing as an understandable (if undesired) response by a woman to irradicate the risk – the newborn baby. At no point does this happen: the women's actions are consistently framed as wrong and criminal. In the early modern period, criminalisation is ramped up and women face incredibly harsh punishments: effectively, death for concealing a pregnancy and birth. While during the nineteenth century and into the twentieth century, women's actions were criminalised as either murder with a commuted death sentence or a lesser offence such as concealment of birth and later infanticide. One of the reasons attempts to amend homicide laws and create an infanticide offence were unsuccessful on numerous occasions prior to 1922 was a wider belief that to enact an offence which would mitigate the death sentence would effectively encourage women to kill their children (Ward, 2002). It is also significant that the infanticide legislation was introduced in order to facilitate convictions, as it was perceived women were getting away with murder (through a not-guilty verdict or concealment conviction). Furthermore, the law was framed around the individual woman's disturbance of the balance of her mind, which leads to the third consistency in legal approach across the period – individualisation of responsibility.

To recognise the women's actions of killing a newborn child as a legitimate response to avert the risk posed to them by a pregnancy (although not necessarily an ideal response), society, the state, and the law would need to acknowledge the wider social circumstances that cause newborn child killing. Such a response would require a shift from individual responsibility to an assessment of the social circumstances that lead women to kill infants following birth, which, as noted at the end of Chapter 3, is not how criminal law functions. Instead, across the entire period, from the late sixteenth century to the early twentieth century, the law has worked to centre responsibility for the deaths solely on the accused woman. The 1624 Act did so by focussing on her immoral sexuality and requiring her to prove the baby was stillborn. At trial, it was common for a woman to rely upon an informal defence that she called for help with the labour, but that it did not come; the consequence being that she laboured alone and no one was there to witness that the child was stillborn.[14] Later, concealment was introduced as an offence of convenience to facilitate the criminalisation of women on account of her hiding the body (Milne, 2019). In the nineteenth and early twentieth centuries, leniency was offered based on women acting in these situations in a form of a frenzy and temporary 'social' madness brought on by her situation. It was this perception of the mental state of the infanticidal woman which culminated in the introduction of the Infanticide Act 1922, legislated to focus on the perception of individual mental disturbance as a basis for women's homicidal acts.[15]

By noting the consistencies that operate across the historical time period examined in this chapter, we can see that criminal law and criminal justice responses to women suspected of killing newborn children have the same motivational factors – to hold women individually responsible for their attempts to remedy the negative consequence of their 'deviant' sexuality. To make this argument is not to suggest that, across the period, individual legal professionals, politicians, and members of the public did not perceive that the women had done wrong by killing the child. Nor am I attempting to argue that there was no concern for infant life

---

[14]Other informal defences included preparing linens for the birth, see Loughnan (2012).

[15]As Brennan and Milne (forthcoming) outline, this mental disturbance was not considered akin to insanity but closer to provocation or intoxication. See also Ward (1999).

during this period, as changing perceptions of child welfare certainly influenced public sentiments towards infanticidal women.[16] However, a persistent feature of these cases is a wider perception that these women should never have been pregnant in the first place, and that, if they had avoided pregnancy, they would not have ended up killing a child. Thus, it is women's sexuality that remains at the heart of these cases. In this sense, we can see criminal and legal responses consistently operating as a social control of women's sexuality and 'appropriate' motherhood throughout the period. What changes as the period progresses is *how* the law and criminal justice operates to socially control sexuality and motherhood. In the sixteenth and seventeenth centuries, a period when punishment was inflicted upon the flesh for a vast array of offences, responses to women were severe in nature and consequence. As we move into and through the nineteenth century, the role of law and mechanism of punishment changed, embodying notions of 'civility' and 'rationality' (Foucault, 1991 [1977]; Wiener, 2004). We can see the response of law and justice as a mechanism of state and social control and regulation that is appropriate, acceptable, and rooted in philosophies of punishment for that time period. But regardless, the nature and basis of the social control remain the same: women should only be having sex with their husbands for the purpose of producing his children.

A Criminal End to a Pregnancy

A connected, but separate, area of law that developed over this time period relates to the legal regulation of ending a pregnancy and 'killing' a foetus – the creation of the offences of procuring a miscarriage and child destruction.[17] Today, both offences are often perceived as a means to protect foetuses from death.[18] However, this is not the root of either piece of legislation. Instead of seeing these offences as a basis for protecting foetuses, we need to consider them in the wider context of regulating which women can be mothers and thus women's sexuality.

Lord Ellenborough's Act 1803 made abortion at any point in the pregnancy a felony, punishable by imprisonment or transportation for up to 14 years for pre-quickening abortions and by death for post-quickening abortions.[19] Note it is the ending of

---

[16]For details of changing attitudes towards children on perceptions of infanticide see, for example, Beckingham (2013), Behlmer (1982), Grey (2009, 2013), and Hendrick (2003).

[17]Procuring a miscarriage is an offence under section 58 of the Offences Against the Person 1861, and child destruction is an offence under section 1 of the Infant Life (Preservation) Act 1929.

[18]See Sheldon (2016) for her analysis of how both offences are used in the contemporary period, mostly to criminalise men who attack pregnant women, but also, as illustrated by this research, applied in instances where women end their own pregnancies. Indeed, as I have argued elsewhere (Milne, 2020), and discuss in Chapter 6, procuring a miscarriage is being used in cases presented here as a proxy for a foetal homicide law.

[19]Quickening is the point at which a woman feels the foetus move, between approximately 15 and 17 gestational weeks.

the pregnancy that is the offence, not the killing of the foetus.[20] While some may argue this distinction is only semantics, it remains important, as will become clear. Prior to the nineteenth century, abortion had been a common law offence when committed post-quickening. While mostly regarded as a matter for the Ecclesiastic Courts, the law was infrequently, inconsistently, and sporadically applied, implying a tolerance of the practice of ending a pregnancy (Dickens, 1966; Francome, 1986; Keown, 1988); that it was not seen as a moral or legal wrong; and that, prior to the nineteenth century, it played an important role in the regulation of fertility (McLaren, 1984).

Codification of the offence of ending a pregnancy and inclusion of pre-quickening abortions in the statute should not be seen through a lens of contemporary attitudes towards foetal life, but rather as a means through which medical men were able to exert their influence and control as a process of recognition of their role as professionals. Their argument, that only they had the skills and knowledge to determine which abortions should be allowed and those that should be illegal, assisted in a rise in their professional status and helped facilitate their aim to eliminate rival practitioners such as midwives (Keown, 1988).[21] Furthermore, the inclusion of abortion in the 1803 Act is noted to be procedural and was intended to remove inconsistencies in law (McLaren, 1984; Potts et al., 1977).[22]

The wording of the 1803 legislation has led scholars, such as Angus McLaren (1984), to argue that it focussed on those who provided abortion; designed to protect women from being killed in the process of an abortion gone wrong: 'thereby to murder, or thereby to cause and procure the Miscarriage of any Woman'. It was not until the enactment of the 1861 Offences Against the Person Act that women could be prosecuted for self-abortions under statute.[23] While historians have argued that women could be prosecuted under common law (Keown, 1988), so few prosecutions occurred that it is not possible to confirm if women were ever the focus of criminal sanctions due to ending their pregnancy, as argued by Bernard M. Dickens (1966). Limited parliamentary debate occurred around the passing of the 1861 Act, so it is unclear why pregnant women were named as potential offenders under this law. Generally, scholars agree that the historical purpose of the law was to prevent or condemn harm from coming to pregnant women and the intentional destruction of foetal life (Dickens, 1966; Keown, 1988). Nevertheless, legal scholar Glanville

---

[20]Romanis (2020a) also highlights this point.

[21]Eradication of women practitioners from pregnancy and childbirth 'medical' practice is well documented in both the United Kingdom and the United States, with midwives and women in the community who assisted pregnant women labelled as dangerous and untrained. See Ehrenreich and English (1978), Leavitt (1986), Oakley (1984), Reagan (1997), and Wertz and Wertz (1989).

[22]McLaren (1984) argues that the abortion statute was an unexpected consequence of the repeal of the 1624 Act – to balance the perceived reduction in harshness of the law concerning the death of illegitimate newborn children, Ellenborough created a stringent abortion law. The perceived need for the legislation occurred within the context of the Ecclesiastic Courts being nearly moribund, and common law courts refusing to try such cases.

[23]Section 58.

Llewelyn Williams (1958) argues that the former purpose was of most importance, as the concern was not for the unborn child, but for the injury done to women as a result of the actions of an unskilled abortion provider.

Regardless of the focus of criminalisation being upon women or abortion providers, we need to contextualise the codification of abortion as a further element of the control and regulation of women's sexuality. The adoption of abortion into criminal legislation had the impact of limiting women's ability to control their fertility by using abortion as contraception: a regular practice during the early modern period (McLaren, 1984). As Carla Spivack (2007) argues, any concern for the 'criminality' of abortion in secular and Ecclesiastic courts during the early modern period occurred in the context of a wider focus on illegitimacy and sex outside of the confines of marriage: abortion facilitated both by allowing the unwanted product of the 'immoral' sexual act to be eradicated prior to spontaneous birth. Tightening of regulations and controls as to who could provide abortions during the nineteenth century can also be seen as a means of regulating women's sexuality, as it was men – medical professionals who would have been almost exclusively male – who, after 1803, had the power and legal rights to determine which women should be allowed to legally end a pregnancy.

The enactment of the Infant Life (Preservation) Act 1929 needs to be seen in a similar light. The legislation created the offence of child destruction:

> [...] any person who, with intent to destroy the life of a child capable of being born alive, by any wilful act causes a child to die before it has an existence independent of its mother, shall be guilty of felony, to wit, of child destruction, and shall be liable on conviction thereof on indictment to penal servitude for life.[24]

This offence is still in force today. In addition to being an indictable offence, on charges of murder, manslaughter, infanticide, and procuring a miscarriage, a jury can return an alternative verdict of child destruction.[25] Analysis by Sally Sheldon (2016) indicates that child destruction has never been used as intended. The statute developed out of the desire to close a legal loophole – an infant killed while part of its body was still in the birth canal, following spontaneous labour, could not be the victim of murder, as, at the time of killing, it was not living an independent existence and thus was not a reasonable creature in *rerum natura* (Coke, 1644 [1681], pp. 50–51). Nor would the offence of procuring a miscarriage be committed as labour was not induced (Davies, 1937). Concern about the legal loophole during the latter half of the nineteenth and early twentieth centuries arose in the same context as concern that justice was not being done in cases of newborn child murder, because accused women were acquitted, convicted of concealment, or had their sentence commuted. The perception was that women

---

[24]Section 1(1).

[25]A jury can also return a verdict of guilty of procuring a miscarriage following an indictment for child destruction.

were exploiting the loophole by waiting until their labour started spontaneously and then killing the child before it was fully born (Graves, 2006). While there is limited evidence that women were actively engaging in this practice, concern was sufficient to legislate against it and so ensure the women would be convicted of an offence carrying the same tariff as infanticide – life imprisonment.

Both procuring a miscarriage and child destruction need to be seen as legal measures to limit women's decision-making about reproduction and so, like legal regulation of newborn child killing, part of wider controls and regulations of who can and should be mothers and thus of women's sexuality. By limiting means to dispose of the unwanted/unallowed consequences of sex with someone other than your husband – an illegitimate foetus/baby – the state is using the law to control who women have sex with and when. The message of this array of offences – child destruction, concealment of birth, infanticide, and procuring a miscarriage – is that women cannot hide the consequences of their 'immorality' and so the best and right approach is to not have sex outside of your marriage bed. Such an approach in law delegitimises women's access to mechanisms to control their fertility, which in turn assists in the maintenance of social norms, the status quo, and thus patriarchy.

As feminists have argued, to allow women to regulate their own reproduction – when they have children, how many, how far apart the age gap between their children – has the consequence of calling into question the basic ordering of society (Gordon, 1986). The fundamental structures of patriarchal society are shaken, if not destroyed, through women, and only women, having control and regulation of their own reproduction. Reproductive control removes the notion that to have children is natural, as pregnancy can be controlled and halted through contraception (including abortion), and it is not an inevitable outcome of sexual activity. Consequently, the notion that a woman's place is in the home, caring for children, and thus she should be denied access to elements of social and cultural life outside of the home – political voice and representation, education, equal employment on the basis of equal pay and opportunities of progression, a life beyond domesticity and male control – ceases to be a valid and logical conclusion of social and cultural life. Feminists such as Linda Gordon made these arguments in relation to campaigns to decriminalise abortion in the 1970s, 1980s, and 1990s. Anti-abortion campaigns reflect wider social anxieties, particularly those held by men, about women's reproductive autonomy: the removal of men's control over their wives and family and the extent to which abortion, and contraception in general, facilitates women's sexual independence (Faludi, 1992).[26] As illustrated above, the points may, however, be applied to how laws surrounding pregnancy and newborn child killing can be and have been conceptualised.

The Unending Danger of Women's Sexuality

As already noted, the law has historically, and still today in England and Wales, considered the 'child' that is not born – the foetus – as distinct from the child that

---

[26]For an excellent summary of feminist arguments about abortion, see Amery (2020).

is born. One is a person in law, the other is not. Scholars such as Gerard Casey (2005) and Clarke D. Forsythe (1986) have argued that historically the born alive rule was for evidential purposes, as it was incredibly difficult, if not impossible, to prove that violence towards the body of the pregnant woman, including the taking of 'poisons', would cause the death of the foetus; thus, there is an inability to prove causation for homicide. It is beyond the scope of this book to engage in a debate about the legal theory surrounding the continued existence of the born alive rule, although see Emma Cave (2004) and Jennifer Temkin (1986) for their discussions.[27] Regardless, the law has seen, and continues to see, the foetus and a born child as distinct. Consequently, the nature of the crimes committed 'against' the foetus differs from those committed against the newborn child, at least in theory (see Chapter 6). However, while the foetus/baby are considered legally distinct, women who have the potential to become mothers when they should not be – when they have had sex with a man who is not their husband – have not been seen as legally distinct, regardless of the stage at which and means by which they 'end' the pregnancy. By this, I mean that whether she has killed a foetus *in utero* or a newborn child *ex utero*, either partially or fully born, her actions are viewed conceptually as equivalent – acting to address the consequences of her sexual immorality. In ending the life of the foetus/infant, she is deemed to be attempting to readdress the 'problem' caused by her sexual acts outside of marriage – the illegitimate child. The menu of offences enacted over the period of the late sixteenth century to the early twentieth century provided means to capture women's acts of ending the unwanted pregnancy at any stage, from conception to post-birth. Thus, while the born alive rule holds significance in criminal law for how the actions of accused women are labelled, in reality, each offence provides a means to punish women who challenge gender, sex, and sexuality norms by having sex when it is deemed they should not, and so becoming a 'mother' when it is deemed they should not. Each offence removes any form of legitimacy for a woman to control her fertility and so enable independent decisions over her sexuality. The extent to which criminal law has been deployed to regulate and control women's ability to have sex and prevent motherhood when unwanted/unauthorised indicates the centrality of this element of regulation of women. It is this point that I want to focus upon in the conclusion of this chapter.

As I have argued, historically, the responses to women who became pregnant outside of their marriage bed and then acted to rid themselves of the unauthorised foetus/baby came from a number of different laws. Each law was distinct and a product of the historical period in which it was enacted and so needs to be understood in its historical context.[28] Nevertheless, as I have outlined, the different laws

---

[27]There are also practical implications of criminalising women whose behaviour is deemed to harm or kill the foetus, as well as the newborn child, as will be discussed in Chapter 6.

[28]Sheldon (2016) has made this point in relation to the offence of procuring a miscarriage, arguing that this offence would not be created today but remains in the structures of criminal law and the regulation of the medical procedure of abortion.

are connected by concerns over and responses to appropriate motherhood and sexuality. It is this notion of women's appropriate sexuality and motherhood that also shrouds contemporary cases of suspicious perinatal death. As I have argued in Chapters 3 and 4, one focus in the criminal hearings of women suspected of causing the death of foetuses/newborn children is upon the role of the women as 'good' mothers and 'appropriate' pregnant women, with a direct connection between the two: the good mother is the appropriate pregnant woman who puts the welfare of the foetus first and manages risk accordingly. However, a further element of the court hearings lies in concern over the women's behaviour, in terms of their ability to become pregnant – over her sexuality and the consequences of that sexuality.

First, in a number of cases, discussion is heard as to how the woman became pregnant. For example, as noted in previous chapters, Hannah's relationship with the man who impregnated her is characterised as inappropriate by all members of the court, reflecting the views of Hannah's family:

> It seems that she started a relationship with a Mr [boyfriend] in [date]. This became a sexual relationship, but the relationship was not considered by the defendant's family as being an acceptable relationship, and in fact in [date] the defendant became pregnant and Mr [boyfriend], it would appear, paid for the pregnancy to be terminated. (Hannah, prosecution opening)
>
> ...
>
> and it is perhaps in those [family/childhood] circumstances little wonder that she sought solace in the unsuitable arms of Mr [boyfriend]. I say unsuitable, he was found on the DNA database, he presumably has a record, I know not. (Hannah, defence mitigation)

In cases where the women became pregnant as a consequence of sexual activity with a man who was not/is not their partner, this is discussed as a relevant factor. For example, in Nicole's case:

> Her partner, Mr T, became suspicious that there had been a relationship or was a relationship. I've set out the reasons why he became suspicious. He was told however by the defendant that such relationship as there was was not sexual and that she wouldn't mix with the man again. However, as a result of her relationship with Mr V, the defendant became pregnant. Mr V knew of her pregnancy and knew that he was the father. (Nicole, prosecution opening)

Similarly, in Hayley's case, where the affair is presented as of importance to the case as it is perceived to explain why Hayley wanted an abortion, the defence present this response:

> And her words, far more eloquent than anything I can submit to any Court, when I asked her this morning, was to say this to her husband, [name], and her children, 'I am so sorry for my selfish act'. (Hayley, defence mitigation)

It is not made clear whether the selfish act is the illegal abortion, the pregnancy, or the affair.

In other cases, the notion that the women were having sex at all is commented upon. For example, in Sally's case:

> Thereafter you led what can only be referred to as a chaotic and dysfunctional lifestyle, in the course of which you became pregnant on a number of occasions. (Sally, judge sentencing)

The judge later refers to Sally as being 'promiscuous'. Similarly, in Tanya's case, during sentencing, the judge makes the following reference to the sexual encounter that resulted in Tanya becoming pregnant:

> I don't need to resolve the precise circumstances of this baby's conception. It is plain to me from what you said to [psychiatrist] that however much you may have flirted with this man, you felt forced into having sex with him, although he may not have realised this. I need say no more about it, but it was not something that you remembered with anything other than revulsion. (Tanya, judge sentencing)

Previously, during the hearing, evidence was presented by the prosecution that Tanya had told a psychiatrist she had not wanted to have sex with the man, who was 21 years old while she was 16. Her defence barrister stressed the fact that Tanya's belief that she was raped was 'how it felt in her own mind rather than in any way seeking to suggest now that it was in fact a criminally properly indictable rape' (Hannah, defence mitigation). Nevertheless, the suggestion by the judge in sentencing is that Hannah's sexuality was inappropriate – leading a man on and then being unhappy with the consequences of her 'flirtatious' behaviour.

In each of these examples, for different reasons, the women's sexuality is remarked upon: Hannah, because her partner was considered unsuitable by her family; Hayley and Nicole, because the men were not their established partner/husband; Sally and Tanya, because it was considered questionable whether they should have been having sex at all due to their age and life circumstances. In each case, there is a suggestion, and very little more than that, that the women should not have been having this sex in the first place – if they had not been having sex, then the pregnancy would not have existed and so they would not have committed the crimes they pleaded guilty to.

This idea that women's sexuality is only legitimate for the purpose of procreation is one that continues to haunt contemporary society. We can see this belief reflected in ideas around abortion – the 'shame' women feel, or it is deemed women *should* feel, for wanting to terminate the outcome of sex that was for a purpose other than having a baby (Bommaraju et al., 2016; Hoggart, 2017; Kumar et al., 2009). The continued significance given to the myth of 'virginity' also illustrates such a belief (Blank, 2007; Fanghanel et al., 2021; Noor, 2019). The idea is also present in narratives relating to women's enjoyment of sex, rather than it being something that they endure in order to have a baby, or so that men can enjoy having sex (Pillai, 2020; Weiss, 2018).[29] The narrative of the 'slut' embodies the principle – the idea that only a woman who is sexually immoral will enjoy sex and want to have it. 'Pure' women, 'virtuous' women, 'good' women would not act in such a way. Such ideas reinforce rape myths and can make it very hard for women to refuse sex on the terms set out by their male partner (Madriz, 1997; Thomas et al., 2016). The notion of sex solely for the purpose of procreation, and the right type of procreation (within marriage), is not one that is confined to the history books.

The second area of concern raised in the hearings about women's sexuality and potential to become pregnant focusses on their ability to hide the pregnancy from the community around them. For example, in sentencing Alice, the judge notes 'there was a degree of concealment of the child from the authorities' as an aggravating factor. As Alice abandoned the baby very soon after birth, it would appear that the judge is referring to the pregnancy and foetus when he talks about concealment of the 'child'. A similar concern is raised about a woman's ability to conceal knowledge of her pregnancy in Fiona's case: in this instance due to the impact upon her parents:

PROSECUTION: Following the discovery the photographs of the bags and drawstring bag, in particular, were released to the local media groups. Your Lordship will see, at paragraph 8, that Mr and Mrs [name] watched the news bulletin and had the conversation that I have there put before your Lordship. I do not know whether your Lordship needs to be reminded of it. Following that conversation …

JUDGE: In essence, she agreed that the baby was hers and she was responsible for the death.

PROSECUTION: Yes, my Lord, that is absolutely …

JUDGE: And it must have been a very difficult situation for her and a very difficult situation for her parents. (Fiona, prosecution opening)

---

[29]For example, a campaign arose in 2019 that women should go on a 'sex strike' in protest against the American state of Georgia introducing the 'heartbeat' rule for abortion, widely critiqued as such action is based on the premise that sex is something only 'given' to men for male pleasure and enjoyment (Lister, 2019).

This theme is also present in Imogen's case, with a focus on her actions of hiding the pregnancy and 'deceit' towards her family, including her husband, who impregnated her:

> However, this, your Honour, was a cold, calculated and deceitful series of acts borne out by a web of lies that she has perpetrated from day one, back in 2013, and it continued when the body of that young child, her child, was discovered unceremoniously dumped in the drain at the rear of her parents' property in this town. She deceived, your Honour, not only those closest to her, but she maintained this tissue of lies for several months thereafter, and your Honour would be forgiven for concluding that she has acted irresponsibly and inappropriately from the moment she knew she was with child, and there are a series of text messages, your Honour, which I will open which were sent to family members, in particular her mother, which will show the nature of the deceit that I have merely touched upon at this stage
>
> ...
>
> She maintained, your Honour, that [her husband] knew nothing about the pregnancy and that she had rather adept at simply concealing with clothing and excuses about health the fact that her stomach was growing. (Imogen, prosecution opening)

There is also a focus on the ability of women to hide the existence of the child by not seeking assistance in labour and delivery and then hiding the body:

> Secondly the prosecution relies on a strand of evidence showing the defendant knew that the baby was alive. Look at her not calling for help, the only explanation for which, says the prosecution, is an intention to kill. That the baby should die. (Jessica, judge summing up)
>
> The victim was killed by her mother, and her mother, having killed the baby, took limited but definite steps to conceal what she had done. Had there been no visit by the defendant to the hospital on the following day or the day after that, it is perfectly possible that the bin in which the body was kept would have been put into the communal waste and then disposed of with nobody being any the wiser, Bethany having given wholly contradictory accounts of whether or not she was pregnant and, if so, to what extent. One may sensibly suppose that without having her crime being discovered by the hospital, she would have claimed some later miscarriage, and nobody would have been any the wiser. (Bethany, judge sentencing)

The notion of women purposefully not seeking help during birth echoes criminal hearings of the past, where the focus was upon whether women purposefully hid themselves away, supposedly to allow them to kill the child and then claim it was stillborn and/or to dispose of the body in secret.

The final aspect of these cases that reflects historical concerns over the sexuality of accused women connects to the prosecution's ability to prove the child was born alive and thus that a homicide offence had been committed. As outlined above, this was a key feature of criminal cases throughout the period of the sixteenth to twentieth centuries. While medical testing is far more advanced today, and so the ability to prove live birth is easier, it remains a challenge:

> That baby later found, the pathological medical evidence says that it is not possible to prove when that baby died, how that baby died, whether that baby was born alive, and there would not necessarily be any signs of stillbirth, even if, despite what [prosecution barrister] has just said to you, even if it'd been found immediately afterwards. (Elizabeth, defence closing)

The impact of concealing the body of an infant on the ability to determine live birth and cause of death is noted as a specific element of Lily's offending:

> These offences, and I refer particularly first of all to the offences relating to the birth [concealment of birth and a lawful and decent burial], are serious because it means that the authorities can never establish in circumstances such as this what has happened to the child, and that is something that everybody is entitled to know about, and the seriousness of the offence is that by doing what you did, that could not happen. (Lily, judge sentencing)

However, as I have argued in relation to the offence of concealment of birth (Milne, 2019), and Imogen Jones and Muireann Quigley (2016) have argued in relation to preventing a lawful and decent burial, other offences exist to capture the wrongdoing of hiding a corpse to prevent discovery of further criminal behaviour: disposal of a corpse with intent to obstruct or prevent a coroner's inquest when there is a duty to hold one[30] and perverting the course of justice.[31] Therefore, the offence of concealment is not needed to capture the wrong of hiding a dead body to conceal criminal behaviour and to facilitate prosecutions; although concealment would be far easier to prove than either of the alternative offences. Nevertheless, the perceived 'danger' of women being able to hide their potential wrongdoing continues to be a feature of cases of suspected perinatal homicide.

---

[30] *R* v. *Purcy* [1934] 24 Cr App R 70.
[31] *R* v. *Williams* [1991] 92 Cr App R 158. See Jones and Quigley (2016) for detailed analysis of how both offences could be applied to individuals who conceal a dead body. Both offences have a maximum life sentence.

Table 5.1.   Live Births by Age of Mother and Registration Type.

	Number	Percentage of All Live Births
Joint registrations – same address	214,026	32.57
Joint registrations – different address	69,719	10.61
Sole registrations	34,064	5.18

From 'Lewd' Women to Bad Mothers

Sexuality continues to be a core element of cases of suspected perinatal homicide. As illustrated above, a connection is made between women becoming pregnant when they should not be – at a time when they are not prepared to put the foetus first and become the responsible pregnant woman – and their sexuality. However, today, we cannot reasonably say that there is significant legal concern surrounding women who become pregnant following 'fornication' and thus considered to be 'lewd'. In 2018, almost half, 48.37%, of all live born infants were born to parents who were not married or in a civil partnership at the time of the birth. Furthermore, as Table 5.1 shows, almost 16% of all infants were born to parents who live apart or are sole parents (Office for National Statistics, 2019).

Nevertheless, the continued focus on sexuality and the 'correctness' of being pregnant highlighted in these cases takes us back to points I have discussed earlier in this book: specifically the idea that pregnant woman should act to put the 'baby' first and so be the 'good' mother. In this context, the message suggested in the criminal hearings is that if you have no intention of being a good mother then you should keep your legs firmly shut! Thus, today, the connection between cases of suspected perinatal homicide and concern over women's sexuality is indirect.

A further clear distinction between criminal justice responses to these cases in the contemporary period, compared to the historical responses, is how foetuses and children are conceptualised. As outlined in Chapter 4, children, and by extension foetuses, are seen to be priceless and precious (Ariès, 1965; Zelizer, 1994). In making this point, I am not arguing that children were never seen in such a light in previous centuries, but it was a less prominent understanding held about children compared to today, particularly in relation to the unborn. So, the purpose and focus of prosecutions and criminalisation have shifted, from punishing the lewd woman who attempts to hide the product of her sinful sexuality through an illegal abortion or secret murder of a newborn child, to the punishment of the irresponsible pregnant woman who fails to adopt the role of the 'good' mother to act in the best interests of her 'baby'. The menu of offences has not changed – child destruction, concealment of birth, infanticide, and procuring a miscarriage – but the incentive to punish this manifestation of a deviant woman has. It is the use of these offences in contemporary cases, and the role of prosecutions, to which I turn next. As we will see in Chapter 6, applying the menu can have devastating consequences for women and their foetuses/infants.

Chapter 6

Mothers in Law II: Foetus First

> If I was to say to you that my initial approach is to see this case somewhere in the calendar of offences of being between man-slaughter and murder, you will see that I am thinking in terms of a very substantial period of imprisonment.
>
> ...
>
> I am not with you on either point I am afraid to say, as I have read these papers carefully. The view I take is this was a deliberate calculated decision to break the law in relation to a child which she would have anticipated could have been born alive within the next few days. (Hayley, judge to defence barrister during mitigation)

So far in this book, I have outlined how women suspected of causing the death of their foetuses/newborn children are understood and represented. Rather than their experience of pregnancy being seen as a crisis, they are perceived to be act-ing deceitfully and intentionally hiding their pregnancies to conceal criminality. They are also judged next to ideals of motherhood; expected to be the 'good' mother simply by the existence of the pregnancy and that, consequently, they will act as the 'responsible' pregnant woman, putting the needs of the foetus first. I have also outlined the legal principle of the born alive rule that continues to oper-ate in England and Wales, at least in principle. In Chapter 5, I then illustrated how the laws relating to suspected perinatal homicide came into being, and that prosecutors now have a menu of offences to 'choose' from when attempting to prosecute women.

In this chapter, I am going to focus on the non-homicide offences and the con-victions against women where there is no evidence that the infant was born alive. So, I am focussing on the cases where the 'victim' of the women's actions – the foetus – had no legal personality.[1] In focussing on the application of such offences in the prosecutorial menu – specifically concealment of birth and procuring a

---

[1]In so much as there is no evidence of live birth.

Criminal Justice Responses to Maternal Filicide: Judging the Failed Mother, 127–144
Copyright © 2021 by Emma Milne
Published by Emerald Publishing under an Exclusive Licence
doi:10.1108/978-1-83909-620-420211008

miscarriage[2] – I illustrate that the way criminal law is being applied in these cases negates the legal principle of the born alive rule and legal personhood. Within these cases, the law is being used to facilitate the criminalisation of women who are deemed to have failed to put the foetus first – to be the 'responsible' pregnant woman and so the 'good' mother. Thus, I conclude that the offences of concealment of birth and procuring a miscarriage are being used as proxies for foetal homicide laws. By presenting this analysis, I am not claiming that the offences have been misapplied in these cases or that miscarriages of justice have occurred. In each case, the law has been applied to the letter. Instead, my intention is to illustrate that the menu of offences facilitates the criminalisation of women in almost all circumstances, whether evidence of live birth or not. And so, criminal justice is working to hold women to account for their failings as 'bad' mothers and 'irresponsible' pregnant women. To assist in this analysis, I briefly turn to legal jurisdictions in the United States, where many states have enacted laws to protect foetal life and well-being. As will become clear from analysis of the situation in American states, protecting foetuses in law, and so holding women criminally liable for their acts or omissions while pregnant, has significant consequences for both women and their foetuses.

The Vanishing Line of Birth and the Secret Victim

At the time of writing (September 2020), NICE – the National Institute for Health and Care Excellence (2020) – asked for responses to its consultation on draft quality standards for foetal alcohol spectrum disorder. The quality standards include the following:

> *Statement 1*: Pregnant women are given advice not to drink alcohol during pregnancy at their first contact appointment.

> *Statement 2*: Pregnant women have information on their alcohol consumption recorded throughout their pregnancy.

Recorded levels of consumption of alcohol during pregnancy would be transferred to the records of the child, once born. Putting aside the issues of informed consent of the pregnant woman, which are substantial,[3] it is the formalisation of monitoring women's behaviour while pregnant, and use of collected information to make assessments of the health outcomes of the foetus post-birth, that are of

---

[2]Homicide offences are not included in this section as, within such cases, clear evidence of live birth allows for prosecution of offences relating to the behaviour of the women after the child has been born; so negating the 'harm' that may, or may not, have resulted as a consequence of behaviour by the women during pregnancy.

[3]It is not made clear in the consultation documents if women will be informed as to how any information they disclose will be recorded and used, or if they will be provided with an opportunity to state if they want this information to be collected and then used (Romanis et al., 2020b).

significance in the context of this study. While there is currently limited scope for women to be held liable for behaviour when pregnant that may result in harm to the foetus and subsequently born child, either criminally or in tort,[4] such a move by the body that provides national guidance and advice 'to improve health and social care' is alarming. One of the potential consequences of recording the level of alcohol consumed by women while pregnant, and then transferring the 'data' to the health record of the born child, is that it creates a body of information that could potentially be used as 'evidence' in the future, thus assisting, inadvertently perhaps, in opening the door to women facing criminal and/or civil liability for their actions and/or omissions while pregnant.

'And why not!?' you may say. Why should a woman who has caused harm to her foetus who then becomes a born alive child, or who causes death to the foetus before birth, not face criminal sanctions and punishment for the harms inflicted on the unborn? If we hold women criminally liable for their actions or omissions which cause harm or death to their born children, as we do if they have responsibility for that child,[5] why would we not hold women criminally liable for what they do to their 'children' who have not yet been born?

As English and Welsh criminal law currently stands, the born alive rule acts as the invisible line between the foetus having no legal personality (prior to live birth and separate existence) and legal personality (after separate existence is achieved). Consequently, the line of birth marks the point when a foetus/child can be the 'victim' of a criminal offence: prior to separate existence, the foetus cannot be a victim of crime, while after separate existence, the born child can be a victim, as with all other people of any age. The one notable exception here

---

[4]The born alive rule currently prevents this form of liability. Women's lack of criminal liability was most recently confirmed in the civil case of *CP (A Child)* v. *First-Tier Tribunal (Criminal Injuries Compensation)* [2014] EWCA Civ 1554: the Court of Appeal refused the claim by CP (A Child) for criminal injuries' compensation from the Criminal Injuries Compensation Authority after she was born with foetal alcohol spectrum disorder following her mother's alcohol consumption during pregnancy. CP's claim was that the disability she faces is due to an injury sustained directly from a crime of violence – her birth mother's malicious administering of poison so as to endanger life or inflict grievous bodily harm, an offence under section 23 of the Offences Against the Person Act 1861. Although this was a civil case, if finding for CP and awarding compensation, the Court of Appeal would have been required to rule that CP's birth mother had committed a criminal offence in consuming alcohol while pregnant, and so, CP was a 'victim' of a non-fatal crime against the person. The court ruled against CP as, at the time the alcohol was ingested, CP was not 'any other person', as humans *in utero* do not have legal personality. Upon being born alive, and thus becoming 'any other person' and so capable of being a victim of a crime of violence, the administration of alcohol – the poison – had stopped. Therefore, the crime was never committed against the 'baby' when it had legal personality, and so, the birth mother was not liable. See Cave and Stanton (2016) for discussion of the case. For further discussion of women's liability when pregnant, see Cave (2004).
[5]Children and Young Persons Act 1933, s1.

is the offence of child destruction, discussed in Chapter 5: a criminal offence of killing the child capable of being born alive.[6] However, the invisible line of birth does not mean women[7] are necessarily precluded from criminal liability for their actions or omissions which cause harm to the foetus and result in a child dying after being born alive. As Emma Cave (2004) and Sara Fovargue and José Miola (1998) have argued, women could be held criminally liable if their born alive child dies of injuries sustained *in utero* due to the criminal acts of the pregnant woman. The *Attorney General's Reference* (No. 3 of 1994)[8] ruled that attacking a pregnant woman without intent to kill the foetus could result in a conviction of constructive manslaughter[9] if the child was born alive and subsequently died as a result of the injuries. While there has yet to be a case to determine pregnant women's liability in such a situation, feminist scholars fear that women could be held to a similar level of criminal liability. The foetus' lack of legal personality also does not mean that a pregnant woman has no duty owed to the foetus.[10] Margaret Brazier (1999) has argued that women have a moral responsibility for the child not yet born; however, she concludes that using the law to compel women to act for the betterment of the foetus will result in the abandonment of 'choice for the crudity of compulsion', and so society will have:

> ceased to recognize the pregnant woman's capacity to make her own moral choices for herself and her child. That could be justifiable only if cogent reasons could be advanced for prioritizing the child's interests, and the law could do so in a manner which will realistically achieve that aim. (p. 375)

It is beyond the scope of this book to engage in the legal and philosophical debates as to women's criminal liability and duty to the foetus. Instead, the focus of this chapter is an exploration of how the application of criminal law, in cases of suspicious perinatal deaths, may be working to defeat the principle of the born alive rule; so, providing unofficial legal sanctions of women who are suspected of harming or killing their infants either before or after live birth. While, in theory, the born alive rule is a firm line between legal personhood and non-legal

---

[6]Infant Life (Preservation) Act 1929 (ILPA), s1. As also noted in Chapter 5, the offence of procuring a miscarriage is not an offence against the foetus per se but of ending a pregnancy.

[7]Or other people in the context of third parties who attack pregnant women.

[8][1997] All ER 936; [1998] AC 245.

[9]Constructive manslaughter, or unlawful and dangerous act manslaughter, is a form of involuntary manslaughter that occurs if a crime committed by the defendant, which was intentionally performed in circumstances rendering it dangerous, results in the death of a person. Note that a foetus is not considered 'a person', but the ruling in A-G Ref No. 3 of 1994 means that if the act occurs before live birth, but the death of the child occurs after it is born alive, then this can be a crime of manslaughter.

[10]With thanks to Dr Mark Dsouza for a lively and informative debate on this point at the Society for Legal Scholars annual conference, 2020.

personhood,[11] this is not the case in practice. To outline how laws are being applied as proxies for foetal homicide law, I turn to discussions of the women's actions in cases of convictions for concealment of birth and procuring a miscarriage.

The Continued Convenience of Concealment of Birth

As discussed in Chapter 5, over 86 years ago, D. Seaborne Davies (1937, p. 213) argued that the offence of concealment of birth was a 'convenient stop-gap', as it allowed for the prosecution of women who were suspected of killing newborn children but who could not be convicted of murder due to a lack of evidence of live birth. As I have argued elsewhere, the offence continues to be used in this manner: to facilitate convictions when it is suspected women have killed their born alive infants, but the decomposed state of the body means that it is not possible to determine whether the child was born alive and the subsequent cause of death (Milne, 2019). For example, in Lily's case, the judge summarised the suspicions:

> There has been a veiled suggestion in the case, and I put it no higher than that, that there may have been something suspicious about the birth and your subsequent behaviour. You were never charge [*sic.*] of course with any homicide, but what can be said is that you were already the mother of three children and you have cared for children subsequently and cared well, and I dismiss any suggestion, veiled or otherwise, that there was something sinister about your birth of the child and procuring its birth. (Lily, judge sentencing)

Similarly, in Imogen's case, the time between the birth and discovery of the body meant it was impossible to tell if the baby was born alive. Despite the offence of concealment of birth having nothing to do with the cause or nature of the death of the baby, the prosecution provided substantial detail of the injuries caused to the baby's body:

> Cause of death could not be ascertained. In addition, fracture to the skull, this is the depression of eight to seven centimetres, and described as having numerous radiating arms from the point of impact. However, your Honour will have noted the engineer [who discovered the body] went in with a shovel and it could not be ascertained what had caused that injury, be it pre or post-mortem. Fracture to ribs, possible fracture to ribs. This may have been caused by the position of the infant.
>
> …
>
> In relation to the injury to the skull, your Honour, I say only this, and I contained it at para.14K. This would not be expected as a result of a standard vaginal delivery. Had such an injury been

---

[11]Whether the foetus is a 'person' continues to be hotly contested; see Scott (2002) for a summary of the debate. This discussion is beyond the scope of this book.

sustained in life it most certainly would have been severe enough to lead to death, but due to the decomposition of the baby's body, it was not possible to determine whether the child was live at birth or a still born. There were indicators of what is described as squamous in the lungs that may indicate foetal distress, and it is that foetal distress which could be or which may be consistent with a child more likely to be born still born. (Imogen, prosecution opening)

The suggestion presented here is that it is not unreasonable to believe that Imogen had taken steps to kill the baby, but that there is simply no evidence to prove this.

In Olivia and Michael's case, the suggestion that both defendants may be culpable for more than concealing the dead body is made in one of the defendants pre-sentencing reports. While the judge clearly dismisses the suggestion, the fact that the point is raised illustrates the idea that concealment cases indicate further wrongdoing.

PROSECUTION:	The pathology report, I've disclosed it to my learned friend, indicates that the child was eight weeks premature and as I've already said there's no further charges because we are just not able to know given it was eight weeks premature whether it was stillborn or whether it died during the birth of anything else.
JUDGE:	Well, this is why I asked you at the beginning because it seems to me to be an important matter. In the report for Michael there's a reference to it almost being an aggravating feature that the child might have been alive at some point, but that doesn't seem to be an aggravating feature. To try to revive the child as he said he did is not what this case is about.
PROSECUTION:	It's not, no.
JUDGE:	So, either the child was stillborn or died very soon after it was born and there's no evidence that it's death, if that's the case, is the responsibility of either of these two defendants.
PROSECUTION:	No.
JUDGE:	I think it's really important we focus on what it is that they have done. So, it's as you say them concealing the birth with the upsetting and undignified way in which it happened.

PROSECUTION: Yes. That really is the offence: concealing the birth and the body being disposed in the manner that it was. (Olivia and Michael, prosecution opening)

As noted in Chapter 4, the conduct of the women convicted of concealment is also discussed in the context of their behaviour while pregnant, especially their failure to mitigate the risk to the foetus or the actions or inactions that put the foetus at risk. The judge's remarks, while sentencing Sally – focussing on Sally's behaviour while pregnant which had the potential to cause harm to the foetus – provide the clearest examples of such judgements:

> [...] whilst the circumstances and reasons for the stillborn births will never fully be able to be established, your chaotic lifestyle choices, including alcohol abuse and promiscuity at the time of your pregnancies was such as to put the good health of any unborn child at risk. (Sally, judge sentencing)

Similar sentiments are vocalised during Imogen's trial, in relation to her failure to prepare for the birth of the baby, as the judge states:

> We shall never know whether his life might have been saved had you sought proper medical attention at the time of his birth. Many would describe your conduct as wicked. You wanted to conceal your pregnancy. You wanted to conceal the birth and the death of your son. Your conduct was truly deplorable. (Imogen, judge sentencing)

The suggestion, in both cases, is that the women, through their actions or inactions, bear some responsibility for the death of the foetuses/babies. As there is neither the evidence nor scope within the law to capture such behaviour as criminal offences, these comments remain extraneous to their convictions. Nevertheless, the inclusion of the comments does indicate that the women's 'failure' to ensure the survival of their foetuses, and to safeguard the well-being of their 'children', were considered key elements of their conduct, even if not specifically the behaviour they have been criminalised for.

When Is an Abortion Not an Abortion?

The offence of procuring a miscarriage applies from the point when an embryo adheres to the lining of a woman's uterus (approximately 6–10 days after fertilisation, which itself could be up to 7 days after the woman last had sex) through to spontaneous labour. As noted in Chapter 5, it is the ending of the pregnancy and not the killing of a foetus that is the focus of this offence. Under section 58 of the Offences Against the Person Act 1861 (hereafter OAPA), the law does not distinguish between unlawful procuring of a miscarriage at any gestational stage. However, as Sally Sheldon (2016) argues, to understand criminal legal regulation of abortion, we must read section 58 of the OAPA in conjunction with the Abortion Act 1967. In so doing, the conclusion drawn is that abortion is not a moral wrong in need of criminalisation at any stage of gestation. Instead, the law criminalises the ending of a pregnancy when conducted outside of the medical parameters of the Abortion Act:[12] the law determines the termination of a pregnancy to be a serious wrong warranting criminalisation when not carried out under medical supervision. The requirement for abortions to occur under medical supervision is 'in line with the best medical practice of the 1960s', when abortion could only be conducted through medical procedure (rather than medication) and illegal abortions posed significant health risks to pregnant women (Sheldon, 2016, p. 356). An abortion is only legal if two doctors agree it meets the requirements of the Abortion Act and thus can go ahead, and Sheldon concludes that the Abortion Act provides 'socially acceptable' reasons why a woman would be allowed to discontinue a pregnancy. The message of the law is one of medical paternalism, as women are deemed to be relatively incapable of making a morally significant decision about their pregnancies. Sally Sheldon (1997) has long argued that the law has always refused to recognise that women have a fundamental right to decide to terminate a pregnancy. Instead, the law advocates that doctors are the best people to determine if a woman should be allowed an abortion. And if a woman conducts an abortion outside of this legally sanctioned medical regime, then she is committing a criminal offence, punishable by life imprisonment.

Sheldon's point is well made, and of great importance for the development of social and legal regulations of women's bodies and reproductive autonomy.[13] However, when we take a look at the women who have been convicted of the offence of procuring a miscarriage, it becomes apparent that their cases are distinct, not because of their actions of illegally ending a pregnancy but because of the decision by criminal justice professionals to intervene and criminalise their conduct. Most prosecutions under section 58 of the OAPA have been of men who have assaulted pregnant women or secretly administered abortifacients with the intention of ending the pregnancy (Sheldon, 2016). From the research I have conducted, it would appear that only two women have been convicted of the offence; their cases are analysed here – Hayley and Sophie. In both cases, women ordered misoprostol via the internet: the drug is used to start labour and expel the foetus from the uterus.

---

[12]The Abortion Act provides exemption from prosecution under the OAPA, s58, if the abortion is performed in specific therapeutic circumstances, whereby two registered medical practitioners are of the opinion that 'the pregnancy has not exceeded its twenty-fourth week and that the continuance of the pregnancy would involve risk, greater than if the pregnancy were terminated, or injury to the physical or mental health of the pregnant woman or any existing children of her family (s1(1)(a)), or 'the termination is necessary to prevent grave permanent injury to the physical or mental health of the pregnant woman' (s1(1)(b)), or 'continuance of the pregnancy would involve risk to the life of the pregnant woman, greater than if the pregnancy were terminated' (s1(1)(c)), or 'that there is a substantial risk that if the child were born it would suffer from such physical or mental abnormalities as to be seriously handicapped' (s1(1)(d)).

[13]There is now a nation-wide campaign to decriminalise abortion, spearheaded by the British Pregnancy Advisory Service, We Trust Women (n.d.). A number of attempts to decriminalise abortion through Private Members Bills have been heard in Parliament. For discussion of this, see Fanghanel et al. (2021) and Sheldon and Wellings (2020b).

As I have argued elsewhere (Milne, 2020), in Hayley's case, her actions are seen not as the ending of a pregnancy, but as the killing of a foetus. Several times during her sentencing hearing, the judge equates Hayley's actions to homicide:

> This is not charged as murder, and I would be wrong to treat it as such, as a matter of law. Equally it is not manslaughter, nor is it akin to it, because the termination here was deliberately caused with a view to terminating the life of an unborn child. It is not akin to causing death by dangerous driving either, with its maximum sentence of 14 years, but once again I have to bear in mind the nature of the calculated intentionality here. As matters stand in English law, none of those offenses could be committed in relation to an unborn child, but the seriousness of the criminality here is that, at whatever stage life can be said to begin, the child in the womb was so near to birth that in my judgment all right thinking people would consider this offense more serious than that of unintentional manslaughter or any offense on the calendar other than murder. (Hayley, judge sentencing)

The judge continually refers to the foetus as a 'child', including stating that '[t]his is a child who, on the face of it, prospectively was capable of being born alive in the next few days ...'; thus, further equating Hayley's actions to the killing of a live born child. Moreover, Hayley was initially sentenced to 12 years' imprisonment, which was reduced by the Court of Appeal, judging that Hayley's culpability lay in her 'extinguishing of a life about to begin'.

Similarly, in Sophie's case, the foetus is referred to as a 'child', being noted by the prosecution as having been named. Furthermore, the prosecution intimate that it is Sophie's actions of taking the abortifacients that led to the death of the foetus. Throughout the hearing, the foetus is referred to as a 'baby':

> PROSECUTION: The conclusion was that it was very likely he was still born. My Lord, I won't go into the details of the post-mortem.
>
> JUDGE: No.
>
> PROSECUTION: Save to say that the cause of death was antenatal foetal hypoxia, and that was the consequence of the self-administration of misoprostol.
>
> JUDGE: Yes.
>
> PROSECUTION: There was no indication that there was any naturally occurring trigger for labour or delivery, and at that gestation a normally formed foetus, which he was otherwise, would be expected to survive with appropriate and timely medical treatment. (Sophie, prosecution opening)

A key distinction between Hayley's and Sophie's cases is how their culpability is discussed. One of the main factors lingered upon in Hayley's case is that, due to consultation with medical professionals, she would have known the gestational stage of her pregnancy, and it is argued that she took the abortifacients knowing that spontaneous labour could have occurred at any moment:

> But for the drugs intentionally taken, however, there is no reason to believe that you would not have been delivered of a healthy boy. Had he been safely born within a matter of days and you had then killed him, you would be facing a charge of murder. (Hayley, judge sentencing)

In contrast, Sophie is seen by the judge to be less culpable for the same actions (illegally ending a pregnancy) due both to not knowing the exact stage of her pregnancy and to her pregnancy not being as far progressed as Hayley's:

> The case has nothing to do with the general morality or otherwise of terminating the lives of unborn foetus's [*sic*.], the law in this country is quite clear. As you must be fully aware, no doubt in line with your internet searches and not in any event, it was open to you to seek a termination of your pregnancy on the NHS at any stage before 24 weeks gestation, although as the deadline approached it would obviously be more difficult for doctors to sign the necessary certificates. At 24 weeks gestation a foetus has a fair chance of survival if born prematurely. Your child, at 32 to 34 weeks gestation, had a very good chance of survival. It had no chance once you administered this drug. Outside the circumstances comprehended by the Abortion Act, the law does not permit the administration of a poison with intent to procure miscarriage at any stage of a foetus's development, but I mention the gestation dates to place your case in context.
>
> …
>
> In [Hayley's][14] case the abortifacient was administered close to term, making the case more serious than yours because the defendant there was fully aware of the position. (Sophie, judge sentencing)

The assessment made here, that culpability increases with the gestational stage of the foetus, is contrary to the legal provision of the OAPA, s58, which makes procuring a miscarriage illegal at any point in the pregnancy following implantation in the uterine wall. There is no mitigation in the OAPA based on the woman being unaware of the gestational stage of her pregnancy: procuring a miscarriage is an offence at any stage unless conducted within the parameters of the Abortion Act

---

[14]Name of case changed to maintained confidentiality.

(with the authorisation of two doctors). Even within the parameters of the Abortion Act, there is no time limit placed on when a termination of a pregnancy will cease to be allowed under certain conditions.[15] If a pregnancy causes the risk of 'grave injury to the physical or mental health of the pregnant woman' or 'the continuance of the pregnancy would involve risk to the life of the pregnant woman, greater than if the pregnancy were terminated', then a termination can legally be conducted under sections 1(1)(b-c) of the Abortion Act, at any point of gestation.[16] Similarly, if the termination is being conducted due to foetal abnormalities, then there is no time limit placed on the legality of this conduct by medical professionals under s1(1)(d). While there is legal provision for women to obtain late-term abortions, this does not mean that they are easy or even possible to access for reasons other than foetal abnormality – confirmed in conversations I have had with members of the British Pregnancy Advisory Service public relations team.

There is evidence to suggest that, each year, many women attempt to access, or do successfully access, illegal abortions. While only two women have faced prosecution for illegal abortions in England and Wales, evidence of seizure of abortifacients being delivered by mail to women across the United Kingdom would suggest that numerous women are procuring their own miscarriages, outside of medical guidance, without facing criminal charges (Kirby, 2017). In support of her Bill to decriminalise abortion, Member of Parliament Dame Diana Johnson presented comments from women who had illegally obtained and consumed abortifacients from the organisation *Women on Web*, none of whom have faced criminal prosecution.[17] Research by Abigail R. A. Aiken et al. (2018) concludes that despite legal provisions to access abortions in Great Britain,[18] many women struggle to obtain legal abortions due to access barriers, including long waiting

---

[15]With thanks to Dr Sheelagh McGuinness for reminding me of this important point in relation to the cases analysed here.

[16]It should be noted here that, in such instances, terminating the pregnancy under these grounds may not result in the death of the foetus. For example, if a woman needed a life-saving operation due to injuries sustained, and such an operation was not compatible with continuation of the pregnancy, then a caesarean section may be conducted with the foetus being delivered and then treated for conditions related to prematurity. However, in such instances, the Abortion Act is not needed to protect medical professionals from prosecution under OAPA, s58, as the wording of the statute means that it has always been the 'unlawful' administering of 'poison or other noxious thing' or 'use [of] any instrument or other means whatsoever' with intent to procure the miscarriage of a woman that has been an offence; thus, suggesting that, in specific circumstances, procuring a miscarriage has been legal for medical professionals. *Bourne* [1939] 1 KB 687 confirmed previous common law that a medical professional who terminates a pregnancy conducted with the intention to preserve the life of the pregnant woman was not committing an offence under s58. Furthermore, the ruling confirmed that the concept of preserving life included both physical and mental health.

[17]Hansard [HC Deb] 13 March 2017, Diana Johnson MP, vol. 623, col. 26–28.

[18]At the time Aiken et al. were writing, in 2018, abortion was illegal in most circumstances in Northern Ireland.

times, distance to clinics, work or childcare commitments, lack of eligibility for free NHS services, and prior negative experiences of abortion care. Women also reported privacy concerns, including lack of confidentiality of services, perceived or experienced stigma, and preferring the privacy and comfort of using pills at home. Furthermore, some women struggled to access legal abortions due to controlling circumstances, including partner violence and partner/family control. Home-use of abortion medication following a phone consultation, introduced as a temporary measure during the coronavirus in March 2020, may have temporarily alleviated some of these difficulties. The classification of the 'home of a pregnant woman', as being an authorised place for the purpose of termination of a pregnancy under section 1 of the 1967 Act for an early medical abortion, was decided by the Government on 30 March 2020 (Department of Health and Social Care, 2020b). However, the measure is currently time limited – expiring either on the day on which the temporary provisions of the Coronavirus Act 2020 expire or at the end of the two-year period beginning with the day on which they were made, whichever is earlier – so this option may not be available to women in the long term.[19]

There are numerous reasons why prosecutions of women obtaining illegal abortions are not regularly sought, including that the police may be unaware that the offence is being committed and evidence may be limited. Nevertheless, the ability to track mail and internet searches would facilitate a prosecution for, at the very least, procuring an abortifacient,[20] if not for an illegal termination of a pregnancy. It appears, however, that there is little appetite to prosecute women seeking early medical abortions through illegal means. As Sally Sheldon (2016) argues, prosecutions tend to be reserved for terminations of pregnancies in the very late stages of gestation and for non-consensual abortions (often involving a third party attacking a pregnant woman). Lack of prosecutions of women who terminate non-viable pregnancies, which still kill the foetus, would suggest that criminal law serves no purpose in regulating such action. In light of this, what is the driver for prosecuting women such as Hayley and Sophie – those who illegally end viable pregnancies? The conclusion presented during both criminal hearings is that the actions of the women resulted in the 'killing' of a 'child'. Such a conclusion distorts what they actually did and were convicted of – taking medication to bring their pregnancies to an end. The death of the foetus/infant[21] was a consequence in each case; nevertheless, technically, it is not the death of the foetus/child for which either woman is criminalised. While in the strictest sense of the law the

---

[19]Furthermore, even under this delivery mechanism, some women will still struggle to access legal abortions due to the need for the medication to be dispensed to a woman's home: women who are homeless, women with unsettled immigration status who may not wish to reveal where they are living, women living in abusive and controlling situations, for example.

[20]OAPA, s59.

[21]In Hayley's case, it is not known if the foetus died *in utero* or was born alive and died after birth.

prosecutions brought against both women are correctly applied, as they did both take steps to end their pregnancies; in reality, and as is made clear in the discussion of their actions during their court hearings, it is the death of the foetus/child that is identified as their wrongdoing.

I have argued elsewhere that it is perhaps incorrect to view the actions of Hayley and Sophie as illegal abortions (Milne, 2020), and that the offence of procuring a miscarriage is not the best means under which to criminalise their behaviour. When comparing Hayley's and Sophie's actions to 'typical' abortions that occur in England and Wales each year, we can see them as distinct and in opposition to most abortions. Abortion is a common medical procedure that one in three women in the United Kingdom will experience at least once in her lifetime (Edwards, 2015).[22] The vast majority of terminations, 82%, are conducted before the 10th week of gestation. Abortions that occurred at or after the 24th week of pregnancy totalled 279 in 2019; 0.1% of the legal abortions that occurred (Department of Health and Social Care, 2020a). Therefore, I have argued that the distinction between Hayley's and Sophie's actions and 'typical' abortions means that we *potentially* ought to see their actions as the killing of a foetus/child, not the ending of a pregnancy (Milne, 2020). As already outlined, homicide is precisely how members of the court are interpreting the women's actions – the homicide of the foetus. However, due to the requirements of the born alive rule, homicide of a foetus is not a crime under English and Welsh law.[23] Thus, as with the offence of concealment of birth, procuring a miscarriage is being used as an unofficial foetus homicide offence. Both offences are being used to criminalise women's behaviour and thus apply criminal sanctions that are deemed to put the

---

[22]Previously, I have cited the National Health Service (2020a) advice and guidance on abortion, but information about the frequency with which women access abortion has been removed from the website, for some reason.

[23]Arguably, an exception here is the offence of child destruction, which, due to the possible life sentence attached to the offence, could be seen as a form of a foetal homicide law. As outlined in Chapter 5, when enacted, the law was not envisaged to protect foetuses while *in utero*; instead, it was created to capture women suspected of killing their foetus/infant after labour had begun but before the child was a legal person. In Hayley's case, the judge questioned why she had not been convicted of child destruction, and the prosecution argued it was due to the inability to prove the child had died prior to living a separate existence (the body of the child was never found, so it was not possible to determine whether live or stillbirth occurred). A charge of child destruction is not discussed in Sophie's case. One of the elements of ILPA, that has an impact on how it can be applied in cases of suspected foetal killing, is the need to prove that the woman's conduct (or that of any other person charged) was done 'with intent to destroy the life of a child capable of being born alive'. In cases of concealment as outlined above, this would be very difficult to demonstrate. Similarly, in cases of procuring a miscarriage, an argument could be made that the women were intending to end their pregnancies, not to kill the child capable of being born alive. A discussion of the connection of the ILPA and foetal protection is needed but is beyond the scope of this book.

life of the foetus at risk. The offences are not being applied incorrectly, but they are, nevertheless, being used to obtain convictions in lieu of actually being able to punish women for harming or killing their foetuses. As a consequence, the invisible line of birth that signifies whether legal personhood has been obtained, or not, has lost its legal significance in cases of suspicious perinatal death. Instead, we see a desire to punish 'bad' mothers and 'irresponsible' pregnant women, resulting in the application of existing criminal law due to the lack of availability of foetal homicide laws.

Foetal Protection in the United States

A natural conclusion of the arguments I have just made may be to advocate for the protection of foetuses in law – the creation of foetal homicide laws. Enacting such legal protection for the foetus could mean that criminal justice might *officially* sanction women for causing harm or death to their foetuses. No longer would prosecutors need to *unofficially* defeat the principle of the born alive rule; they could hold women to account for harm to the foetus through official mechanisms. However, before we amend the law and officially scrap the principle of the born alive rule as a mechanism for limiting liability, it is important that we consider the potential consequences of such a legal development.[24] To do so, I turn to the United States, where, in most states, foetuses are now protected under criminal law. As I will outline, such legal developments have had *dramatic* consequences on the health and well-being of both pregnant women and foetuses and so has had a significant impact on women's rights. Here I draw on arguments I have made in relation to the impact of the foetus-first mentality and the application of criminal law (Milne, 2020).

In the United States, at least 38 states now have laws protecting foetuses,[25] and at least 29 of these states apply their laws to the early stages of pregnancy (Murphy, 2014; National Conference of State Legislatures, 2018). In almost half of all states, the pregnant woman is specifically exempt from prosecution under foetal protection laws. This maternal exemption reflects the fact that most foetal homicide laws developed out of a desire to protect pregnant women and their unborn children from attack by third parties, allowing for a perpetrator of such violence to be punished for harm to the woman and her foetus (see Flavin, 2009; Ramsey, 2006). In four further states, Andrew S. Murphy (2014) argues, it is unlikely

---

[24]In some American states, the born alive rule is still in place and foetuses are granted protection in law by, for example, declaring the foetus a potential victim of homicide; see Murphy (2014) for details of how different states have approached foetal protection. Thus, the born alive rule itself does not necessarily offer women protection from criminal liability.

[25]Within the literature, scholars often refer to 'foetal homicide laws'. However, as argued here, protection of foetuses stretches beyond homicide offences, and so, I argue that 'foetal protection laws' is a more appropriate term to capture the development of law in American states from 1970 onwards.

that pregnant women could be prosecuted for causing the death of their own foetus due to the wording of the legislation. However, other states are silent on whether or not a pregnant woman could be held liable. Murphy concludes that this leaves the possibility of criminal proceedings being brought against women to individual prosecutors, who, evidence would suggest, have demonstrated a willingness to advocate for a broad interpretation of such statutes so as to incorporate the pregnant woman as a potential offender of these 'crimes'.

As a consequence of these developments of foetal protection laws in the United States, over 413 women were arrested, detained, and forced to have medical treatment under the basis of protecting the health and well-being of foetuses between 1973 and 2005 (Paltrow & Flavin, 2013).[26] Women have been arrested and sometimes imprisoned following a belief that a stillbirth or miscarriage occurred due to the woman intentionally acting to end the pregnancy; so considered a case of foeticide (Hayes, 2010; Newman, 2010).[27] There are also reported cases of women facing a criminal investigation after they have declined to follow medical advice in relation to their pregnancy, and the foetus has been stillborn (BBC News, 2004; Thomson, 2004). Women have faced criminal justice involvement in cases where their baby has been born alive and then died shortly after birth, and medical professionals and law enforcers have deemed that the actions of the woman while pregnant caused the death of the child.[28] Women have also faced homicide convictions in instances where injury inflicted on their body (either by themselves or by a third party) resulted in their survival but the death of the foetus (Hunt, 1995; Pilkington, 2012; Stockman, 2019) and in instances where pregnant woman have tested positive for illegal substances, even where there is little or no evidence that the drug use caused harm or death to the foetus/child (Bassett, 2014; Pilkington, 2015). The law has not been applied equally, with Lynn M. Paltrow and Jeanne Flavin's study illustrating that 59% of those detained were women of colour, with black women making up 52%. Regardless of race and ethnicity, the women were also overwhelmingly economically disadvantaged.

Feminists in the United States have been very critical of foetal protection laws, in part because of the consequences they have upon access to legal abortion, due to the foetus being determined to be a legal 'person' – an autonomous entity with rights equivalent and in opposition to the rights of the pregnant woman (Bhattacharjee, 2002; Brown, 2005; Johnsen, 1989; MacKinnon, 1991; Paltrow, 1999). While it has been argued that providing the foetus with legal personality would not be a significant-enough legal challenge alone (Ely, 1973; Lynch, 1995), concerns have been raised that legal protection for the foetus will contribute to a

---

[26]These figures are based on a review of newspaper reports, so should be considered an underestimate.

[27]This includes the case of Christine Taylor, who fell down the stairs while pregnant.

[28]Jennifer Jorgensen was convicted of manslaughter after she crashed her car while pregnant and was deemed to have been driving recklessly; the baby was born alive and later died of her injuries. Jorgensen's conviction was overturned on appeal to the Supreme Court of New York, *People* v. *Jorgensen*, 41 N.E.3d 778, 779 (N.Y. 2015).

pro-life ideology that portrays abortion as immoral within a wider message of the 'culture of life' (Sanger, 2006).

Beyond rights and access to abortion, foetal protection laws are argued to be discriminatory towards women and to interfere with women's rights. For a state to sanction a woman for behaviour because she is pregnant (e.g. for using drugs while pregnant, considering drug use is often not illegal for people while not pregnant)[29] is depriving women of their rights *because of* their pregnancy status. The sanction would not be imposed if the woman was not pregnant.[30] Accordingly, this is a distinct form of sex-based discrimination, based on women's bodily functions as women: their capacity to become pregnant and to carry a foetus. Dawn Johnsen (1989) argues that such state prescription of behaviour deprives women of the right to control their lives during pregnancy – a fundamental right of liberty and privacy, as guaranteed by the Constitution of the United States, and specifically the Fourteenth Amendment.[31] Women have the right to refuse medical intervention and to be free from criminal or civil liability for their conduct during pregnancy based on the common law and constitutional rights of privacy, bodily integrity, and personal decision-making. These rights include freedom from the coercion of medical treatment, freedom of choice for a family life, the right to self-determination, the right to non-subordination, freedom from bodily invasion, and appropriation of the body for the purpose of another (the foetus). And yet, many American states have demonstrated that they are prepared to prioritise the protection of the foetus over the pregnant woman's rights to bodily autonomy and integrity (Bordo, 2003; Flavin, 2009; Gallagher, 1987).

Such implications for women's rights could *perhaps* (and I emphasise perhaps, considering how devastating these changes to law have been for women's rights) be justified if criminal law and justice intervention to protect foetuses was seen to result in a substantial benefit for unborn children. However, the evidence we have from the United States shows limited benefit, if not a downright detriment to foetal health and well-being. In contrast to what is often argued, it is not so easy to determine that the actions of pregnant women have a substantial negative impact on the foetus. For example, in instances where illegal substances have been consumed and the pregnancy ends in a miscarriage or stillbirth, frequently the cause of foetal death is unknown (Frank et al., 2001; Kampschmidt, 2015; Ondersma et al., 2000).

The socio-economic background of the pregnant woman has a greater impact on maternal and foetal health than maternal behaviour, specifically deprivation, which has a drastic impact upon women's decisions about their health and life during pregnancy, such as whether they can afford to access healthcare (Fentiman, 2006).

---

[29]Whereas possession and dealing of illegal substances often are.
[30]See my discussion of drug use in pregnancy, and illegal abortions in Alabama and Indiana, USA, respectively (Milne, 2020).
[31]Women in the United Kingdom are afforded such protection under the Human Rights Act 1998.

Even when there is clear evidence that maternal behaviour caused harm to the foetus, it is still not necessarily the case that legal sanctions against women will improve the well-being of the foetus. In fact, legal sanctions can lead to worse foetal outcomes as women avoid medical care due to a fear that they will be reported to the police, and lack of prenatal care is a leading factor in poor pregnancy outcomes (American College of Obstetricians and Gynecologists, 2014; Boudreaux & Thompson, 2015; Center for Reproductive Rights, 2000). Finally, there is evidence that women in the United States have sought legal abortions in order to escape prosecution under foetal protection laws (Murphy, 2014). Thus, attempts to 'protect' foetuses are, in some instances, resulting in negative health outcomes for them or even death.

Instead of protecting foetuses, feminists have argued that foetal protection laws act as 'a state legitimized form of motherhood' (Cherry, 2007, p. 198), criminalising the behaviour of women who are deemed to not meet the expectations set by the state – to not be the 'good' mother and 'responsible' pregnant woman (Milne, 2020). In making these arguments, feminists reject the notion that the state criminalises women to protect foetuses. As Rickie Solinger (2005) argues, if the state valued women and children, then it would fund necessary medical treatment for pregnant women, such as drug rehabilitation, and assist women to achieve good health during pregnancy. Instead, state intervention says far more about the 'type' of woman that the state deems *should* be a mother (Flavin, 2009; Roberts, 1997). State-sponsored coercion of pregnant women's behaviour 'compels women who desire children to reorganize their lives in accordance with judicially defined norms of behavior' (Johnsen, 1989, p. 612). Furthermore, as is evident from the findings of Lynn M. Paltrow and Jeanne Flavin (2013), and as with pretty much all criminal justice intervention, foetal protection laws are applied discriminatorily, with poor women and women of colour overrepresented among those arrested or subject to equivalent deprivations of liberty. As outlined in Chapter 3, such women have the fewest resources to meet the requirements of the myths of motherhood and are policed more heavily than women in stronger socio-economic situations.

As illustrated by cases from the United States, laws protecting foetuses from harm or death have very real and damaging implications for women and their rights, as well as negative consequences for foetuses. Therefore, when thinking about England and Wales, while we may find the behaviour of Hannah, Imogen, Lily, Olivia, Sally, and Sophie abhorrent, we need to think long and hard as to whether protecting the foetus through law, criminal and civil, is truly the right approach to these cases and to wider concerns about the health of born children due to the actions of pregnant women. As illustrated by cases from the United States, the consequences of protecting foetuses in law are significant and can be hugely damaging. Proposals to change the NICE guidance on foetal alcohol spectrum disorder, as well as other public health messages outlined in Chapter 4, illustrate a dedication to the principles of foetal protection. Taking the next step and enshrining that into law is likely to have devastating consequences for women, particularly in cases of crisis pregnancies. As I have outlined in this chapter, and in previous chapters, it is easy enough to criminalise women for failing to be the 'good' mother and the 'appropriate' pregnant woman. I am, thus, very nervous about any attempts to make it even easier by introducing *official* foetal protection laws. In the final chapter, I will outline wider implications of prioritising the foetus over the pregnant woman, and what this approach tells us about the position of women in society.

Chapter 7

Redressing Gendered Harm: The Role of Criminal Law and Criminal Justice

How should we, as a society, understand and respond to women who are suspected of causing the death of their foetus or newborn child? Specifically, what role should criminal law and criminal justice play in our approach? As I have outlined across the chapters of this book, the response of criminal law and justice has been individualistic: focussed on the women as single entities and their actions as individualised behaviour. This is the function and role of criminal law. It is how it is designed to work – to hold the 'rational man' to account for his actions, negating the wider social, political, economic, and cultural circumstances that contextualise his actions (Norrie, 2014). But how does such an approach to understanding criminality (read: behaviour deemed to require criminal sanction) fare in relation to suspicious perinatal deaths and accused women?

As I have argued, women who are suspected of causing the death of their newborn child/foetus are in exceptionally vulnerable situations. Their lives are such that a pregnancy is considered an intolerable threat to their existence: it causes them a crisis. And the crisis results in the women consciously or unconsciously determining that they cannot actively respond to the pregnancy (seek medical care to end the pregnancy, if an available option, and/or to assist with continuation of the pregnancy and plans for labour and delivery). Thus, they come to be in a situation whereby they are labouring and giving birth alone, and, at some point around the time of birth, the foetus/baby dies.

The temptation to see these cases as an individual 'problem' – a reproductive dysfunction – is clearly substantial; this is the approach taken by many scholars assessing women's experiences of crisis pregnancy and cases of neonaticide. Furthermore, as illustrated in the analysis of the cases presented here, the approach of the courts is also to focus on the individual 'problem' of the women, expressing their behaviour as an example of the 'bad' and/or failed mother, and the 'irresponsible' pregnant woman, or by pathologising their actions. These responses reflects the 'mad' or 'bad' approach that many feminists have identified in criminal law and justice responses to 'criminal' women (Carlen, 1983; Milne & Turton, 2018; Morrissey, 2003; Worrall, 1990). By portraying these women as unmotherly monsters, the focus of the criminal law and justice response is on the individual women and their failure. However, to focus on the woman and her actions alone is to miss

Criminal Justice Responses to Maternal Filicide: Judging the Failed Mother, 145–159
Copyright © 2021 by Emma Milne
Published by Emerald Publishing under an Exclusive Licence
doi:10.1108/978-1-83909-620-420211009

the myriad and substantial influences and impacts of society in constructing and contributing to circumstances that lead to the 'crimes' of women suspected of newborn child or foetal killing.

As I illustrated in Chapter 2, the cases need to be understood in the context of the women's lives. It is precisely because of their wider social circumstance – their vulnerabilities – that they experience a crisis pregnancy. Poverty, deprivation, emotional and physical abuse and violence, sexual violence, and general life conditions can leave a woman feeling a pregnancy is an illegitimate 'option' for her. If not for these experiences, the pregnancy as a crisis may not have occurred for these women, and so, their 'criminal' acts may not have occurred either.

Moreover, beyond the individual reasons why women feel unable to accept their pregnancy and address it, there are wider social elements that feed into how pregnancy and motherhood are experienced and perceived. As outlined in Chapter 3, the myths of motherhood and ideologies of womanhood as synonymous with 'good' motherhood – inherent, natural, unquestioning – play a significant part in how we perceive the role of women as mothers and how we understand pregnancy. To become pregnant, or even for there to be a possibility of becoming pregnant, is to be assumed to adopt the role of the 'good' mother and to embrace child-rearing as 'child-centred, expert-guided, emotionally absorbing, labour-intensive, and financially expensive' (Hays, 1996, p. 8). To be this woman, to be the 'good' mother, is to put the foetus first, regardless of the circumstances and consequences of the pregnancy. As outlined in Chapter 4, the foetus-first mentality manifests itself in a very specific way in Anglo-American society. To be the 'good' mother is to be the 'responsible' pregnant woman: to manage any risk to the foetus, including any risks perceived to be caused by the self (alcohol consumption, stress, eating brie, etc.). To fail to do this – to be 'in conflict' with the foetus and to not put its needs first – is to 'fail' as a mother.

However, not all women are 'meant' to be mothers. By this, I mean that society has always, historically and today, placed limits on those women for whom motherhood is considered to be an illegitimate option. Historically, marriage was a key factor in determining if a woman's pregnancy and her role as a mother was deemed to be legitimate, as outlined in Chapter 5. And, as I explored in Chapters 4 and 6, in the contemporary period, the 'illegitimacy' of motherhood for certain women can clearly be noted from government policy, media coverage and commentary, public health guidance, and the implementation of criminal law through criminal justice policy and practice. Large swathes of the population are deemed to be 'illegitimate' in their role as mothers due to their current situations and circumstances: specifically, younger women, older women, disabled women, poorer women, women who consume controlled substances, women who consume alcohol,[1] single women, women from

---

[1] Previously, I would have said women who consume 'too much' alcohol but, considering the NICE guidance discussed in Chapter 6, now any alcohol appears to be 'too much', despite the paucity of evidence to support this public health guidance of abstinence while pregnant (Thom et al., 2020).

minoritised ethnic communities.[2] The perception of the illegitimacy of these women as mothers impacts not only how they are treated when they become pregnant or following birth but also how their sexuality is approached. For example, contemporary public health guidance around alcohol and pregnancy frames all women of reproductive age as potential mothers and constructs a 'choice' between drinking alcohol and having sex (Thom et al., 2020; see also, guidance from the Centers for Disease Control and Prevention, 2016). Some sex education practices, in the United States in particular but not exclusively, have also focussed on abstinence-only approaches, advocating it is the only sure and fast way to prevent teen pregnancy, despite the approach clearly not working to reduce pregnancy rates in young people (Perrin & DeJoy, 2003; Sanger, 2006). Steps have been taken to limit the capacity of 'undesirable' women from reproducing (drug users, poorer women, women who have previously neglected or abused children, for example). In both the United States and the United Kingdom, charities have worked to give financial incentives to women who consume controlled substances if they agree to be surgically sterilised (BBC News, 2010; Bois, 2018; Paltrow, 2012);[3] programmes in the United Kingdom to assist women who have lost multiple infants to care at birth often require the woman to take long-acting reversible contraceptives (LARCs) to be eligible: 'help' will only be provided if the woman limits her reproductive capacity (Cox, 2012); and in the United States, there is a long history of forced and non-consensual sterilisation of women of colour and First Nation women (Gordon & Gordon, 2002; Nelson, 2003; Reagan, 1997). There are also examples of women in the United States being denied release from prison unless they agree to take LARCs, women of colour being most likely to be targeted by this criminal justice response (Flavin, 2009; Goodwin, 2020; Oberman, 1992). So it is not difficult to conclude that policies to limit motherhood for certain women continue to be rooted in class and race.

As we can see, experiences of pregnancy, and responses to women's pregnancies and potential to become pregnant, are heavily imbued with social controls and regulations that dictate 'appropriate' and 'inappropriate', or 'legitimate' and 'illegitimate', motherhood. And yet, when women respond to negate an illegitimate pregnancy, when they respond in line with societal messages that their pregnancies are inappropriate (due to being the consequence of an extra-marital affair,

---

[2]Anxieties over these groups of women (as well as others not noted) becoming pregnant have also been reflected in previous centuries, particularly in relation to poor women and women from minoritised ethnic communities, so this is not a new element of the myths of motherhood and regulation of sex and reproduction.

[3]This policy, and the actions of medical professionals who then go on to sterilise drug-using women, is in contrast to the challenges that other women have faced when they have requested to be sterilised; being told by doctors that they cannot access the procedure as they might regret it one day. As with all areas of 'policing pregnancy' discussed in this book, it is women from minoritised ethnic communities and poorer women who face the brunt of such policies and are the target of the rhetoric of 'undesirable reproducers'.

due to her family believing the man who impregnated her was of 'bad sorts', due to her being considered too young, due to her being at risk of being beaten or killed by an abusive partner, for example), the focus and blame are placed entirely and squarely upon those women and the 'wrongfulness' of their behaviour.

It is this focus on individual blame that has resulted in the construction of the 'menu of offences' that I have referred to throughout this book. As I outlined in Chapter 5, the menu developed from historical concerns about protecting male lineage, so discouraging women from engaging in sexual practice outside of marriage. As today, her actions to redress the consequences of her 'deviant' sexuality – to eradicate an unauthorised pregnancy/newborn child through abortion or newborn child killing – were focussed on by criminal law and criminal justice, as well as by political, medical, and legal professional men who created, supported, and enforced the law. It was her individual behaviour that became the focus of criminal law, criminal justice, and society, with criminalisation based on her immorality and the 'wrongness' of her behaviour. The punishment enacted to redress the wrongfulness of her actions manifested itself differently in line with the ideology of punishment that operated at that time; whether through harsh means as with the 1624 Act, or an allowed leniency as through the Infanticide Act 1922. Nevertheless, it is the individual woman who had to pay the price for acting to be rid of a pregnancy that society made clear to her could not exist.

Today, the menu of offences continues to offer a selection of chargeable crimes to capture women's behaviour through criminal law, regardless of when or how the foetus died. As I outlined in Chapter 6, the legal principle of the born alive rule is being negated by application of offences such as concealment of birth and procuring a miscarriage. The focus of legal professionals during the court hearings, through presentation and assessment of the women's 'failings' to put the well-being of the foetus first and so putting the foetus at risk, indicates that the offences are being used as unofficial foetal homicide laws. One of the key conclusions of this research is that the born alive rule is, in practice, no longer in operation in cases of suspected newborn child killing. While the label attached to the criminality may change, and the level of punishment available is different, the principle of being able to criminalise the behaviour of the woman exists, regardless of the evidence to support live birth and the cause of death. The message of criminal law and justice responses to women is clear: we have the means and incentives to criminalise your actions.[4] So, as in the past, the conclusion that

---

[4]Although it should be noted that the existence of certain laws and the application of law is not a complete process of legitimation. As Fyfe (1991) argues, laws are often ignored and broken, and do not necessarily reflect public sentiments. Brennan (2018b) makes this point in relation to infanticide, arguing that social pressures allowed for the defeat of homicide laws prior to the enactment of the Infanticide Act in Ireland. With regard to the current study, I would actually conclude that it is the desire to criminalise and punish accused women that means the born alive rule is being ignored; thus, law is being stretched beyond the limits intended.

women should draw, as well as wider society, is that if you do not intend to act like a mother – to put the foetus first – then it is best you do not have sex, so you do not risk becoming pregnant.[5]

Women, Crime, and Agency

As noted above, this is not the first study to conclude that women are being held individually responsible for actions that are a result of wider social structures and discriminatory practices.[6] However, as noted in Chapter 3, such analysis often results in the claim that to see women's offending behaviour as a consequence of social and structural disadvantage is to remove their agency – to essentially conclude that women do not behave as moral actors who are making decisions about their offending behaviour (Allen, 1987; Edwards, 1984; Morris & Wilczynski, 1993). A desire by feminist scholars, to show that women are moral agents and

---

[5]Such an ideology also operates around abortion; even those that take place in the earliest stages of pregnancy. Abortion stigma and 'shame' are still alive and well (Bommaraju et al., 2016; Hoggart, 2017; Kumar et al., 2009), with legal abortion continuing to be conceptualised as a 'necessary evil' to prevent women from seeking illegal abortions to 'solve' an unwanted pregnancy. The natural conclusion of such a position is that there is something 'wrong' with women having sex for reasons other than procreation, or that they were careless with their non-functional (read: sex for reasons other than baby-making), pleasure-driven sexual encounter(s). Instead, abortion could be conceptualised in a sex-positive manner: as one of many forms of contraception that allow women to engage in sex as they wish, without the burdensome consequences of pregnancy. Similar narratives can be seen around 'emergency contraception', sometimes referred to as 'plan-B'. The notion that it is 'plan-B' suggests that there was a 'plan-A' that either went wrong or the woman 'failed' to put into practice, so she needs 'emergency' medication to solve the 'problem' caused by her non-productive sex. The expense and difficulties of accessing emergency contraception further reinforce the idea that something has gone wrong and that there needs to be a punitive element to accessing this form of birth control to 'discourage' women – from what, it is not entirely clear, but I suspect from non-productive sex. In 2016, the British Pregnancy Advisory Service (2016; n.d.) launched a campaign to reform access to, and cost of, emergency contraception. The campaign, 'Just Say Non!', advocated lower cost and easier access to the medication, highlighting that, for the same amount of money British pharmacies charge for the medication (£30), a woman could jump on the Eurostar, enjoy an afternoon in Paris and buy the medication, which costs 7€.

[6]This is by no means an experience held by women alone. Other social disadvantages that result from other aspects of identity – race and class as clear examples – also exemplify criminal law and justice responses as individualistic, rather than elements of structural oppression. It is also really important to remember that the application of criminal law and justice upon women is not experienced equally, with women from minoritised ethnic communities and poorer women increasingly likely to be criminalised and to experience harsher punishments than their wealthier, white sisters. Thus, an intersectional approach is required.

do make conscious decisions about their offending has, argues Laureen Snider (2003), resulted in harsher criminal justice responses to women who offend; the logic of the argument is that if women are equal to men and equally capable, then they should be treated equally, thus punished as harshly as men.[7] The conclusion of the Corston Report, that *equal* treatment between men and women in punishment and penalty does not need to mean the *same* treatment, has mostly fallen on deaf ears (Annison et al., 2015; Birkett, 2016; Corston, 2007; Milne et al., 2018), and we continue to see a growth in the number of women imprisoned and repeatedly imprisoned following reoffending. The connection between the concept of individual agency and the punishment of women – who are generally exceptionally disadvantaged and have significant vulnerabilities – continues to hound both feminist research and the application of law and justice.

It is beyond the scope of this book to find a solution to the issue of agency versus the social context of women's offending, and I would not do justice to the debate by attempting to address it in any substantial way here. However, the cases of offending behaviour I have assessed here, and other cases of suspected perinatal killing, add further evidence to the conclusion that the debate is not and should not be seen as a dichotomy. It is not that women either have agency and therefore made a decision to end the life of the foetus/child or that their actions or inactions occurred as a consequence of wider factors and so they had no option and thus lacked agency; the debate cannot be that simple. When a woman's back is against the wall and she can see only bad options (including deciding to negate/ignore/deny the pregnancy in the hope that it goes away), we cannot think of this as her having 'choices'. And to do so would be to lose sight of the concept of what it means to 'choose'.

Clearly, one of the reasons why we continue to face this false notion of women's 'agency' in choosing behaviour deemed criminal comes from how the criminal justice system and criminal law was designed and constructed – by men and for men (Lacey, 1998; MacKinnon, 2005; Naffine, 1990; Smart, 1998). In her groundbreaking and influential work, Robin West (1988) clearly outlines that the construction of the Rule of Law is based on the values and fears of dominant men. Men value autonomy and so fear annihilation, but they also long for attachment and dread alienation. Their construction of their desired state and internalised fears come from their lived experiences of seeking autonomy from abusive/domineering fathers, teachers, and bullies and through dreading alienation arising from childhood memories of their mother, experiences of rejection, and 'continuing inability to introspect, converse, or commune with the natural world, including the natural world of others' (West, 1988, p. 64). As a consequence, the Rule of Law, which is masculine and patriarchal, is designed to protect from annihilation and to facilitate and protect the principle of autonomy. The result is that the law and principles of justice have little to no ability to conceptualise, protect, and readdress the harms experienced by women, most of whom have a fundamentally different experience of life compared to men (Conaghan, 1996). Women's lived

---

[7]This is not a direct argument made by feminist scholars but is a possible conclusion that can be drawn and has been drawn by politicians and professionals working in the criminal justice system.

experiences of pregnancy, motherhood, and heterosexual sex, which are made compulsory for many women through social structures, mean that women often value intimacy, fearing separation, but also long for individualisation and dread invasion/intrusion (West, 1988). Being pregnant and breastfeeding both require a literal connection between woman and child, and so, a woman is unable to be an individual; she is quite literally connected to another human, be it a foetus that is inside her, an infant suckling her breast, or a man who has penetrated her with his penis. An example of how the construction of the Rule of Law, in line with men's lived experiences, leaves women not only unprotected by law, but also harmed by it, can be seen in the legal regulation of abortion. As West argues, for women, the fear of an unwanted foetus comes from the risk to the body's integrity, that the existence of the foetus and, later, the born child will result in her ceasing to be or never becoming herself. Thus, for women, the right to an abortion is on the basis of a form of self-defence – protection of the invasion and loss of the self. For men, who mostly have the lived experience of being separate, this makes little to no sense, as their view of self-defence is based on the principle of fear of annihilation, and a foetus, as a vulnerable, helpless being, cannot annihilate anyone. When thinking about and using West's theory of the Rule of Law it is important to note that her work has been criticised for being essentialising, assuming one women's experience shared by all. As Angela P. Harris (1990) outlines the experiences of women are shaped by more than simply their biological sex.

In Chapter 4, I analysed the nature of the gendered harms of pregnancy, which are negated by society and criminal justice, and so women's actions of neutralising the risks posed by the existence of their pregnancy/the foetus/newborn child are considered delegitimate and, thus, criminal. West's analysis also allows us to consider why criminal law and justice continue to view women's 'criminal' acts in terms of moral agency, rejecting the possibility of social and cultural context as the basis of criminal behaviour. The position of the men in society who, historically and still today, control and influence the Rule of Law and criminal justice (white, middle- and upper-class, educated, heterosexual, able-bodied men) is such that it is difficult for them to appreciate the harms of an 'illegitimate' or 'unauthorised' pregnancy. Similarly, those women who have the ability to control and influence law and justice also, generally, hold significant privilege and wealth; thus, they are, potentially, similarly unable to appreciate the dangers of 'invasion' due to having the money and power to negate the damage and harm of such an experience of pregnancy. This argument, coupled with Karen Brennan's (2018a) theory of infanticide law as paternalistic, facilitating leniency to limit calls for changes to discriminatory social structures that cause newborn child killing (see Chapters 4 and 5), further complicates the notion of the dichotomy of women's agency to offend, versus the social context of women's offending. It is not simply about whether a woman has agency or not. By looking at the system of criminal law and justice we can see that the system does not allow her agency. To truly have agency, to truly have choice, to truly be 'free' to make a decision as to how to respond to a pregnancy, and to then be judged fairly and equally as a 'reasonable (wo)man' requires an overhaul of the system. None of this is possible while women live within the grip and under the weight of patriarchy.

The Role of Criminal Law and Criminal Justice

So, what is the way forward? Where could we go from here? An overthrowing of patriarchy and masculine law is unrealistic, at least in the short term. Changes to the oppressive system of heteronormative, racist, capitalist, patriarchy will occur through incremental changes; if you believe change is possible at all. So, we need some fixes in the meantime to attempt to address the gendered injustice of criminal law and criminal justice towards women suspected of foetal or newborn child killing. We also need to consider what role criminal law and justice are playing here and what is the aim of the law in focussing on these 'offenders' and the criminalisation of their conduct.

I have argued elsewhere that the offence of concealment of birth is outdated and should be consigned to the history books (Milne, 2019). The legislation was designed to capture women for 'crimes' that could not be proven (such as homicide of a newborn child) or for behaviour that is not actually criminal but is popularly deemed deviant and 'wrong' (failure as both a 'mother' and pregnant woman). Any actual wrongdoing that is identifiable in the actions of the women convicted of concealment can be captured by other provisions in criminal law – inappropriate disposal of a body,[8] failure to register a birth or stillbirth,[9] or hiding a corpse to prevent discovery of further criminal behaviour, such as obstructing or preventing a coroner's inquest or perverting the course of justice.[10] Thus, on the principles of just outcomes for women, it is time to remove this discriminatory piece of statute. Similarly, there is now strong support for the decriminalisation of abortion, premised on the basis that the legislation is outdated, hinders medical professionals in providing the best care for women, and that women should be trusted to make their own decisions about their bodies (Sheldon, 2016; *We Trust Women*, n.d.). As Rebecca J. Cook (2014, p. 347) argues, 'Through criminal prohibition, a state is signaling conditions in which abortion is criminally wrong, reflecting the historical origin of crime in sin that can and should be punished'. The continued existence of both these offences serves to demarcate women as distinct from men: that women cannot be trusted to exert control over their bodies and their lives without the intervention of the law.

As a society, we may deem that we want to protect the foetus in law more so than is currently provided by the Infant Life (Preservation) Act 1929. We may also decide that there is limited justification for the continuance of the principle of the born alive rule. However, as outlined in Chapter 6, and I and others have argued elsewhere (Bordo, 2003; Flavin, 2009; Gallagher, 1987; Johnsen, 1989; Milne, 2020; Murphy, 2014; Paltrow & Flavin, 2013), protecting the foetus in law

---

[8]See Jones and Quigley (2016) who outline the wrongfulness of inappropriate disposal of a body and the criminal offences that capture this wrongful behaviour.
[9]Births and Deaths Registration Act 1953, ss1-2 and 36, punishable by a fine of up to £200.
[10]*Purcy* [1934] 24 Cr App R 70; *Williams* [1991] 92 Cr App R 158. See Jones and Quigley (2016) for detailed analysis of how both offences could be applied to individuals who conceal a dead body.

can have truly horrendous consequences for women and their rights – in both principle and practice. We need to think long and hard about providing the foetus with legal protection: we need to truly consider *why* we want to imbue the foetus with legal rights. In engaging in these discussions, we particularly need to keep at the forefront of our minds that women do not enjoy equality with men, and across women most hold other intersecting identities that increase their potential to experience discrimination and the hardships of life. Thus, any move to legally prohibit the behaviour of women while they are pregnant will almost certainly increase, not decrease, inequalities faced.

Of the conduct of women suspected of killing newborn children or late-term foetuses, one factor that cannot be overlooked is the victim of their actions – a human who has died or almost died in the cases of abandonment. I have discussed the concept and flow of risk throughout this book. In popular thought, the risk to the foetus is often seen as greater than the risk to the woman – the foetus is at risk of death, while the risks the woman faces are of lesser consequence than death.[11] This is a significant point and reinforces the notion that it is 'right' to control and regulate women to 'save' foetuses. However, as I have outlined in Chapter 4, I see a flaw in the binary of this argument (foetus vs woman),[12] as women's experiences of pregnancy in these cases (as well as more generally) reflect how society conceptualises pregnancy and motherhood. Thus, it is not about individual women and individual foetuses but social structures. Furthermore, as I have emphasised throughout this book, the threats and risks to women need to be conceptualised more broadly than as they are when pitted against a foetus' risk of death. In some of the cases discussed here, it is not too extreme to state that the woman might have been at risk of death due to her pregnancy status: many women are.[13] But more than this, the notion that death is the worst possible outcome misses the point. Conceptualising annihilation as the greatest threat humans face feeds a patriarchal and masculine view of the world (West, 1988), so failing to appreciate the harms that women experience as a consequence of pregnancy.

As has been explored in this book, the complexity of how foetuses, as humans, are conceptualised in English and Welsh law plays a significant role in the cases examined: *in utero* and so with limited protection under law, or as a legal subject who has been born alive. Certainly, there is a key point here that, once born alive, a baby is a person and so the Crown Prosecution Service needs to approach the case as in any other unlawful killing.[14] Recognition of children as victims is

---

[11]With thanks to Dr Karen Brennan for raising this point in our discussions of risk, criminal law, and pregnancy.
[12]Many others are also heavily critical of the notion of the maternal–foetal conflict; see, for example, Chavkin (1992); Lyerly et al. (2009); Oberman (2000); and Romanis et al. (2020a).
[13]Pregnancy is noted to be a time when women are increasingly likely to experience violence and abuse from a partner or former partner (Tuerkheimer, 2006).
[14]With thanks to Phil Bates for highlighting this point during our discussions of this work.

an important element of the criminal justice process in these cases and one that cannot be overlooked or negated. Historically, children have been seen to be less important than adults, to be the property of their parents or guardians and so needing less protection under law and by the state. As such ideas changed, and the concept of state intervention to protect children developed, laws surrounding child labour, care for children, and violence and 'punishment' of children have developed. Similarly, the development of the principle of children having rights, in and of themselves, is significant. These rights are not negated by the age of the child nor by the simple fact that they are under the age of majority. Children's rights are not subject to the perspectives of their parents, so children do not have the right to life because their parent deems it so; it is a right held by them as an independent human and is not conditional on others.[15]

As explored in Chapter 4, children are also a powerful symbol in our society, representing innocence, the newness of life, the future, purity. Consequently, they are held in a special place in popular thought, at least in theory: in the United Kingdom there were 4.2 million children living in poverty in 2018/2019,[16] which begs the question as to whether concern for children moves beyond symbolism, specifically for the state and government. Nevertheless, one of the consequences of the wider social idea of the child, and by connection, the foetus, and views that they are 'precious', is that their victimisation can be said to have eclipsed that of other people who are killed. The 'newness' of the newborn child or foetus seems to exacerbate this idea, giving these victims a prioritisation and a focus as 'special'; thus, a status reserved for few others.[17] The concept of the 'innocent' and 'vulnerable' child/foetus hangs heavy over cases of suspected perinatal homicide, as well as over cases whereby the behaviour of pregnant women is perceived to have the potential to harm the foetus (Milne, 2020). The 'special' place reserved for newborn/foetal victims is illustrated in a number of the court case hearings:

> But, your Honour, on behalf of the investigating team, and it took a lot of effort, both emotional effort in this case, they are certainly pleased that [baby] has now, and that is how they have referred to this baby boy throughout, has now been laid to rest. (Imogen, prosecution opening)

---

[15]See Unicef UK (n.d.) for *The United Nations Convention on the Rights of the Child* and Flekkoy (1997) for an overview of the rights of the child.

[16]Statistics from Child Poverty Action Group (2020), who draw on data from the Households Below Average Income (HBAI) Statistics: statistics on the number and percentage of people living in low-income households for financial years 1994/1995 to 2018/2019, Tables 4a and 4b. Department for Work and Pensions, 2020.

[17]The newness of a newborn child also reflects social anxieties around early death and the popular myth that we all have the ability and right to live to old age (with thanks to Dr Elizabeth Chloe Romanic for this point). As with other arguments presented in this chapter, the 'right' to live to old age is not afforded equally and is denied to many people due to deprivation they experience. Many of the hardships of life are a consequence of structural disadvantages that result due to race, class, and other intersecting identities.

Similarly, in Olivia and Michael's case, public concern for the 'victim'[18] was highlighted by the judge, in response to Olivia's barrister saying the case had been hard for her family due to media attention:

> Well, it is a legitimate public concern because the child had a life, albeit very briefly, and it's a matter of great public concern. They are going to have to accept that. (Olivia and Michael, judge response during defence mitigation for Olivia)

Further public concern was highlighted later, in sentencing:

> You, Olivia, I accept, did not know until very late on and for the same reason, had little time to prepare for such a fundamental event. However, what then happened can only really be described as offensive to right-thinking people and to have shown a disregard for the sanctity of a dead baby. For that baby to be put in a bag and thrown over a bridge is just an appalling thought for anyone to contemplate. (Olivia and Michael, judge sentencing)

The 'horror' of the victimhood of the newborn child/foetus seems to be experienced and understood as being even greater when the 'perpetrator' is the 'mother'. This perception is clearly expressed in the transcripts, as outlined in Chapter 3. The belief that underpins the discussions and presentation of evidence in these cases is that motherhood is natural and innate to women, and that women who are suspected of newborn child or foetal homicide are either unnatural or have somehow defied nature by their actions or inactions that have caused harm to their 'child', before, during, or after birth. Consequently, the women defendants are perceived to have failed to protect their 'child', including from themselves. The women are not seen as exerting a right to self-protection from invasion by and under threat of the foetus.

As I have outlined in this book, one of the realities of cases of suspicious perinatal death is that the accused woman appeared to hold a belief that the pregnancy could not exist: the existence of the pregnancy and foetus/newborn child was perceived as posing a risk to her life, her well-being, and, potentially, her safety (discussed in Chapter 2). This is an argument that has been embraced by feminist activists in relation to access to, and legality of, abortion: the principle that women should not be subjugated by another human due to the protection of that 'person's' right to exist over her rights to freedom and bodily autonomy (Johnsen, 1989; MacKinnon, 1989; Petchesky, 1990; Purdy, 1990). This is also the argument presented by Robin West (1988), outlined above – abortion is about self-defence, protection from invasion. However, this is not how abortion is seen

---

[18] As Olivia and Michael were convicted of concealment of birth – a miscellaneous crime against society – then there was, arguably, no individual 'victim' of their criminal acts. However, this is clearly not the view of the court, as expressed in the quote.

by wider society, specifically in the context of the laws regulating abortion in Great Britain, outlined in Chapter 6. As argued by Rosalind Pollack Petchesky (1990),[19] feminists' arguments that abortion is one aspect of wider concern for women's reproductive freedom were lost from the rhetoric and public understanding of abortion. Instead, abortion continues to be viewed as a necessary evil by most people.

The self-defence argument appears to have even less support when the 'innocent victim' is a late-term foetus *in utero* or in the process of delivery or a born alive child. Thus, a pregnancy that does not end with a legal abortion exemplifies one of the very few instances whereby a human is expected to put the well-being and needs of another person above their own,[20] regardless of the woman's perceived unacceptability of the existence of that other human and the impact on her bodily autonomy and rights. Once the child is born, a number of the ethical issues are resolved due to the two humans no longer being physically connected. However, the ideologies of motherhood that are held by society mean that the born child can continue to pose significant risks to a woman: society's belief that a woman has an imperative to mother a child she births is incredibly difficult to overcome. If a woman perceives that mothering that child poses a significant risk to her well-being and self, then the issue of self-defence remains. However, the notion of accused women acting in self-defence is not even recognised as a possibility or potential interpretation of events by criminal law, criminal justice professionals, or wider society. As I outlined in Chapter 4, the concept of perceived risk to the woman caused by a crisis pregnancy is null and void. So, we are left with a situation whereby a woman is required to put the needs of another before her desire and need to protect herself. If she does not put the foetus first, then, as outlined in this book, the law and criminal justice use the menu of offences to criminalise her actions and impose criminal sanctions upon her. Therefore, we can conclude that greater legal protection is given to the life of a human that is not yet born (or is newly born) than to a woman's ability to protect herself from harm that she perceives will be inflicted by society and/or individuals around her.

The foetus or newborn child is a human who has not existed in the world outside of another person: he/she has no history, does not speak or understand any of the languages of our species, does not materially contribute to society, is often not known or cared about by any other person (beyond abstract thought), and, arguably, cannot be considered to be the equivalent in terms of the intellectual,

---

[19]Discussing the situation in America but also relevant to the UK context.

[20]Minkoff and Paltrow (2004) make this argument in relation to women forced to undergo a caesarean section following a court order: if a born child needed a bone marrow transplant to survive, and the only available donor was the child's father, it would never be considered an acceptable intervention by the state to legally compel that man to donate. But states seem prepared to violate the rights of pregnant women to not have their bodies subjugated by another. As they conclude, 'the State has now endowed the fetus with greater rights than its living siblings and, for that matter, any born person of any age' (Minkoff & Paltrow, 2004, p. 1235).

moral, or social and cultural value of the woman whose body they are within or have just been expelled from. Stating these points does not deny the humanness of the foetus or newborn child. I hold the belief that foetuses are human, but that such a perception of their ontology does not mean they should necessarily be considered as holding the same position of importance and value in society as the pregnant woman: foetuses are humans but not equivalent humans to pregnant women (for a detailed discussion of this position, see Furedi, 2016).[21]

In problematising the significance of a newborn child to the wider world I am not attempting to argue that we, as a society, should not recognise them as humans and as potential victims. Nor am I arguing criminal law should not recognise crimes against them.[22] That being said, it is important to recognise that society appears to provide far greater levels of 'justice' to foetuses/newborn children than to countless other people who die at the hands (directly or indirectly) of another. For example, the rates at which 'perpetrators' of crimes against the foetus/newborn child are criminalised and held to account for their actions/ inactions appears to be far greater than for those who kill other members of society, such as people of colour who are killed while in police custody; people who live in council housing who die in a fire due to poor maintenance of the property; people who have no home who are forced to sleep on our streets and die of exposure and poor health from their living conditions; people who die prematurely due to their impoverished living conditions and poor diet, whose lives have been made harder

---

[21]See Bordo's (2003) analysis of the position of the foetus in society, describing the foetus as a super-subject.

[22]This is particularly the case when a third party acts in a way that causes harm or death to a foetus that is wanted by the pregnant woman, through violence towards or non-consensual administration of an abortifacient. Ramsey (2006) makes this argument in relation to foetal protection laws in the United States, noting that most Americans poll in favour of criminalising people who attack pregnant women and consequently kill the foetus (regardless of intention to harm the foetus). She advocates that, by protesting against the enactment of 'justice' in these cases and the use of foetal homicide laws, feminists risk looking like they advocate for a culture of death – in other words, feminists can be seen to not care at all when foetuses are killed, even when the pregnant woman wanted her 'baby' and is devastated by the loss of her 'child'. However, the fallout of granting foetuses personhood is substantial, as I outlined in Chapter 6, so decisions as to how to recognise the loss of a wanted foetus though unlawful acts by third parties need to be considered very carefully. Hannah Mason-Bish and I have previously explored the possibility of using the model of hate crime policy/legislation to allow for recognition of the harm of foetal loss following violence and aggression towards a pregnant woman (Milne & Mason-Bish, 2019). Such an approach would not directly recognise the foetus as a victim but would allow for an increased sentence to be handed down to a person convicted of a crime after inflicting harm on the pregnant woman that results in the death of, or harm to, the foetus. In seeing the existence of a pregnancy as an aggravating feature for sentencing, then the increased suffering experienced by the victim of the crime (the woman), due to the loss of her foetus, would be recognised and reflected in the sentence.

due to welfare cuts and austerity.[23] These examples of deaths are often described as falling under the banner of 'state crime', committed by state actors, or occurring as a consequence of state policy/approaches to its citizens, and are notoriously difficult to bring to 'justice' (Green & Ward, 2004). While the examples are not directly comparable to suspicious perinatal deaths, it is remarkable to think how quickly the state works to bring a vulnerable woman, who experienced a crisis pregnancy that results in the death of the foetus/newborn child, to 'justice'. Meanwhile, it is over four years since 72 people died in a fire in Grenfell Tower, and, at the time of writing in Autumn 2020, there is yet to be any sign of anyone being brought to 'justice' for the deaths of these people (Booth, 2020).

If we couple this notion of 'selective justice' with the previously discussed point of 'crimes' against children that are, at best, not prevented by the state, and at worst, committed or facilitated by the state,[24] then we are left with this question: Is the criminal law and justice response to women suspected of causing the death of a foetus or newborn child really about protecting 'children', or is it actually about controlling women? As Bridget Hutter and Gillian Williams (1981, p. 9) outline, controls exercised over women who are perceived to be deviant allow society to clarify the concept of 'normal behaviour'. Inevitably, these controls are divisive, emphasising the difference between groups of women. Women's ability to become pregnant is threatening to dominant ideas of masculinity (Bayne, 2011; Romanis et al., 2020a), and, as I outlined in Chapter 5, historically, women's reproductive capacity poses a threat to social order due to the potential to introduce another man's child into *his* family. This notion has a strong legacy that continues to operate today. Take, for example, the continued use of the term 'cuckolding': a man and his adulterous wife. While there is an equivalent term for a woman and her adulterous husband – cuckqueaning – it does not have anywhere near the same level of gravity. Dangers are also posed by a woman's ability to control her fertility, challenging the structures and order of society, the exclusion of women from the public sphere, and facilitation of women's sexuality for procreation alone (Gordon, 1986; Petchesky, 1990). When pregnant, women are further conceptualised as being perilous for society due to the risks they are deemed to pose to the foetus. As Elizabeth Chloe Romanis et al. (2020a) argue, the cultural legacy that the pregnant woman carries the man's child (she is the soil in which the man plants his seed) hangs heavy over obstetric care, feeding the notion of the maternal–foetal conflict. A further dimension of pregnancy

---

[23]For an excellent analysis of deaths in which the state is implicated, watch the lecture by Professor Leslie Thomas QC, appointed Gresham Professor of Law in 2020, *Does the State Really Care When It Kills You?* Available here: https://www.gresham. ac.uk/lectures-and-events/state-killing.

[24]For example, children living in poverty, refusal by the state to pay the child element of child tax credit for more than two children, physical and sexual abuse committed against children who reside in state-run care homes, the overwhelming number of people in prison who were looked after by the state as a child, the imprisonment of child refugees in adult detention centres (Bulman, 2020).

lies in the notion that, when women 'breed', they are replenishing the nation, so their capacity as breeders is not only a threat to individual men but to society as a whole (Foucault, 1998 [1976]; Fyfe, 1991; Weeks, 1981). If women breed with the wrong people or do something that will 'harm the baby' (i.e. enjoy a rare steak and a glass of rioja), then it is the health and strength of the nation they put at risk, as well as the health and strength of their 'husband's legacy'. Equally, Alexandra Fanghanel's (2019) research, into women's experiences of sexual harassment and non-consensual touching while pregnant, indicates the extent to which pregnancy is deemed to be a time when women's bodies are conceptualised as communal bodies – open and available to be touched.

The 'risk' posed by women's impregnable bodies explains why society goes to such great lengths to control and regulate who becomes pregnant, when they become pregnant, how and when they can stop being pregnant, and how they behave while they are pregnant, as presented throughout this book. Women such as those who have been the focus of this study are but one example – an extreme example – of the risks of women and their reproductive bodies. Women who are suspected of killing foetuses/newborn children are women who have become pregnant when they should not be; have concealed/denied their pregnancy, so not providing space for society to control and regulate their behaviour and to ensure the well-being of the foetus; and who reject motherhood of that child in favour of their own needs and well-being. These women are deemed to be inherently dangerous. They challenge the notion that motherhood and 'responsible' pregnancy are inherent and natural – if it was inherent and natural, then they would not act as they have. So, as with so many other examples of the regulation of women's bodies and behaviour (particularly apparent in relation to foetal protection laws), it is far easier for the state to point to the small number of women who come before the courts suspected of causing the death of a foetus/newborn child and punish her as an individual, as an unnatural and evil villain, or a pitiful woman deserving of our sympathy,[25] than to acknowledge the wider social consequences that lead to her actions. To acknowledge the legitimacy of these women in 'disposing' of an unauthorised pregnancy is to confess that society is politically, culturally, and economically skewed to limit the rights and freedoms of all women. Perhaps this is the women's greatest crime – risking exposure of the 'realities' of sex, pregnancy, and motherhood for women.

---

[25]This is particularly true in terms of the application of the offence of infanticide. See Brennan and Milne (forthcoming), Loughnan (2012), Morris and Wilczynski (1993), and Ward (1999).

References

Aiken, A. R. A., Guthrie, K. A., Schellekens, M., Trussell, J., & Gomperts, R. (2018). Barriers to accessing abortion services and perspectives on using mifepristone and misoprostol at home in Great Britain. *Contraception, 97*(2), 177–183. doi:10.1016/j.contraception.2017.09.003

Alder, C. M., & Baker, J. (1997). Maternal filicide: More than one story to be told. *Women & Criminal Justice, 9*(2), 15–39. doi:10.1300/J012v09n02_02

Allen, H. (1987). *Justice unbalanced: Gender, psychiatry, and judicial decisions.* Milton Keynes: Open University Press.

American College of Obstetricians and Gynecologists. (2014). Substance abuse reporting and pregnancy: The role of the obstetrician–gynecologist. January 2011 (Reaffirmed 2014). Retrieved from https://www.acog.org/-/media/Committee-Opinions/Committee-on-Health-Care-for-Underserved-Women/co473.pdf?dmc=1&ts=20170224T0820264139

Amery, F. (2020). *Beyond pro-life and pro-choice: The changing politics of abortion in Britain.* Bristol: Bristol University Press.

Amon, S., Putkonen, H., Weizmann-Henelius, G., Almiron, M. P., Formann, A. K., Voracek, M., Eronen, M., Yourstone, J., Friedrich, M., & Klier, C. (2012). Potential predictors in neonaticide: The impact of the circumstances of pregnancy. *Archives of Women's Mental Health, 15*(3), 167–174. doi:10.1007/s00737-012-0268-0

Annison, J., Brayford, J., & Deering, J. (Eds.). (2015). *Women and criminal justice: From the Corston report to transforming rehabilitation.* Bristol: Policy Press.

Arendell, T. (2000). Conceiving and investigating motherhood: The decade's scholarship. *Journal of Marriage and Family, 62*(4), 1192–1207. doi:10.1111/j.1741-3737.2000.01192.x

Ariès, P. (1965). *Centuries of childhood.* New York, NY: Random House.

Ayres, S. (2007). Who is to shame: Narratives of neonaticide. *William & Mary Journal of Women and the Law, 14*(1), 55–106.

Ayres, S. (2014). When women kill newborns: The rhetoric of vulnerability. In K. Cole (Ed.), *Feminist challenges or feminist rhetorics? Locations, scholarship, discourse* (pp. 83–97). Newcastle upon Tyne: Cambridge Scholars Publishing.

Bacchi, C. (2005). Discourse, discourse everywhere: Subject "agency" in feminist discourse methodology. *NORA – Nordic Journal of Feminist and Gender Research, 13*(3), 198–209. doi:10.1080/08038740600600407

Ballinger, A. (2007). Masculinity in the dock: Legal responses to male violence and female retaliation in England and Wales, 1900–1965. *Social & Legal Studies, 16*(4), 459–481. doi:10.1177/0964663907082731

Barlow, C. (2016). *Coercion and women co-offenders: A gendered pathway into crime.* Bristol: Policy Press.

Barthes, R. (1972). *Mythologies.* London: J. Cape.

Bascom, L. (1977). Women who refuse to believe: Persistent denial of pregnancy. *MCN, American Journal of Maternal Child Nursing, 2*(3), 174–177. doi:10.1097/00005721-197705000-00012

Basilio, M. (1996). Corporal evidence: Representations of Aileen Wuornos. *Art Journal, 55*(4), 56–61. doi:10.2307/777655

Bassett, L. (2014). Judge tosses murder case against Mississippi mom with stillborn baby. *The Huffington Post*, April 3. Retrieved from http://www.huffingtonpost.com/2014/04/03/judge-tosses-mississippi-_n_5086215.html

Bassin, D., Honey, M., & Kaplan, M. M. (Eds.). (1994). *Representations of motherhood*. New Haven, CT: Yale University Press.

Bayne, E. (2011). Womb envy: The cause of misogyny and even male achievement? *Women's Studies International Forum*, *34*(2), 151–160. doi:10.1016/j.wsif.2011.01.007

BBC News. (2004, March 12). Mother charged in caesarean row. Retrieved from http://news.bbc.co.uk/1/hi/world/americas/3504720.stm

BBC News. (2010, October 17). Charity offers UK drug addicts £200 to be sterilised. Retrieved from https://www.bbc.co.uk/news/uk-england-london-11545519

BBC News. (2016, March 9). Teen pregnancy rate continues to fall, ONS figures show. Retrieved from http://www.bbc.co.uk/news/health-35761826

Beattie, J. M. (1986). *Crime and the courts in England, 1660–1800*. Princeton, NJ: Princeton University Press.

Beauvoir, S. (1997 [1949]). *The second sex* (H. M. Parshley, Trans.). London: Vintage.

Beck, U. (1992). *Risk society: towards a new modernity*. London: Sage.

Beckingham, D. (2013). Scale and the moral geographies of Victorian and Edwardian child protection. *Journal of Historical Geography*, *42*, 140–151. doi:10.1016/j.jhg.2013.02.003

Behlmer, G. K. (1982). *Child abuse and moral reform in England, 1870–1908*. Stanford, CA: Stanford University Press.

Beier, K. M., Wille, R., & Wessel, J. (2006). Denial of pregnancy as a reproductive dysfunction: A proposal for international classification systems. *Journal of Psychosomatic Research*, *61*(5), 723–730. doi:10.1016/j.jpsychores.2005.11.002

Bessett, D. (2010). Negotiating normalization: The perils of producing pregnancy symptoms in prenatal care. *Social Science & Medicine*, *71*(2), 370–377. doi:10.1016/j.socscimed.2010.04.007

Beyer, K., McAuliffe Mack, S., & Shelton, J. L. (2008). Investigative analysis of neonaticide: An exploratory study. *Criminal Justice and Behavior*, *35*(4), 522–535. doi:10.1177/0093854807313410

Bhattacharjee, A. (2002). Private fists and public force: Race, gender, and sexuality. In J. M. Silliman & A. Bhattacharjee (Eds.), *Policing the national body: Sex, race, and criminalization* (pp. 1–54). Cambridge, MA: South End Press.

Birkett, G. (2016). "We have no awareness of what they actually do": Magistrates' knowledge of and confidence in community sentences for women offenders in England and Wales. *Criminology & Criminal Justice*, *16*(4), 497–512. doi:10.1177/1748895816632852

Blackstone, W. (1791). *Commentaries on the laws of England* (Vol. 4, 11th ed.). London: T. Cadell.

Blank, H. (2007). *Virgin: The untouched history*. New York, NY: Bloomsbury.

Bloom, L. R. (1998). *Under the sign of hope: Feminist methodology and narrative interpretation*. New York, NY: State University of New York Press.

Bois, P. (2018). This woman pays drug addicts to get sterilized. *The Daily Wire*, January 3. Retrieved from https://www.dailywire.com/news/25334/woman-pays-drug-addicts-get-sterilized-paul-bois

Bommaraju, A., Kavanaugh, M. L., Hou, M. Y., & Bessett, D. (2016). Situating stigma in stratified reproduction: Abortion stigma and miscarriage stigma as barriers to reproductive healthcare. *Sexual & Reproductive Healthcare*, *10*, 62–69. doi:10.1016/j.srhc.2016.10.008

Booth, R. (2020). Grenfell witnesses will not have their evidence used against them. *The Guardian*, February 26. Retrieved from https://www.theguardian.com/uk-news/2020/feb/26/grenfell-witnesses-will-not-have-their-evidence-used-against-them

Bordo, S. (2003). *Unbearable weight: Feminism, western culture, and the body*. Berkeley, CA: University of California Press.

Bortoli, L. D., Coles, J., & Dolan, M. (2013). A review of maternal neonaticide: A need for further research supporting evidence-based prevention in Australia. *Child Abuse Review*, *22*(5), 327–339. doi:10.1002/car.2250

Boston Women's Health Book Collective. (2008). *Our bodies, ourselves: Pregnancy and birth*. New York, NY: Touchstone Book/Simon & Schuster.

Boston Women's Health Book Collective. (2011). *Our bodies, ourselves (40th anniversary)*. New York, NY: Simon & Schuster.

Boudreaux, J. M., & Thompson, J. W. (2015). Maternal-fetal rights and substance abuse: Gestation without representation. *Journal of the American Academy of Psychiatry and the Law Online, 43*(2), 137–140.

Bourget, D., Grace, J., & Whitehurst, L. (2007). A review of maternal and paternal filicide. *Journal of the American Academy of Psychiatry and the Law Online, 35*(1), 74–82.

Braun, V., & Clarke, V. (2006). Using thematic analysis in psychology. *Qualitative Research in Psychology, 3*(2), 77–101. doi:10.1191/1478088706qp063oa

Brazier, M. (1999). Liberty, responsibility, maternity. *Current Legal Problems, 52*(1), 359–391. doi:10.1093/clp/52.1.359

Brennan, K. (2013). "A fine mixture of pity and justice": The criminal justice response to infanticide in Ireland, 1922–1949. *Law and History Review, 31*(4), 793–841. doi:10.1017/s0738248013000436

Brennan, K. (2018a). Murderous mothers and gentle judges: Paternalism, patriarchy, and infanticide. *Yale Journal of Law and Feminism, 30*(1), 139–195.

Brennan, K. (2018b). Social norms and the law in responding to infanticide. *Legal Studies, 38*(3), 480–499. doi:10.1017/lst.2017.20

Brennan, K., & Milne, E. (forthcoming). Mercy for mothers: A socio-historical understanding of the Infanticide Act 1938. *Criminal Law Review*.

Brezinka, C., Brezinka, C., Biebl, W., & Kinzl, J. (1994). Denial of pregnancy: Obstetrical aspects. *Journal of Psychosomatic Obstetrics & Gynecology, 15*(1), 1–8. doi:10.3109/01674829409025623

British Pregnancy Advisory Service. (2016, November 29). Emergency contraception needs urgent review. Retrieved from https://www.bpas.org/about-our-charity/press-office/press-releases/emergency-contraception-needs-urgent-review/

British Pregnancy Advisory Service. (n.d.). Just say non! Retrieved from https://www.justsaynon.org.uk

Brooks-Gardner. (2003). Pregnant women as social problem. In D. R. Loseke & J. Best (Eds.), *Social problems: Constructionist readings* (pp. 188–195). New York, NY: Aldine de Gruyter.

Brown, L. M. (2005). Feminist theory and the erosion of women's reproductive rights: The implications of fetal personhood laws and in vitro fertilization. *American University Journal of Gender, Social Policy & the Law, 13*(1), 87–108.

Brozovsky, M., & Falit, H. (1971). Neonaticide: Clinical and psychodynamic considerations. *Journal of the American Academy of Child Psychiatry, 10*(4), 673–683. doi:10.1016/s0002-7138(09)61765-9

Brubaker, S. J., & Dillaway, H. E. (2009). Medicalization, natural childbirth and birthing experiences. *Sociology Compass, 3*(1), 31–48. doi:10.1111/j.1751-9020.2008.00183.x

Bulman, M. (2020). Child refugees "betrayed" by UK as home office sends them to adult detention centres. *The Independent*, October 23. Retrieved from https://www.independent.co.uk/news/uk/home-news/child-refugees-minors-home-office-adult-detention-report-b1229079.html

Burns, E. R., Farr, S. L., & Howards, P. P. (2015, March 13). Stressful life events experienced by women in the year before their infants' births – United States, 2000–2010. Centers for Disease Control and Prevention, Morbidity and Mortality Weekly Report (MMWR).. Retrieved from https://www.cdc.gov/mmwr/preview/mmwrhtml/mm6409a3.htm

Camperio Ciani, A. S., & Fontanesi, L. (2012). Mothers who kill their offspring: Testing evolutionary hypothesis in a 110-case Italian sample. *Child Abuse & Neglect, 36*(6), 519–527. doi:10.1016/j.chiabu.2012.05.001

Caplan, P. J. (1998). Mother-blaming. In M. Ladd-Taylor & L. Umansky (Eds.), *"Bad" mothers: The politics of blame in twentieth-century America* (pp. 127–144). New York, NY: New York University Press.

Caplan, P. J. (2013). Don't blame mothers: Then and now. In M. Hobbs & C. Rice (Eds.), *Gender and women's studies in Canada: Critical terrain* (pp. 99–103). Toronto: Women's Press.

Caplan, P. J., & Hall-McCorquodale, I. (1985). Mother-blaming in major clinical journals. *American Journal of Orthopsychiatry, 55*(3), 345–353. doi:10.1111/j.1939-0025.1985.tb03449.x

Carlen, P. (1983). *Women's imprisonment: A study in social control.* London: Routledge.

Carlen, P., & Worrall, A. (Eds.). (1987). *Gender, crime and justice.* Milton Keynes: Open University Press.

Carrington, D. (2019). Air pollution "as bad as smoking in increasing risk of miscarriage". *The Guardian,* January 11. Retrieved from https://www.theguardian.com/environment/2019/jan/11/air-pollution-as-bad-as-smoking-in-increasing-risk-of-miscarriage

Casey, G. (2005). *Born alive: The legal status of the unborn child in England and the U.S.A.* Chichester: Barry Rose Law Publishers.

Cave, E. (2004). *The mother of all crimes: Human rights, criminalization, and the child born alive.* Aldershot: Ashgate.

Cave, E., & Stanton, C. (2016). Maternal responsibility to the child not yet born. In C. Stanton, S. Devaney, A.-M. Farrell, & A. Mullock (Eds.), *Pioneering healthcare law: Essays in honour of Margaret Brazier* (pp. 280–291). London: Routledge.

Center for Reproductive Rights. (2000, September). Punishing women for their behavior during pregnancy: An approach that undermines women's health and children's interest. Retrieved from https://www.reproductiverights.org/document/punishing-women-for-their-behavior-during-pregnancy-an-approach-that-undermines-womens-heal

Centers for Disease Control and Prevention. (2016, February 2). More than 3 million US women at risk for alcohol-exposed pregnancy. Retrieved from http://www.cdc.gov/media/releases/2016/p0202-alcohol-exposed-pregnancy.html

Centers for Disease Control and Prevention. (2020a, April 30). Alcohol use in pregnancy. Retrieved from https://www.cdc.gov/ncbddd/fasd/alcohol-use.html

Centers for Disease Control and Prevention. (2020b, April 16). Planning for pregnancy. Retrieved from https://www.cdc.gov/preconception/planning.html

Centers for Disease Control and Prevention. (2020c, June 12). Pregnancy and HIV, viral hepatitis, STD, & TB prevention. Retrieved from https://www.cdc.gov/nchhstp/pregnancy/Default.htm

Centers for Disease Control and Prevention. (2020d, August 13). Pregnancy complications. Retrieved from https://www.cdc.gov/reproductivehealth/maternalinfanthealth/pregnancy-complications.html

Centers for Disease Control and Prevention. (2020e, April 23). Pregnant women and Zika. Retrieved from https://www.cdc.gov/pregnancy/zika/protect-yourself.html

Centers for Disease Control and Prevention. (2020f, April 28). Smoking during pregnancy.. Retrieved from https://www.cdc.gov/tobacco/basic_information/health_effects/pregnancy/index.htm

Centers for Disease Control and Prevention. (2020g, July 15). Substance use during pregnancy. Retrieved from https://www.cdc.gov/reproductivehealth/maternalinfanthealth/substance-abuse/substance-abuse-during-pregnancy.htm

Chadwick, R. J., & Foster, D. (2014). Negotiating risky bodies: Childbirth and constructions of risk. *Health, Risk & Society, 16*(1), 68–83. doi:10.1080/13698575.2013.863852

Chan, W., & Rigakos, G. S. (2002). Risk, crime and gender. *British Journal of Criminology, 42*(4), 743–761. doi:10.1093/bjc/42.4.743

Chavkin, W. (1992). Women and the foetus: The social construction of conflict. In C. Feinman (Ed.), *The criminalization of a woman's body* (pp. 193–202). New York, NY: Harrington Park Press.

Cherry, A. L. (2007). The detention, confinement, and incarceration of pregnant women for the benefit of fetal health. *Columbia Journal of Gender and Law, 16*(1), 149–199.

Child Poverty Action Group. (2020, July). Child poverty facts and figures. Retrieved from https://cpag.org.uk/child-poverty/child-poverty-facts-and-figures

Children's Hospital of Philadelphia. (n.d.). Seat belt safety: Pregnancy. Retrieved from https://www.chop.edu/pages/seat-belt-safety-pregnancy

Chodorow, N. (1978). *The reproduction of mothering: Psychoanalysis and the sociology of gender.* Berkeley, CA: University of California Press.

Cohen, S. (1985). *Visions of social control: Crime, punishment and classification.* Cambridge: Polity.

Coke, E. (1644 [1681]). *The fourth part of the institutes of the laws of England: Concerning the jurisdiction of courts* (6th ed.). London: W. Rawlins.

Collins, P. H. (1994). Shifting the center: Race, class, and feminist theorizing about motherhood. In E. N. Glenn, G. Chang, & L. R. Forcey (Eds.), *Mothering: Ideology, experience, and agency* (pp. 45–66). New York, NY: Routledge.

Collins, P. H. (2000). *Black feminist thought: Knowledge, consciousness, and the politics of empowerment.* New York, NY: Routledge.

Conaghan, J. (1996). Gendered harms and the law of tort: Remedying (sexual) harassment. *Oxford Journal of Legal Studies, 16*(3), 407–431. doi:10.1093/ojls/16.3.407

Conlon, C. (2006, April). Concealed pregnancy: A case-study approach from an Irish setting (crisis pregnancy agency no. 15). Retrieved from http://hdl.handle.net/10147/305217

Cook, R. J. (2014). Stigmatized meanings of criminal abortion law. In R. J. Cook, J. N. Erdman, & B. M. Dickens (Eds.), *Abortion law in transnational perspective: Cases and controversies* (pp. 347–369). Philadelphia, PA: University of Pennsylvania Press.

Corston, J. (2007, March 13). The Corston report: A review of women with particular vulnerabilities in the criminal justice system. Retrieved from http://webarchive.nationalarchives.gov.uk/+/http://www.homeoffice.gov.uk/documents/corston-report/

Cox, P. (2012). Marginalized mothers, reproductive autonomy, and "repeat losses to care". *Journal of Law and Society, 39*(4), 541–561. doi:10.1111/j.1467-6478.2012.00599.x

Craig, M. (2004). Perinatal risk factors for neonaticide and infant homicide: Can we identify those at risk?. *Journal of the Royal Society of Medicine, 97*(2), 57–61. doi:10.1258/jrsm.97.2.57

Crenshaw, K. (1989). Demarginalizing the intersection of race and sex: A black feminist critique of antidiscrimination doctrine, feminist theory and antiracist politics. *University of Chicago Legal Forum, 1989*(1), 139–168.

Crown Prosecution Service. (2019, November 6). Sentencing dangerous offenders. Retrieved from https://www.cps.gov.uk/legal-guidance/sentencing-dangerous-offenders

Curry, T. J. (2011). Shut your mouth when you're talking to me: Silencing the idealist school of critical race theory through a culturalogical turn in jurisprudence. *Georgetown Journal of Law & Modern Critical Race Perspective, 3*(1), 1–38.

d'Orbán, P. T. (1979). Women who kill their children. *British Journal of Psychiatry, 134*(6), 560–571. doi:10.1192/bjp.134.6.560

Dally, A. (1982). *Inventing motherhood: The consequences of an ideal.* London: Burnett.

Davies, D. S. (1937). Child-killing in English law. *Modern Law Review, 1*(3), 203–223. doi:10.1111/j.1468-2230.1937.tb00018.x

Davis-Floyd, R. (1992). *Birth as an American rite of passage.* Berkeley, CA: University of California Press.

Davis-Floyd, R. (2001). The technocratic, humanistic, and holistic paradigms of childbirth. *International Journal of Gynecology & Obstetrics, 75*(S1), 5–23. doi:10.1016/s0020-7292(01)00510-0

Department for Education. (2019, February 21). Working together to safeguard children 2018. Retrieved from https://www.gov.uk/government/publications/working-together-to-safeguard-children-2

Department of Health and Social Care. (2020a, September 4). Abortion statistics for England and Wales: 2019. Retrieved from https://www.gov.uk/government/statistics/abortion-statistics-for-england-and-wales-2019

Department of Health and Social Care. (2020b, March 30). Temporary approval of home use for both stages of early medical abortion. Retrieved from https://www.gov.uk/government/publications/temporary-approval-of-home-use-for-both-stages-of-early-medical-abortion-2

Dhar, D. (2020, January 14). *Women's unpaid care work has been unmeasured and under-valued for too long. Essays on equality*. London: The Global Institute for Women's Leadership, King's College. Retrieved from https://www.kcl.ac.uk/news/womens-unpaid-care-work-has-been-unmeasured-and-undervalued-for-too-long

Dickens, B. M. (1966). *Abortion and the law*. London: Macgibbon & Kee.

Dill, B. T. (1988). Our mothers' grief: Racial ethnic women and the maintenance of families. *Journal of Family History, 13*(4), 415–431. doi:10.1177/036319908801300404

Disclosure and Barring Service. (n.d.). About us. Retrieved from https://www.gov.uk/government/organisations/disclosure-and-barring-service/about

Douglas, S. J., & Michaels, M. W. (2005). *The mommy myth: The idealization of motherhood and how it has undermined all women*. New York, NY: Free Press.

Dowd, N. E. (1997). In *defense of single-parent families*. New York, NY: New York University Press.

Downes, J., Kelly, L., & Westmarland, N. (2014). Ethics in violence and abuse research – A positive empowerment approach. *Sociological Research Online, 19*(1), 29–41. https://doi.org/10.5153/sro.3140

Dulit, E. (2000). Girls who deny a pregnancy: Girls who kill the neonate. In A. H. Esman (Ed.), *Annals of the American society for adolescent psychiatry* (Vol. 25, pp. 219–236). Hillsdale, MI: The Analytic Press.

Eaton, M. (1986). *Justice for women? Family, court and social control*. Milton Keynes: Open University Press.

Edwards, G. (2015). 1 in 3 women has an abortion, and 95% don't regret it – So why are we so afraid to talk about it?. *The Independent*, July 16. Retrieved from https://www.independent.co.uk/life-style/health-and-families/features/1-3-women-have-abortion-and-95-don-t-regret-it-so-why-aren-t-we-talking-about-it-10392750.html

Edwards, S. S. M. (1984). *Women on trial: A study of the female suspect, defendant, and offender in the criminal law and criminal justice system*. Manchester: Manchester University Press.

Edwards, S. S. M. (2016). Loss of self-control: When his anger is worth more than her fear. In A. Reed & M. Bohlander (Eds.), *Loss of control and diminished responsibility: Domestic, comparative and international perspectives* (pp. 79–96). London: Routledge.

Ehrenreich, B., & English, D. (1978). *For her own good: 150 years of the experts' advice to women*. Garden City, NY: Anchor Press.

Ehrenreich, B., & English, D. (2010). *Witches, midwives, and nurses: A history of women healers* (2nd ed.). New York, NY: Feminist Press at the City University of New York.

Ely, J. H. (1973). The wages of crying wolf: A comment on Roe V. Wade. *Yale Law Journal, 82*(5), 920–949. doi:10.2307/795536

Faludi, S. (1992). *Backlash: The undeclared war against American women*. London: Vintage.

Fanghanel, A. (2019). *Disrupting rape culture: Public space, sexuality and revolt*. Bristol: Bristol University Press.

Fanghanel, A., Milne, E., Zampini, G. F., Banwell, S., & Fiddler, M. (2021). *Sex and crime*. London: Sage.

Feeley, M. M., & Simon, J. (1992). The new penology: Notes on the emerging strategy of corrections and its implications. *Criminology, 30*(4), 449–474. doi:10.1111/j.1745-9125.1992.tb01112.x

Feeley, M. M., & Simon, J. (1994). Actuarial justice: The emerging new criminal law. In D. Nelken (Ed.), *The futures of criminology* (pp. 173–201). London: Sage.

Fentiman, L. C. (2006). The new fetal protection: The wrong answer to the crisis of inadequate health care for women and children. *Denver University Law Review*, *84*(2), 537–600.

Fineman, M. A. (1995a). Images of mothers in poverty discourse. In M. A. Fineman & I. Karpin (Eds.), *Mothers in law: Feminist theory and the legal regulation of motherhood* (pp. 205–223). New York, NY: Columbia University Press.

Fineman, M. A. (1995b). Preface. In M. Fineman & I. Karpin (Eds.), *Mothers in law: Feminist theory and the legal regulation of motherhood* (pp. ix–xiii). New York, NY: Columbia University Press.

Fineman, M. A. (2008). Vulnerable subject: Anchoring equality in the human condition, the essay. *Yale Journal of Law & Feminism*, *20*(1), 1–24.

Fineman, M. A., & Thomadsen, N. S. (1991). *At the boundaries of law: Feminism and legal theory*. London: Routledge.

Flavin, J. (2009). *Our bodies, our crimes: The policing of women's reproduction in America*. New York, NY: New York University Press.

Flekkoy, M. G. (1997). *The participation rights of the child: Rights and responsibilities in family and society*. London: Jessica Kingsley.

Fletcher, J.C. (1981). The Fetus as Patient: Ethical Issues. *JAMA, 246*(7), 772–773. doi: 10.1001/jama.1981.03320070056028.

Foodsafety.gov. (2019, April 1). People at risk: Pregnant women. Retrieved from https://www.foodsafety.gov/risk/pregnant/chklist_pregnancy.html

Forcey, L. R. (1994). Feminist perspectives on mothering and peace. In E. N. Glenn, G. Chang, & L. R. Forcey (Eds.), *Mothering: Ideology, experience, and agency* (pp. 335–376). New York, NY: Routledge.

Ford, S. (2018). Many women maybe unaware of correct seatbelt use while pregnant. *Nursing Times*, May 11. Retrieved from https://www.nursingtimes.net/news/policies-and-guidance/many-women-maybe-unaware-of-correct-seatbelt-use-while-pregnant/7024459.article

Forsythe, C. D. (1986). Homicide of the unborn child: The born alive rule and other legal anachronisms. *Valparaiso University Law Review*, *21*(3), 563–630.

Foucault, M. (1991 [1977]). *Discipline and punish: The birth of the prison* (A. Sheridan, Trans.). London: Penguin Books.

Foucault, M. (1992 [1985]). *The history of sexuality, vol. 2: The use of pleasure* (R. Hurley, Trans.). London: Penguin Books.

Foucault, M. (1998 [1976]). *The will to knowledge: The history of sexuality*, volume *1* (R. Hurley, Trans.). London: Penguin Books.

Fovargue, S., & Miola, J. (1998). Policing pregnancy: Implications of the attorney-general's reference (no. 3 of 1994). *Medical Law Review*, *6*(3), 265–296. doi:10.1093/medlaw/6.3.265

Fox, B., & Worts, D. (1999). Revisiting the critique of medicalized childbirth: A contribution to the sociology of birth. *Gender & Society*, *13*(3), 326–346. doi:10.1177/089124399013003004

Francome, C. (1986). *Abortion practice in Britain and the United States*. London: Allen & Unwin.

Frank, D.A., Augustyn, M., Knight, W.G., Pell, T., & Zuckerman, B. (2001). Growth, Development, and Behavior in Early Childhood Following Prenatal Cocaine Exposure: A Systematic Review. *JAMA, 285*(12), 1613–1625. doi:10.1001/jama.285.12.1613

Frederick, A. (2015). Between stigma and mother-blame: Blind mothers' experiences in USA hospital postnatal care. *Sociology of Health & Illness*, *37*(8), 1127–1141. doi:10.1111/1467-9566.12286

Friedman, S. H., Cavney, J., & Resnick, P. J. (2012). Mothers who kill: Evolutionary underpinnings and infanticide law. *Behavioral Sciences & the Law*, *30*(5), 585–597. doi:10.1002/bsl.2034

Friedman, S. H., & Friedman, J. B. (2010). Parents who kill their children. *Pediatrics in Review*, *31*(2), 10–16. doi:10.1542/pir.31-2-e10

Friedman, S. H., Heneghan, A., & Rosenthal, M. (2007). Characteristics of women who deny or conceal pregnancy. *Psychosomatics, 48*(2), 117–122. doi:10.1176/appi.psy.48.2.117

Friedman, S. H., Horwitz, S. M., & Resnick, P. J. (2005). Child murder by mothers: A critical analysis of the current state of knowledge and a research agenda. *American Journal of Psychiatry, 162*(9), 1578–1587. doi:10.1176/appi.ajp.162.9.1578

Friedman, S. H., & Resnick, P. J. (2009). Neonaticide: Phenomenology and considerations for prevention. *International Journal of Law and Psychiatry, 32*(1), 43–47. doi:10.1016/j.ijlp.2008.11.006

Furedi, A. (2016). *The moral case for abortion.* London: Palgrave Macmillan.

Fyfe, W. (1991). Abortion Acts: 1803 to 1967. In S. Franklin, C. Lury, & J. Stacey (Eds.), *Off-centre: Feminism and cultural studies* (pp. 160–174). London: Harper Collins.

Gallagher, J. (1987). Prenatal invasions & interventions: What's wrong with fetal rights. *Harvard Women's Law Journal, 10,* 1–8.

Garey, A. I. (1999). *Weaving work and motherhood.* Philadelphia, PA: Temple University Press.

Garey, A. I., & Arendell, T. (2001). Children, work, and family: Some thoughts on "mother-blame". In R. Hertz & N. L. Marshall (Eds.), *Working families the transformation of the American home* (pp. 293–303). Berkeley, CA: University of California Press.

Garland, D. (2000). The culture of high crime societies. *British Journal of Criminology, 40*(3), 347–375. doi:10.1093/bjc/40.3.347

Garland, D. (2001). *The culture of control: Crime and social order in contemporary society.* Oxford: Oxford University Press.

Gathings, M. J., & Parrotta, K. (2013). The use of gendered narratives in the courtroom. *Journal of Contemporary Ethnography, 42*(6), 668–689. doi:10.1177/0891241613497748

Gewirtz, P. D. (1996). Narrative and the rhetoric in the law. In P. Brooks & P. D. Gewirtz (Eds.), *Law's stories: Narrative and rhetoric in the law* (pp. 2–13). New Haven, CT: Yale University Press.

Gillis, J. R. (1997). *A world of their own making: A history of myth and ritual in family life.* Oxford: Oxford University Press.

Glenn, E. N. (1994). Social construction of mothering. In E. N. Glenn, G. Chang, & L. R. Forcey (Eds.), *Mothering: Ideology, experience, and agency* (pp. 1–29). New York, NY: Routledge.

Glenn, E. N., Chang, G., & Forcey, L. R. (Eds.). (1994). *Mothering: Ideology, experience, and agency.* New York, NY: Routledge.

Gonçalves, T., Macedo, M., & Conz, J. (2014). Non-psychotic denial of pregnancy: A psychoanalytical comprehension. *Inter-American Journal of Psychology, 48*(1), 23–29. doi:10.30849/rip/ijp.v48i1.242

Goodwin, M. (2020). *Policing the womb: Invisible women and the criminal costs of motherhood.* Cambridge: Cambridge University Press.

Gordon, L. (1986). Who is frightened of reproductive freedom for women and why? Some historical answers. *Frontiers: A Journal of Women Studies, 9*(1), 22–26. doi:10.2307/3346125

Gordon, L., & Gordon, L. (2002). *The moral property of women: A history of birth control politics in America* (3rd ed.). Chicago, IL: University of Illinois Press.

Gowing, L. (1997). Secret births and infanticide in seventeenth-century England. *Past & Present, 156*(1), 87–115. doi:10.1093/past/156.1.87

Graves, D. C. (2006). "... in a Frenzy While Raving Mad": Physicians and parliamentarians define infanticide in Victorian England. In B. H. Bechtold & D. C. Graves (Eds.), *Killing infants: Studies in the worldwide practice of infanticide* (pp. 111–136). Lewiston: Edwin Mellen Press.

Graycar, R., & Morgan, J. (2002). *The hidden gender of law* (2nd ed.). Leichhardt: Federation Press.

Green, C. M., & Manohar, S. V. (1990). Neonaticide and hysterical denial of pregnancy. *British Journal of Psychiatry, 156*(1), 121–123. doi:10.1192/bjp.156.1.121

Green, P., & Ward, T. (2004). *State crime: Governments, violence and corruption.* London: Pluto Press.

Gregg, R. (1995). *Pregnancy in a high-tech age: Paradoxes of choice.* New York, NY: New York University Press.

Grey, D. J. R. (2009). "More ignorant and stupid than wilfully cruel": Homicide trials and "baby-farming" in England and Wales in the Wake of the Children Act 1908. *Crimes and Misdemeanours: Deviance and the Law in Historical Perspective, 3*(2), 60–77.

Grey, D. J. R. (2013). "Liable to very gross abuse": Murder, moral panic and cultural fears over infant life insurance, 1875–1914. *Journal of Victorian Culture, 18*(1), 54–71. doi:10.1080/13555502.2012.740847

Grey, D. J. R. (2014). "The agony of despair": Pain and the cultural script of infanticide in England and Wales, 1860–1960. In R. Boddice (Ed.), *Pain and emotion in modern history* (pp. 204–219). London: Palgrave Macmillan.

Halberstam, J. (2010). The pregnant man. *The Velvet Light Trap, 65*(1), 77–78. doi:10.1353/vlt.0.0082

Halliday, S. (2016). *Autonomy and pregnancy: A comparative analysis of compelled obstetric intervention.* London: Routledge.

Hanmer, J., & Saunders, S. (1984). *Well-founded fear: A community study of violence to women.* London: Hutchinson London.

Hannah-Moffat, K., & O'Malley, P. (2007). *Gendered risks.* London: Routledge-Cavendish.

Hardy, M. (2017). In defence of actuarialism: Interrogating the logic of risk in social work practice. *Journal of Social Work Practice, 31*(4), 395–410. doi:10.1080/02650533.2017.1394828

Harper, E. A., & Rail, G. (2012). "Gaining the right amount for my baby": Young pregnant women's discursive constructions of health. *Health Sociology Review, 21*(1), 69–81. doi:10.5172/hesr.2012.21.1.69

Harris, A. P. (1994). Foreword: The jurisprudence of reconstruction. *California Law Review, 82*(4), 741–785. doi:10.2307/3480931

Hayes, K. (2010). Did Christine Taylor take abortion into her own hands?. *CBS News,* March 2. Retrieved from http://www.cbsnews.com/news/did-christine-taylor-take-abortion-into-her-own-hands/

Hays, S. (1996). *The cultural contradictions of motherhood.* New Haven, CT: Yale University Press.

Helén, I. (2004). Technics over life: Risk, ethics and the existential condition in high-tech antenatal care. *Economy and Society, 33*(1), 28–51. doi:10.1080/0308514032000176720

Hendrick, H. (2003). *Child welfare: Historical dimensions, contemporary debates.* Bristol: Policy Press.

Henham, R. (2001). *Sentence discounts and the criminal process.* Aldershot: Ashgate.

Hequembourg, A. L., & Farrell, M. P. (1999). Lesbian motherhood: Negotiating marginal-mainstream identities. *Gender & Society, 13*(4), 540–557. doi:10.1177/089124399013004007

Higginbotham, A. R. (1989). "Sin of the age": Infanticide and illegitimacy in Victorian London. *Victorian Studies, 3*(3), 319–337.

HM Revenue & Customs. (2020, August 19). Guidance: Child tax credit: Support for a maximum of 2 children. Retrieved from https://www.gov.uk/guidance/child-tax-credit-exceptions-to-the-2-child-limit

Hoffer, P. C., & Hull, N. E. (1981). *Murdering mothers: Infanticide in England and New England, 1558–1803.* New York, NY: New York University Press.

Hoggart, L. (2017). Internalised abortion stigma: Young women's strategies of resistance and rejection. *Feminism & Psychology, 27*(2), 186–202. doi:10.1177/0959353517698997

Home Office. (2016, April 21). Historical crime data. Retrieved from https://www.gov.uk/government/statistics/historical-crime-data

Home Office. (2020, July 17). Police recorded crime and outcomes open data tables. Retrieved from https://www.gov.uk/government/statistics/police-recorded-crime-open-data-tables

Howe, A. (1987). "Social injury" revisited: Towards a feminist theory of social justice. *International Journal of the Sociology of Law, 15*(4), 423–438.

Hrdy, S. B. (2000). *Mother nature: A history of mothers, infants, and natural selection.* New York, NY: Ballantine Books.

Hunt, L. (1995). Abortion most desperate. *The Independent*, March 21. Retrieved from http://www.independent.co.uk/life-style/abortion-most-desperate-1612131.html

Hutter, B., & Williams, G. (1981). Controlling women: The normal and the deviant. In B. Hutter & G. Williams (Eds.), *Controlling women: The normal and the deviant* (pp. 9–39). London: Croom Helm in association with the Oxford University Women's Studies Committee.

Jackson, B. S. (1996a). "Anchored narratives" and the interface of law, psychology and semiotics. Legal and criminological psychology. *Legal and Criminological Psychology, 1*(1), 17–45. doi:10.1111/j.2044-8333.1996.tb00305.x

Jackson, D., & Mannix, J. (2004). Giving voice to the burden of blame: A feminist study of mothers' experiences of mother blaming. *International Journal of Nursing Practice, 10*(4), 150–158. doi:10.1111/j.1440-172X.2004.00474.x

Jackson, M. (1996b). *New-born child murder: Women, illegitimacy and the courts in eighteenth-century England.* Manchester: Manchester University Press.

Jenkins, A., Millar, S., & Robins, J. (2011). Denial of pregnancy: A literature review and discussion of ethical and legal issues. *Journal of the Royal Society of Medicine, 104*(7), 286–291. doi:10.1258/jrsm.2011.100376

Jeremy, D. (2008). The prosecutor's rock and hard place. *Criminal Law Review*, (12), 925–936.

Johnsen, D. (1989). From driving to drugs: Governmental regulation of pregnant women's lives after Webster. *University of Pennsylvania Law Review, 138*(1), 179–215. doi:10.2307/3312183

Johnston, D. D., & Swanson, D. H. (2003). Invisible mothers: A content analysis of motherhood ideologies and myths in magazines. *Sex Roles, 49*(1), 21–33. doi:10.1023/a:1023905518500

Johnston, D. D., & Swanson, D. H. (2006). Constructing the "good mother": The experience of mothering ideologies by work status. *Sex Roles, 54*(7–8), 509–519. doi:10.1007/s11199-006-9021-3

Jones, I., & Quigley, M. (2016). Preventing lawful and decent burial: Resurrecting dead offences. *Legal Studies, 36*(2), 354–374. doi:10.1111/lest.12117

Jones, J. (2003). *Medea's daughters: Forming and performing the woman who kills.* Columbus, OH: Ohio State University Press.

Kampschmidt, E.D. (2015). Prosecuting Women for Drug Use During Pregnancy: The Criminal Justice System Should Step out and the Affordable Care Act Should Step Up. *Health Matrix: Journal of Law-Medicine, 25*, 487–512.

Kaplan, E. A. (1992). *Motherhood and representation: The mother in popular culture and melodrama.* London: Routledge.

Kaplan, R., & Grotowski, T. (1996). Denied pregnancy. *Australian and New Zealand Journal of Psychiatry, 30*(6), 861–863. doi:10.3109/00048679609065056

Kelly, L., Burton, S., & Regan, L. (1994). Researching Women's lives or studying women's oppression? Reflections on what constitutes feminist research. In M. Maynard & J. Purvis (Eds.), *Researching women's lives from a feminist perspective* (pp. 27–48). London: Taylor & Francis.

Kent, J. (1973). Attitudes of members of the house of commons to the regulation of "personal conduct" in late Elizabethan and early Stuart England. *Historical Research*, *46*(113), 41–71. doi:10.1111/j.1468-2281.1973.tb01478.x

Keown, J. (1988). *Abortion, doctors and the law: Some aspects of the legal regulation of abortion in England from 1803 to 1982*. Cambridge: Cambridge University Press.

Kilday, A.-M. (2013). *A history of infanticide in Britain, c.1600 to the present*. Basingstoke: Palgrave Macmillan.

King, W. J. (2014). Punishment for bastardy in early seventeenth-century England. *Albion*, *10*(2), 130–151. doi:10.2307/4048339

Kingma, E., & Porter, L. (2020). Parental obligation and compelled caesarean section: Careful analogies and reliable reasoning about individual cases. *Journal of Medical Ethics*. doi:10.1136/medethics-2020-106072

Kirby, J. (2017). Women turning to illegal abortion pills in rising numbers, charity warns. *The Independent*, February 15. Retrieved from http://www.independent.co.uk/news/uk/home-news/abortion-pill-access-online-illegal-decriminalise-woman-british-pregnancy-advisory-service-danger-a7580566.html

Knopoff, K. A. (1991). Can a pregnant woman morally refuse fetal surgery? *California Law Review*, *79*(2), 499–540. doi:10.2307/3480692

Kumar, A., Hessini, L., & Mitchell, E. M. H. (2009). Conceptualising abortion stigma. *Culture, Health & Sexuality*, *11*(6), 625–639. doi:10.1080/13691050902842741

Lacey, N. (1998). *Unspeakable subjects: Feminist essays in legal and social theory*. Oxford: Hart Publishing.

Lane, K. (2008). The medical model of the body as a site of risk: A case study of childbirth. In J. Low & C. Malacrida (Eds.), *Sociology of the body: A reader* (pp. 157–164). Don Mills: Oxford University Press.

Lazarus, E. S. (1994). What do women want? Issues of choice, control, and class in pregnancy and childbirth. *Medical Anthropology Quarterly*, *8*(1), 25–46. doi:10.1525/maq.1994.8.1.02a00030

Leavitt, J. W. (1986). *Brought to bed: Childbearing in America, 1750 to 1950*. Oxford: Oxford University Press.

Letherby, G. (1994). Mother or not, mother or what? *Women's Studies International Forum*, *17*(5), 525–532. doi:10.1016/0277-5395(94)00038-7

Letherby, G. (2003). *Feminist research in theory and practice*. Buckingham: Open University Press.

Lister, K. (2019). Yes, sex strikes have been successful. But not because women simply withheld sex. *iNews*, May 15. Retrieved from https://inews.co.uk/opinion/comment/sex-strikes-georgia-abortion-heartbeat-law-alyssa-milano-291127

Lloyd, A. (1995). *Doubly deviant, doubly damned: Society's treatment of violent women*. London: Penguin Books.

Longhurst, R. (2001). *Bodies: Exploring fluid boundaries*. London: Routledge.

Loughnan, A. (2012). The "strange" case of the infanticide doctrine. *Oxford Journal of Legal Studies*, *32*(4), 685–711. doi:10.1093/ojls/gqs017

Lupton, D. (1999a). *Risk and sociocultural theory: New directions and perspectives*. Cambridge: Cambridge University Press.

Lupton, D. (1999b). Risk and the ontology of pregnant embodiment. In D. Lupton (Ed.), *Risk and sociocultural theory: New directions and perspectives* (pp. 59–85). Cambridge: Cambridge University Press.

Lupton, D. (2011). "The best thing for the baby": Mothers' concepts and experiences related to promoting their infants' health and development. *Health, Risk & Society*, *13*(7–8), 637–651. doi:10.1080/13698575.2011.624179

Lupton, D. (2012a). *Medicine as culture: Illness, disease and the body* (3rd ed.). Los Angeles, CA: Sage.

Lupton, D. (2012b). "Precious cargo": Foetal subjects, risk and reproductive citizenship. *Critical Public Health*, *22*(3), 329–340. doi:10.1080/09581596.2012.657612

Lyerly, A. D., Lisa, M. M., Elizabeth Mitchell, A., Lisa, H. H., Rebecca, K., Miriam, K., & Margaret Olivia, L. (2009). Risk and the pregnant body. *Hastings Center Report, 39*(6), 34–42. doi:10.1353/hcr.0.0211

Lynch, J. J. (1995). Posterity: A constitutional peg for the unborn. *American Journal of Jurisprudence, 40*(1), 401–405. doi:10.1093/ajj/40.1.401

Macfarlane, A. (1980). Bastardy and its comparative history. In P. Laslett, K. Oosterveen, & R. M. Smith (Eds.), *Bastardy and its comparative history* (pp. 71–85). London: Edward Arnold.

MacKinnon, C. A. (1989). *Toward a feminist theory of the state.* Cambridge, MA: Harvard University Press.

MacKinnon, C. A. (1991). Reflections on sex equality under law. *Yale Law Journal, 100*(5), 1281–1328. doi:10.2307/796693

MacKinnon, C. A. (2005). *Women's lives, men's laws.* Cambridge, MA: Belknap Press of Harvard University Press.

Madriz, E. (1997). *Nothing bad happens to good girls: Fear of crime in women's lives.* Berkeley, CA: University of California Press.

Makhlouf, F., & Rambaud, C. (2014). Child homicide and neglect in France: 1991–2008. *Child Abuse & Neglect, 38*(1), 37–41. doi:10.1016/j.chiabu.2013.08.016

Marshall, J. (2012). Concealed births, adoption and human rights law: Being wary of seeking to open windows into people's souls. *Cambridge Law Journal, 71*(2), 325–354. doi:10.1017/s0008197312000517

Martin, E. (1987). *The woman in the body: A cultural analysis of reproduction.* Boston, MA: Beacon Press.

Maynard, M., & Purvis, J. (2013). *Researching women's lives from a feminist perspective.* London: Taylor & Francis.

McGlynn, C., Rackley, E., & Houghton, R. (2017). Beyond "revenge porn": The continuum of image-based sexual abuse. *Feminist Legal Studies, 25*(1), 25–46. doi:10.1007/s10691-017-9343-2

McKenzie, G., Robert, G., & Montgomery, E. (2020). Exploring the conceptualisation and study of freebirthing as a historical and social phenomenon: A meta-narrative review of diverse research traditions. *Medical Humanities, 46*(4), 512–524. doi:10.1136/medhum-2019-011786

McLaren, A. (1984). *Reproductive rituals: The perception of fertility in England from the sixteenth century to the nineteenth century.* London: Methuen.

Mendelson, S. H., & Crawford, P. (1998). *Women in early modern England: 1550–1720.* Oxford: Oxford University Press.

Meteyard, B. (1980). Illegitimacy and marriage in eighteenth-century England. *Journal of Interdisciplinary History, 10*(3), 479–489. doi:10.2307/203189

Meyer, C. L., & Oberman, M. (2001). *Mothers who kill their children: Understanding the acts of moms from Susan Smith to the "prom mom".* New York, NY: New York University Press.

Michalowski, S. (1999). Court-authorised caesarean sections – The end of a trend? *Modern Law Review, 62*(1), 115–127. doi:10.1111/1468-2230.00194

Miller, L. J. (2003). Denial of pregnancy. In M. G. Spinelli (Ed.), *Infanticide: Psychosocial and legal perspectives on mothers who kill* (pp. 81–104). Washington, DC: American Psychiatric Pub.

Milne, E. (2019). Concealment of birth: Time to repeal a 200-year-old "convenient stop-gap"? *Feminist Legal Studies, 27*(2), 139–162. doi:10.1007/s10691-019-09401-6

Milne, E. (2020). Putting the fetus first – Legal regulation, motherhood, and pregnancy. *Michigan Journal of Gender & Law, 27*(1), 149–211. doi:10.36641/mjgl.27.1.putting

Milne, E., Brennan, K., South, N., & Turton, J. (Eds.). (2018). *Women and the criminal justice system: Failing victims and offenders?* London: Palgrave Macmillan.

Milne, E., & Mason-Bish, H. (2019). Protecting pregnant women through hate crime policy. Paper presented at the European Society of Criminology Annual Conference, Ghent, Belgium.

Milne, E., & Turton, J. (2018). Understanding violent women. In E. Milne, K. Brennan, N. South, & J. Turton (Eds.), *Women and the criminal justice system: Failing victims and offenders?* (pp. 119–139). London: Palgrave Macmillan.

Milstein, K. K., & Milstein, P. S. (1983). Psychophysiologic aspects of denial in pregnancy: Case report. *The Journal of Clinical Psychiatry, 44*(5), 189–190.

Minkoff, H., & Paltrow, L. M. (2004). Melissa Rowland and the rights of pregnant women. *Obstetrics & Gynecology, 104*(6), 1234–1236. doi:10.1097/01.AOG.0000146289.65429.48

Mitchison, R., & Leneman, L. (1998). *Girls in trouble: Sexuality and social control in rural Scotland 1660–1780*. Edinburgh: Scottish Cultural Press.

Morris, A., & Wilczynski, A. (1993). Rocking the cradle: Mothers who kill their children. In H. Birch (Ed.), *Moving targets: Women, murder, and representation* (pp. 198–217). London: Virago.

Morrissey, B. (2003). *When women kill: Questions of agency and subjectivity*. London: Routledge.

Murphy, A. S. (2014). A survey of state fetal homicide laws and their potential applicability to pregnant women who harm their own fetuses. *Indiana University Maurer School of Law, 89*(2), 847–843.

Murphy Tighe, S., & Lalor, J. G. (2016). Concealed pregnancy: A concept analysis. *Journal of Advanced Nursing, 72*(1), 50–61. doi:10.1111/jan.12769

Naffine, N. (1990). *Law and the sexes: Explorations in feminist jurisprudence*. Sydney: Allen & Unwin.

National Advocates for Pregnant Women. (2018, June 18). Challenge to Wisconsin's "Unborn Child Protection Act". Retrieved from https://www.nationaladvocatesforpregnantwomen.org/challenge-to-wisconsins-unborn-child-protection-act/

National Conference of State Legislatures. (2018, January 5). State laws on fetal homicide and penalty – Enhancement for crimes against pregnant women. Retrieved from http://www.ncsl.org/research/health/fetal-homicide-state-laws.aspx

National Health Service. (2009, June 17). Pregnancy warning for older women. Retrieved from https://www.nhs.uk/news/pregnancy-and-child/pregnancy-warning-for-older-women/

National Health Service. (2018a, April 12). Diabetes and pregnancy. Retrieved from https://www.nhs.uk/conditions/pregnancy-and-baby/diabetes-pregnant/

National Health Service. (2018b, April 4). Epilepsy and pregnancy. Retrieved from https://www.nhs.uk/conditions/pregnancy-and-baby/epilepsy-pregnant/

National Health Service. (2018c, April 12). High blood pressure (hypertension) and pregnancy. Retrieved from https://www.nhs.uk/conditions/pregnancy-and-baby/hypertension-blood-pressure-pregnant/

National Health Service. (2018d, March 6). Where to give birth: The options. Retrieved from http://www.nhs.uk/conditions/pregnancy-and-baby/pages/where-can-i-give-birth.aspx

National Health Service. (2019a, January 31). Illegal drugs in pregnancy. Retrieved from https://www.nhs.uk/conditions/pregnancy-and-baby/illegal-drugs-in-pregnancy/

National Health Service. (2019b, November 7). Stop smoking in pregnancy. Retrieved from https://www.nhs.uk/conditions/pregnancy-and-baby/smoking-pregnant/

National Health Service. (2020a, April 24). Abortion. Retrieved from https://www.nhs.uk/conditions/abortion/

National Health Service. (2020b, January 29). Drinking alcohol while pregnant. Retrieved from https://www.nhs.uk/conditions/pregnancy-and-baby/alcohol-medicines-drugs-pregnant/

National Health Service. (2020c, April 16). Foods to avoid in pregnancy. Retrieved from https://www.nhs.uk/conditions/pregnancy-and-baby/foods-to-avoid-pregnant/

National Health Service. (2020d, February 14). Have a healthy diet in pregnancy. Retrieved from https://www.nhs.uk/conditions/pregnancy-and-baby/healthy-pregnancy-diet/

National Health Service. (2020e, January 20). Overweight and pregnant. Retrieved from https://www.nhs.uk/conditions/pregnancy-and-baby/overweight-pregnant/

National Health Service. (2020f, January 21). Planning your pregnancy. Retrieved from https://www.nhs.uk/conditions/pregnancy-and-baby/planning-pregnancy/

National Institute for Health and Care Excellence. (2014, December 3). Nice confirms midwife-led care during labour is safest for women with straightforward pregnancies. Retrieved from https://www.nice.org.uk/news/press-and-media/midwife-care-during-labour-safest-women-straightforward-pregnancies

National Institute for Health and Care Excellence. (2020, August 20). Fetal alcohol spectrum disorder. Retrieved from https://www.nice.org.uk/guidance/indevelopment/gid-qs10139/consultation/html-content-3

National Institute of Diabetes and Digestive and Kidney Diseases. (2018, December). Thyroid disease & pregnancy. Retrieved from https://www.niddk.nih.gov/health-information/endocrine-diseases/pregnancy-thyroid-disease

Nelson, J. (2003). *Women of color and the reproductive rights movement.* New York, NY: New York University Press.

Newman, A. (2010). Pregnant? Don't fall down the stairs. *Rewire,* February 15. Retrieved from https://rewire.news/article/2010/02/15/pregnant-dont-fall-down-stairs/

Nirmal, D., Thijs, I., Bethel, J., & Bhal, P. S. (2006). The incidence and outcome of concealed pregnancies among hospital deliveries: An 11-year population-based study in South Glamorgan. *Journal of Obstetrics & Gynaecology, 26*(2), 118–121. doi:10.1080/01443610500443303

Noor, P. (2019). "Now I have to check your hymen": The shocking persistence of virginity tests. *The Guardian,* December 9. Retrieved from https://www.theguardian.com/lifeandstyle/2019/dec/09/hymen-virginity-tests-us-ti

Norrie, A. (2014). *Crime, reason and history: A critical introduction to criminal law* (3rd ed.). Cambridge: Cambridge University Press.

O'Malley, P. (1992). Risk, power and crime prevention. *Economy and Society, 21*(3), 252–275. doi:10.1080/03085149200000013

O'Malley, P. (2000). Uncertain subjects: Risks, liberalism and contract. *Economy and Society, 29*(4), 460–484. doi:10.1080/03085140050174741

O'Malley, P. (2004). *Risk, uncertainty and government.* London: GlassHouse.

Oakley, A. (1974). *Woman's work: The housewife, past and present.* New York, NY: Pantheon.

Oakley, A. (1984). *The captured womb: A history of the medical care of pregnant women.* Oxford: Basil Blackwell.

Oakley, A. (1993). *Essays on women, medicine and health.* Edinburgh: Edinburgh University Press.

Oberman, M. (1992). The control of pregnancy and the criminalization of femaleness. *Berkeley Journal of Gender, Law & Justice, 7*(1), 1–12.

Oberman, M. (1996). Mothers who kill: Coming to terms with modern American infanticide. *American Criminal Law Review, 34*(1), 1–110.

Oberman, M. (2000). Mothers and doctors' orders: Unmasking the doctor's fiduciary role in maternal-fetal conflicts. *Northwestern University Law Review, 94*(2), 451–503.

Oberman, M. (2003). Mothers who kill: Cross-cultural patterns in and perspectives on contemporary maternal filicide. *International Journal of Law and Psychiatry, 26*(5), 493–514. doi:10.1016/s0160-2527(03)00083-9

Office for National Statistics. (2018, February 8). Sexual offences in England and Wales: Year ending March 2017. Retrieved from https://www.ons.gov.uk/

peoplepopulationandcommunity/crimeandjustice/articles/sexualoffencesinenglandandwales/yearendingmarch2017

Office for National Statistics. (2019, December 6). Births by parents' characteristics. Retrieved from https://www.ons.gov.uk/peoplepopulationandcommunity/birthsdeathsandmarriages/livebirths/datasets/birthsbyparentscharacteristics

Office for National Statistics. (2020, July 22). Births in England and Wales: 2019. Retrieved from https://www.ons.gov.uk/peoplepopulationandcommunity/birthsdeathsandmarriages/livebirths/bulletins/birthsummarytablesenglandandwales/2019

Office on Women's Health. (2018a, June 6). Preconception health. Retrieved from https://www.womenshealth.gov/pregnancy/you-get-pregnant/preconception-health

Office on Women's Health. (2018b, December 27). Weight, fertility, and pregnancy. Retrieved from https://www.womenshealth.gov/healthy-weight/weight-fertility-and-pregnancy

Old Bailey Proceedings Online. (1675, April). Trial of woman (T16750414-3). Version 8.0. Retrieved from www.oldbaileyonline.org

Old Bailey Proceedings Online. (1677, April). Trial of woman (T16770425-3). Version 8.0. Retrieved from www.oldbaileyonline.org

Olson, G. (2014). Narration and narrative in legal discourse. In P. Hühn, J. C. Meister, J. Pier, & W. Schmid (Eds.), *Handbook of narratology* (pp. 371–383). Berlin: Walter de Gruyter.

Ondersma, S. J., Simpson, S. M., Brestan, E. V., & Ward, M. (2000). Prenatal drug exposure and social policy: The search for an appropriate response. *Child Maltreatment, 5*(2), 93–108. doi:10.1177/1077559500005002002

Paltrow, L. M. (1999). Pregnant drug users, fetal persons, and the threat to Roe V. Wade. *Albany Law Review, 62*(3), 999–1056.

Paltrow, L. M. (2012). Is it ethical to suggest that some women need incentives to use contraception or to be sterilized? *Addiction, 107*(6), 1047–1049. doi:10.1111/j.1360-0443.2012.03816.x

Paltrow, L. M., & Flavin, J. (2013). Arrests of and forced interventions on pregnant women in the United States, 1973–2005: Implications for women's legal status and public health. *Journal of Health Politics, Policy and Law, 38*(2), 299–343. doi:10.1215/03616878-1966324

Perrin, K., & DeJoy, S. B. (2003). Abstinence-only education: How we got here and where we're going. *Journal of Public Health Policy, 24*(3), 445–459. doi:10.2307/3343387

Petchesky, R. P. (1987). Fetal images: The power of visual culture in the politics of reproduction. *Feminist Studies, 13*(2), 263–292. https://doi.org/10.2307/3177802

Petchesky, R. P. (1990). *Abortion and woman's choice: The state, sexuality, and reproductive freedom*. Boston, MA: Northeastern University Press.

Phelan, J. P. (1991). The maternal abdominal wall: A fortress against fetal health care?. *Southern California Law Review, 65*(1), 461–490.

Phoenix, A. (1991). *Young mothers?* Cambridge: Polity.

Pilkington, E. (2012). Indiana prosecuting Chinese woman for suicide attempt that killed her foetus. *The Guardian*, May 30. Retrieved from https://www.theguardian.com/world/2012/may/30/indiana-prosecuting-chinese-woman-suicide-foetus

Pilkington, E. (2015). Alone in Alabama: Dispatches from an inmate jailed for her son's stillbirth. *The Guardian*, October 7. Retrieved from http://www.theguardian.com/us-news/2015/oct/07/alabama-chemical-endangerment-pregnancy-amanda-kimbrough?CMP=share_btn_link

Pillai, S. (2020). I grew up believing "good" Indian women shouldn't enjoy sex. I was so wrong. *The Huffington Post*, May 15. Retrieved from https://www.huffingtonpost.co.uk/entry/sex-taboo_uk_5ebd53dfc5b6dd652f53807d

Pitt, S. E., & Bale, E. M. (1995). Neonaticide, infanticide, and filicide: A review of the literature. *Journal of the American Academy of Psychiatry and the Law Online, 23*(3), 375–386.

Pollack, S. (1990). Lesbian parents: Claiming our visibility. In J. P. Knowles & E. Cole (Eds.), *Motherhood: A feminist perspective* (pp. 181–194). New York, NY: Haworth Press.

Porter, T., & Gavin, H. (2010). Infanticide and neonaticide: A review of 40 years of research literature on incidence and causes. *Trauma, Violence & Abuse, 11*(3), 99–112. doi:10.1177/1524838010371950

Potts, M., Diggory, P., & Peel, J. (1977). *Abortion*. Cambridge: Cambridge University Press.

Prison Reform Trust. (2017). Counted out: Black, Asian and minority ethnic women in the criminal justice system. Retrieved from http://www.prisonreformtrust.org.uk/Portals/0/Documents/Counted%20Out.pdf

Public Health England. (2018, January 15). Guidance: Teenage pregnancy prevention framework. Retrieved from https://www.gov.uk/government/publications/teenage-pregnancy-prevention-framework

Public Health England. (2019, February 22). Healthy beginnings: Applying all our health. Retrieved from https://www.gov.uk/government/publications/healthy-beginnings-applying-all-our-health/healthy-beginnings-applying-all-our-health

Purdy, L. M. (1990). Are pregnant women fetal containers? *Bioethics, 4*(4), 273–291. doi:10.1111/j.1467-8519.1990.tb00092.x

Putkonen, H., Collander, J., Weizmann-Henelius, G., & Eronen, M. (2007). Legal outcomes of all suspected neonaticides in Finland 1980–2000. *International Journal of Law and Psychiatry, 30*(3), 248–254. doi:10.1016/j.ijlp.2007.03.008

Rackley, E. (2010). The art and craft of writing judgments: Notes on the feminist judgments project. In R. C. Hunter, C. McGlynn, E. Rackley, & B. Hale (Eds.), *Feminist judgments: From theory to practice* (pp. 44–46). Oxford: Hart Publishing.

Ramsey, C. B. (2006). Restructuring the debate over fetal homicide laws. *Ohio State Law Journal, 67*(4), 721–782.

Rapaport, E. (2006). Mad women and desperate girls: Infanticide and child murder in law and myth. *Fordham Urban Law Journal, 33*(2), 527–571.

Raynor, R. (2016). Dramatising austerity: Holding a story together (and why it falls apart …). *Cultural Geographies, 24*(2), 193–212. doi:10.1177/1474474016675564

Reagan, L. J. (1997). *When abortion was a crime: Women, medicine, and law in the United States, 1867–1973*. Berkeley, CA: University of California Press.

Resnick, P. J. (1969). Child murder by parents: A psychiatric review of filicide. *American Journal of Psychiatry, 126*(3), 325–334. doi:10.1176/ajp.126.3.325

Resnick, P. J. (1970). Murder of the newborn: A psychiatric review of neonaticide. *American Journal of Psychiatry, 126*(10), 1414–1420. doi:10.1176/ajp.126.10.1414

Rhoden, N. K. (1986). The judge in the delivery room: The emergence of court-ordered cesareans. *California Law Review, 74*(6), 1951–2030. doi:10.2307/3480420

Rich, A. (1986). *Of woman born: Motherhood as experience and institution*. New York, NY: Norton.

Roberts, D. E. (1995). Racism and patriarchy in the meaning of motherhood. In M. A. Fineman & I. Karpin (Eds.), *Mothers in law: Feminist theory and the legal regulation of motherhood* (pp. 224–249). New York, NY: Columbia University Press.

Roberts, D. E. (1997). *Killing the black body: Race, reproduction, and the meaning of liberty*. New York, NY: Pantheon Books.

Roberts, H. (Ed.). (1981). *Doing feminist research*. London: Routledge.

Romanis, E. C. (2020a). Artificial womb technology and the choice to gestate ex utero: Is partial ectogenesis the business of the criminal law? *Medical Law Review, 28*(2), 342–374. doi:10.1093/medlaw/fwz037

Romanis, E. C. (2020b). Challenging the "born alive" threshold: Fetal surgery, artificial wombs, and the English approach to legal personhood. *Medical Law Review, 28*(1), 93–123. doi:10.1093/medlaw/fwz014

Romanis, E. C., Begovic, D., Brazier, M. R., & Mullock, A. K. (2020a). Reviewing the womb. *Journal of Medical Ethics*, 1–10. doi:10.1136/medethics-2020-106160

Romanis, E. C., Milne, E., Halliday, S., & Cave, E. (2020b, September 21). Responding to challenges in diagnosing fetal alcohol spectrum disorder. Retrieved from https://www.dur.ac.uk/cells/briefing/?itemno=42806

Rose, N. (1993). Government, authority and expertise in advanced liberalism. *Economy and Society*, *22*(3), 283–299. doi:10.1080/03085149300000019

Rose, N. (1996a). The death of the social? Re-figuring the territory of government. *Economy and Society*, *25*(3), 327–356. doi:10.1080/03085149600000018

Rose, N. (1996b). Psychiatry as a political science: Advanced liberalism and the administration of risk. *History of the Human Sciences*, *9*(2), 1–23. doi:10.1177/095269519600900201

Rose, N. (1998). Governing risky individuals: The role of psychiatry in new regimes of control. *Psychiatry, Psychology and Law*, *5*(2), 177–195. doi:10.1080/13218719809524933

Rose, N. (2000). Government and control. *British Journal of Criminology*, *40*(2), 321–339. doi:10.1093/bjc/40.2.321

Roth, R. (2000). *Making women pay: The hidden costs of fetal rights*. Ithaca, NY: Cornell University Press.

Rothman, B. K. (1989). *Recreating motherhood: Ideology and technology in a patriarchal society*. New York, NY: Norton.

Rothman, B. K. (1993). The active management of physicians. *Birth*, *20*(3), 158–159. doi:10.1111/j.1523-536X.1993.tb00443.x

Rothman, B. K. (1994). Beyond mothers and fathers: Ideology in a patriarchal society. In E. N. Glenn, G. Chang, & L. R. Forcey (Eds.), *Mothering: Ideology, experience, and agency* (pp. 139–157). New York, NY: Routledge.

Ruddick, S. (1989). *Maternal thinking: Toward a politics of peace*. Boston, MA: Beacon Press.

Ruhl, L. (1999). Liberal governance and prenatal care: Risk and regulation in pregnancy. *Economy and Society*, *28*(1), 95–117. doi:10.1080/03085149900000026

Rustin, S. (2016). All British women have the right to a caesarean – They're not "too posh to push". *The Guardian*, March 29. Retrieved from https://www.theguardian.com/commentisfree/2016/mar/29/british-women-right-caesarean-too-posh-to-push

Sample, I. (2017). Men are affected by the biological clock as well, researchers find. *The Guardian*, July 2. Retrieved from https://www.theguardian.com/science/2017/jul/02/men-are-affected-by-the-biological-clock-as-well-researchers-find

Sandoz, P. (2011). Reactive-homeostasis as a cybernetic model of the silhouette effect of denial of pregnancy. *Medical Hypotheses*, *77*(5), 782–785. doi:10.1016/j.mehy.2011.07.036

Sanger, C. (1992). M is for the many things. *Southern California Review of Law and Women's Studies*, *1*(1), 15–67.

Sanger, C. (2006). Infant safe haven laws: Legislating in the culture of life. *Columbia Law Review*, *106*(4), 753–829. doi:10.2307/4099469

Schantz, A. (1994). Taking the nature out of mother. In D. Bassin, M. Honey, & M. M. Kaplan (Eds.), *Representations of motherhood* (pp. 240–255). New Haven, CT: Yale University Press.

Scott, R. (2002). *Rights, duties, and the body: Law and ethics of the maternal–fetal conflict*. Oxford: Hart Publishing.

Seal, L. (2010). *Women, murder and femininity: Gender representations of women who kill*. Basingstoke: Palgrave Macmillan.

Sharpe, J. A. (1983). *Crime in seventeenth-century England: A county study*. Cambridge: Cambridge University Press.

Sheldon, S. (1993). "Who is the mother to make the judgment?": The constructions of woman in English abortion law. *Feminist Legal Studies*, *1*(1), 3–22. doi:10.1007/BF01191522

Sheldon, S. (1997). *Beyond control: Medical power and abortion law*. London: Pluto Press.

Sheldon, S. (2015). The regulatory Cliff Edge between contraception and abortion: The legal and moral significance of implantation. *Journal of Medical Ethics*, *41*(9), 762–765. doi:10.1136/medethics-2015-102712

Sheldon, S. (2016). The decriminalisation of abortion: An argument for modernisation. *Oxford Journal of Legal Studies*, *36*(2), 334–365. doi:10.1093/ojls/gqv026

Sheldon, S., & Wellings, K. (2020a). Introduction. In S. Sheldon & K. Wellings (Eds.), *Decriminalising abortion in the UK: What would it mean?* (pp. 1–16). Bristol: Policy Press.

Sheldon, S., & Wellings, K. (Eds.). (2020b). *Decriminalising abortion in the UK: What would it mean?* Bristol: Policy Press.

Sher, J. (2016). *Missed period: Scotland's opportunities for better pregnancies, healthier parents and thriving babies the first time … and every time.* NHS Greater Glasgow & Clyde (Public Health). Retrieved from http://www.nhsggc.org.uk/media/237840/missed-periods-j-sher-may-2016.pdf

Sherr, L., Mueller, J., & Fox, Z. (2009). Abandoned babies in the UK – A review utilizing media reports. *Child: Care, Health and Development, 35*(3), 419–430. doi:10.1111/j.1365-2214.2009.00952.x

Simon, J. (1988). The ideological effects of actuarial practices. *Law & Society Review, 22*(4), 771–800. doi:10.2307/3053709

Singh, S. (2017). Criminalizing vulnerability. *Social & Legal Studies, 26*(4), 511–533. doi:10.1177/0964663916682825

Slayton, R. I., & Soloff, P. H. (1981). Psychotic denial of third-trimester pregnancy. *Journal of Clinical Psychiatry, 42*(12), 471–473.

Smart, C. (1996). Deconstructing motherhood. In E. B. Silva (Ed.), *Good enough mothering? Feminist perspectives on lone motherhood* (pp. 37–57). London: Routledge.

Smart, C. (1998). The woman of legal discourse. In K. Daly & L. Maher (Eds.), *Criminology at the crossroads: Feminist readings in crime and justice* (pp. 21–36). New York, NY: Oxford University Press.

Smith, D. E. (1988). *The everyday world as problematic: A feminist sociology.* Milton Keynes: Open University Press.

Smith, V., Devane, D., & Murphy-Lawless, J. (2012). Risk in maternity care: A concept analysis. *International Journal of Childbirth, 2*(2), 126–135. doi:10.1891/2156-5287.2.2.126

Snider, L. (2003). Constituting the punishable woman. Atavistic man incarcerates postmodern woman. *British Journal of Criminology, 43*(2), 354–378. doi:10.1093/bjc/43.2.354

Solinger, R. (1994). Race and "value": Black and white illegitimate babies, 1945–1965. In E. N. Glenn, G. Chang, & L. R. Forcey (Eds.), *Mothering: Ideology, experience, and agency* (pp. 287–310). New York, NY: Routledge.

Solinger, R. (2005). *Pregnancy and power: A short history of reproductive politics in America.* New York, NY: New York University Press.

Spencer, L., Ritchie, J., O'Connor, W., Morrell, G., & Ormston, R. (2013a). Analysis: Practice. In J. Ritchie, J. Lewis, C. McNaughton Nicholls, & R. Ormston (Eds.), *Qualitative research practice: A guide for social science students and researchers* (2nd ed., pp. 295–345). London: Sage.

Spencer, L., Ritchie, J., Ormston, R., O'Connor, W., & Barnard, M. (2013b). Analysis: Principles and processes. In J. Ritchie, J. Lewis, C. McNaughton Nicholls, & R. Ormston (Eds.), *Qualitative research practice: A guide for social science students and researchers* (2nd ed., pp. 269–293). London: Sage.

Spielvogel, A. M., & Hohener, H. C. (1995). Denial of pregnancy: A review and case reports. *Birth, 22*(4), 220–226. doi:10.1111/j.1523-536X.1995.tb00262.x

Spinelli, M. G. (2001). A systematic investigation of 16 cases of neonaticide. *American Journal of Psychiatry, 158*(5), 811–813. doi:10.1176/appi.ajp.158.5.811

Spinelli, M. G. (2003). Neonaticide: A systematic investigation of 17 cases. In M. G. Spinelli (Ed.), *Infanticide: Psychosocial and legal perspectives on mothers who kill* (pp. 105–118). Washington, DC: American Psychiatric Publishing.

Spinelli, M. G. (2010). Denial of pregnancy: A psychodynamic paradigm. *Journal of American Academy of Psychoanalysis, 38*(1), 117–131. doi:10.1521/jaap.2010.38.1.117

Spivack, C. (2007). To bring down the flowers: The cultural context of abortion law in early modern England. *William & Mary Journal of Women and the Law, 14*(1), 107–152.

Stanko, E. A. (1985). *Intimate intrusions: Women's experience of male violence.* London: Routledge.

Stanko, E. A. (1997). Safety talk: Conceptualizing women's risk assessment as a "technology of the soul". *Theoretical Criminology*, *1*(4), 479–499. doi:10.1177/1362480697001004004

Stanley, L., & Wise, S. (1990). Method, methodology and epistemology in feminist research processes. In L. Stanley (Ed.), *Feminist praxis: Research, theory and epistemology in feminist sociology* (pp. 20–60). London: Routledge.

Stockman, F. (2019). Manslaughter charge dropped against Alabama woman who was shot while pregnant. *The New York Times*, July 3. Retrieved from https://www.nytimes.com/2019/07/03/us/charges-dropped-alabama-woman-pregnant.html

Stormer, N. (2000). Prenatal space. *Signs*, *26*(1), 109–144. doi:10.1086/495569

Strong, T. H. (2000). *Expecting trouble: The myth of prenatal care in America*. New York, NY: New York University Press.

Sudbury, J. (2002). Celling black bodies: Black women in the global prison industrial complex. *Feminist Review*, *70*(1), 57–74. doi:10.1057/palgrave.fr.9400006

Sutherland, J.-A. (2010). Mothering, guilt and shame. *Sociology Compass*, *4*(5), 310–321. doi:10.1111/j.1751-9020.2010.00283.x

Tague, P. W. (2007). Guilty pleas and barristers' incentives: Lessons from England. *Georgetown Journal of Legal Ethics*, *20*(2), 287–320.

Temkin, J. (1986). Pre-natal injury, homicide and the draft criminal code. *Cambridge Law Journal*, *45*(3), 414–429. doi:10.1017/S0008197300118434

The Fawcett Society. (2016, March 8). Parents, work and care: Striking the balance. Retrieved from https://www.fawcettsociety.org.uk/parents-work-and-care-striking-the-balance

Thom, B., Herring, R., & Milne, E. (2020). Drinking in pregnancy: Shifting towards the "precautionary principle". In S. MacGregor & B. Thom (Eds.), *Alcohol, drugs and risk: Framing dangerous classes and dangerous spaces: Historical and cross-cultural perspectives* (pp. 66–87). London: Routledge.

Thomas, E. J., Stelzl, M., & Lafrance, M. N. (2016). Faking to finish: Women's accounts of feigning sexual pleasure to end unwanted sex. *Sexualities*, *20*(3), 281–301. doi:10.1177/1363460716649338

Thomson, L. (2004). Mother is charged in stillbirth of a twin. *Deseret News*, March 12. Retrieved from http://www.deseretnews.com/article/595048573/Mother-is-charged-in-stillbirth-of-a-twin.html?pg=all

Thurer, S. (1993). Changing conceptions of the good mother in psychoanalysis. *Psychoanalytic Review*, *80*(4), 519–540.

Thurer, S. (1994). *The myths of motherhood: How culture reinvents the good mother*. New York, NY: Penguin Books.

Thynne, C., Gaffney, G., O'Neill, M., Tonge, M., & Sherlock, C. (2012). Concealed pregnancy: Prevalence, perinatal measures and socio-demographics. *Irish Medical Journal*, *105*(8), 263–265.

Tuerkheimer, D. (2006). Conceptualizing violence against pregnant women. *Indiana Law Journal*, *81*(2), 667–712.

Understanding Society. (2019, October 22). How women's employment changes after having a child.. Retrieved from https://www.understandingsociety.ac.uk/2019/10/22/how-womens-employment-changes-after-having-a-child

Unicef UK. (n.d.). How we protect children's rights. Retrieved from https://www.unicef.org.uk/what-we-do/un-convention-child-rights/

van Mulken, M. R. H., McAllister, M., & Lowe, J. B. (2016). The stigmatisation of pregnancy: Societal influences on pregnant women's physical activity behaviour. *Culture, Health & Sexuality*, *18*(8), 921–935. doi:10.1080/13691058.2016.1148199

Vellut, N., Cook, J. M., & Tursz, A. (2012). Analysis of the relationship between neonaticide and denial of pregnancy using data from judicial files. *Child Abuse & Neglect*, *36*(7–8), 553–563. doi:10.1016/j.chiabu.2012.05.003

Wagner, M. (2006). *Born in the USA: How a broken maternity system must be fixed to put mothers and infants first*. Berkeley, CA: University of California Press.

180   *References*

Walker, N. (1968). *Crime and insanity in England: Volume 1, the historical perspective.* Edinburgh: Edinburgh University Press.

Walklate, S. (1997). Risk and criminal victimization: A modernist dilemma? *British Journal of Criminology, 37*(1), 35–45. doi:10.1093/oxfordjournals.bjc.a014148

Ward, T. (1999). The sad subject of infanticide: Law, medicine and child murder, 1860–1938. *Social & Legal Studies, 8*(2), 163–180. doi:10.1177/096466399900800201

Ward, T. (2002). Legislating for human nature: Legal responses to infanticide, 1860–1938. In M. Jackson (Ed.), *Infanticide: Historical perspectives on child murder and concealment, 1550–2000* (pp. 249–270). Aldershot: Ashgate.

We Trust Women. (n.d.). Retrieved from https://wetrustwomen.org.uk

Weare, S. (2016). Bad, mad or sad? Legal language, narratives, and identity constructions of women who kill their children in England and Wales. *International Journal for the Semiotics of Law, 30*(2), 201–222. doi:10.1007/s11196-016-9480-y

Webb, S. A. (2009). Risk, governmentality and insurance: The actuarial re-casting of social work. In H.-U. Otto, A. Polutta, & H. Ziegler (Eds.), *Evidence-based practice – Modernising the knowledge base of social work?* (pp. 211–226). Opladen: Barbara Budrich Publishers.

Wee, V. (2011). Patriarchy and the horror of the monstrous feminine. *Feminist Media Studies, 11*(2), 151–165. doi:10.1080/14680777.2010.521624

Weeks, J. (1981). *Sex, politics and society: The regulation of sexuality since 1800.* London: Longman.

Weigel, M. (2016). The foul reign of the biological clock. *The Guardian,* May 10. Retrieved from https://www.theguardian.com/society/2016/may/10/foul-reign-of-the-biological-clock

Weir, L. (1996). Recent developments in the government of pregnancy. *Economy and Society, 25*(3), 373–392. doi:10.1080/03085149600000020

Weir, L. (2006). *Pregnancy, risk and biopolitics: On the threshold of the living subject.* London: Routledge.

Weiss, S. (2018, August 13). 7 subtle ways women are shamed for their sexuality on a daily basis. *Bustle.* Retrieved from https://www.bustle.com/p/7-subtle-ways-women-are-shamed-for-their-sexuality-on-a-daily-basis-10015068

Wells, C. (1998). On the outside looking in: Perspectives on enforced caesareans. In S. Sheldon & M. Thomson (Eds.), *Feminist perspectives on health care law* (pp. 237–257). London: Cavendish Publishing.

Wertz, R. W., & Wertz, D. C. (1989). *Lying-in: A history of childbirth in America.* New Haven, CT: Yale University Press.

Wessel, J., Endrikat, J., & Buscher, U. (2002). Frequency of denial of pregnancy: Results and epidemiological significance of a 1-year prospective study in Berlin. *Acta Obstetricia et Gynecologica Scandinavica, 81*(11), 1021–1027. doi:10.1034/j.1600-0412.2002.811105.x

Wessel, J., Endrikat, J., & Buscher, U. (2003). Elevated risk for neonatal outcome following denial of pregnancy: Results of a one-year prospective study compared with control groups. *Journal of Perinatal Medicine, 31*(1), 29–35. doi:10.1515/JPM.2003.004

Wessel, J., Gauruder-Burmester, A., & Gerlinger, C. (2007). Denial of pregnancy – Characteristics of women at risk. *Acta Obstetricia et Gynecologica Scandinavica, 86*(5), 542–546. doi:10.1080/00016340601159199

West, C., & Zimmerman, D. H. (1987). Doing gender. *Gender & Society, 1*(2), 125–151. doi:10.1177/0891243287001002002

West, R. (1988). Jurisprudence and gender. *University of Chicago Law Review, 55*(1), 1–72. doi:10.2307/1599769

West, R. (1997). *Caring for justice.* New York, NY: New York University Press.

Wheelwright, J. (2002). "Nothing in between": Modern cases of infanticide. In M. Jackson (Ed.), *Infanticide: Historical perspectives on child murder and concealment, 1550–2000* (pp. 270–285). Aldershot: Ashgate.

Wiener, M. J. (2004). *Men of blood: Violence, manliness and criminal justice in Victorian England*. Cambridge: Cambridge University Press.

Wilczynski, A. (1997). *Child homicide*. London: Greenwich Medical Media Ltd.

Williams, C. (2006). Dilemmas in Fetal Medicine: Premature Application of Technology or Responding to Women's Choice? *Sociology of Health & Illness, 28*(1), 1–20. doi: 10.1111/j.1467-9566.2006.00480.x.

Williams, G. L. (1958). *The sanctity of life and the criminal law*. London: Faber and Faber.

World Health Organisation. (n.d.). Maternal, newborn, child and adolescent health. Retrieved from http://www.who.int/maternal_child_adolescent/topics/maternal/maternal_perinatal/en/

Worrall, A. (1990). *Offending women: Female lawbreakers and the criminal justice system*. London: Routledge.

Young, I. M. (1990). *Throwing like a girl and other essays in feminist philosophy*. Bloomington, IN: Indiana University Press.

Zelizer, V. A. R. (1994). *Pricing the priceless child: The changing social value of children*. Princeton, NJ: Princeton University Press.

Index

Note: Page numbers followed by "*n*" indicate footnotes.